DATE DUE

OCT 1 8 2012			
APR 0 9 2013			
GAYLORD			PRINTED IN U.S.A.

ing,
ing,
and
ing

Other McGraw-Hill Books of Interest

Painting, Staining, and Finishing

Tom Philbin

McGraw-Hill

New York San Francisco Washington, D.C. Auckland Bogotá
Caracas Lisbon London Madrid Mexico City Milan
Montreal New Delhi San Juan Singapore
Sydney Tokyo Toronto

Library of Congress Cataloging-in-Publication Data

Philbin, Tom, 1934–
   Painting, staining, and finishing / Tom Philbin.
      p.   cm.
   ISBN 0-07-049730-3.—ISBN 0-07-049731-1 (pbk.)
    1. House painting—Amateurs' manuals. 2. Wood finishing—
Amateurs' manuals. 3. Wall coverings—Amateurs' manuals.
   I. Title.
   TT320.P54   1997
   698'.1—dc21   96-49071
                                       CIP

McGraw-Hill

*A Division of The **McGraw·Hill** Companies*

1 2 3 4 5 6 7 8 9 0 DOC/DOC 9 0 2 1 0 9 8 7

ISBN 0-07-049730-3 (HC)   0-07-049731-1 (PBK)

The sponsoring editor for this book was Zoe G. Foundotos, the editing supervisor was Ruth W. Mannino, and the production supervisor was Pamela Pelton. It was set in Palatino by McGraw-Hill's Professional Book Group composition unit, Hightstown, N.J.

Printed and bound by R. R. Donnelley & Sons Company.

McGraw-Hill books are available at special quantity discounts to use as premiums and sales promotions, or for use in corporate training programs. For more information, please write to the Director of Special Sales, McGraw-Hill, 11 West 19th Street, New York, NY 10011. Or contact your local bookstore.

 This book is printed on recycled, acid-free paper containing a minimum of 50% recycled, de-inked fiber.

Contents

Part 3. Interior Wood Finishing

Part 4. Exterior Preparation

Part 6. Hanging Wall Coverings

Preface

Years ago, when I first started to paint houses, oil-based paint was commonly used, although latex—I think the first brand was Lucite—had started to come on strong.

As I look back, I can only say that paint has come a long way, and it's going to go further. But one thing will never change, at least not in my lifetime: the heart and soul of a paint job will not be the material or the applicators used to put it on—it will be the painter. There will always be a need for someone to put paint on, and do it right.

That is the goal of this book: to provide the professional painter with the knowhow to perform the craft in the best way possible.

Disagreements

Not every painter will embrace every method presented here. What is presented here is informed by the author's opinions as to the best ways to do a particular thing, based not only on personal experience but also on the expertise of various experienced and knowledgeable people, including housepainters, vendors, and just salespeople who have been standing behind counters answering highly detailed paint questions for decades.

In some instances there may not be a right way or a wrong way, but just a way that works for the individual painter. And although a vast number of distinctions are made among products and methods in the book, there may be more than one right way to do something.

For example, one painter may prefer to paint asbestos cement shingles with a $1\frac{1}{2}$-in roller, because with the long fibers drenched with paint everything can be covered with a pass or two. Another painter might feel that using the $1\frac{1}{2}$-in roller is sloppy and that the roller gets awfully heavy. For this painter no more than a $\frac{3}{4}$-in thick roller should be used.

Who's right? I have my own preference (a $\frac{3}{4}$-in roller), but both approaches work.

New Products

The paint industry has taken some giant steps in product improvement since I began painting. Indeed, maxims that I once held to be true, such as that dark paints cover better than light paints, are no longer valid. (Light paints generally cover better than dark ones.)

I have tried to present the vast variety of products that have been introduced and that the painter should know about, as well as the old standbys.

Whenever practical, I have also tried to explain the why of things, because when you understand something deeply you tend to apply the knowledge. For example, understanding the basic formulation of finish paint and why it works and where it doesn't, and where primers work and don't, increases the chances that the right type of product will be used.

I also have given brand names of products. My philosophy as a writer has always been to try not to make a mystery of things to readers. Naming brand names should help accomplish that.

If someone were to ask me what has been the most dramatic advance in product area, I would say—other than the development of water-based products—the development of superior exterior stains. In part, this is due to the number of decks being built in America. According to a representative at the Flood Company some 1.1 million decks are being built each year. That's a lot of raw wood—and a lot of wood to maintain.

Also, use of cedar for siding (as well as decks) has become more prevalent. I don't know what the percentages are, but certainly much more cedar is being used than in the past. And cedar has to be maintained.

Indeed, in terms of knowhow, probably the most significant conclusions for the industry are the guidelines by the Department of Agriculture's Forest Products Laboratory as to when to coat raw wood exposed to weather. For years, painters understood that wood should weather out before being stained or painted. The Forest Products Laboratory around 1992 issued their conclusions to the contrary. Apparently, these results have not reached all painters or their customers. These findings are very important, and should be emphasized.

Coverage (As It Were)

The book covers all aspects of interior and exterior paint from the products available, to the techniques used in preparation and painting, to a presentation of a wide variety of potential problems (both the reasons behind the problems and the solutions). Quite a few problems are covered.

There is also a section on wallpapering, which discusses the products available, methods of hanging various kinds, and dealing with any problems that might arise.

All told, I believe this book will be a useful addition to the professional painter's library. Good luck!

Tom Philbin

Acknowledgments

The heart and soul of most books is research, the quality of information an author is able to come by. I was fortunate in being able to pick the brains of a variety of people for this book, and I particularly want to thank the individuals and organizations whose names follow:

Ken Walker, painter and paperhanger; Debbie Fedasiuk; Tony Bucco, Behr Process; Bob Hartig, painter and paperhanger; Marty Duffy, USG; Catherine Philbin; Shelly Walk, Sandy Moran, and Scott Baron, Dutch Boy Paints; Len Hickerson, painter; Tom Hardy, Hyde Tools; Fran Calpin, UGL; Graco; Bob Valentino, Scrub-a-Dub-Industries; Julie Colbourne, Bio-Wash; John Mackey, Padco; George Washington and Mike McEnroe, Flood Company; Ginger Mainey; Commercial Painters Supply; Larry Rasmussen, painter and paperhanger; Wooster Brush Co.; and Purdy Brush. Finally, my thanks again to all those great librarians at the Harborfields Public Library.

PART 1
The Basics

1
Tools, Equipment, and Materials

A variety of tools and equipment of varying quality are available for painting jobs, but for the professional the byword should be *quality*. It makes little sense to buy tools of inferior quality because such items can interfere with the quality of the job produced as well as make the task more difficult and time-consuming. For example, bargain-basement roller sleeves will not hold as much paint as good-quality sleeves, will make application more difficult, will likely shed fiber (resulting in a waste of valuable time in clearing away the fiber), and will not produce the best-looking result. All told, twice as much time is spent on a job, and it is done only half as well.

This chapter discusses the items that the professional should always have as well as various special supplies that may come in handy on a variety of jobs. Standard and specialty paints are covered in Chaps. 2 and 7.

Paint Applicators and Related Equipment

Rollers

It is no small wonder that rollers are so popular. They can be used to paint large, flat surfaces in half the time that (or less than) it would take using a brush. It is also estimated that a roller fully loaded with paint—it will not drip while being taken from the tray and applied to the wall—can cover 32 ft^2. It is estimated that with a roller 2 to 4 times more paint is used than with a brush in the same amount of time.

Some terminology should be explained here. When one speaks of rollers, one is normally talking about an assembly made up of two separate components: the roller handle and the part that holds the roller cover, or the sleeve. But when one speaks of how a roller performs, the sleeve is usually being referred to.

Rollers (or roller sleeves) are available for use, as brushes are, with solvent as well as water-based paints.

In selecting a quality sleeve, there are a number of things to look at.

Anatomy of a Sleeve.   The sleeve, or roller cover, consists of a core, some type of fiber (also called *pile*), a backing for the fiber, and the adhesive that joins the fiber backing to the core. The core of the roller may be made of plastic, phenolic-impregnated kraft paper, or cardboard.

The phenolic cores are best. In manufacturing them, kraft paper is spiraled into a tube, and then the tube is immersed in pressure tanks containing phenolic resins. Phenolic cores are best because they are not readily affected by being constantly dipped in liquid—water or solvent. They keep their shape indefinitely.

Plastic cores are good, but they soften when exposed to certain solvents.

The least desirable is a third type, fiber or cardboard, which comes apart fairly quickly once it is saturated with solvent. It will last long enough to paint one room at most.

Fabric Types.   The fabric or fiber on roller covers is either synthetic, such as dacron, nylon, polyester, and orlon, or natural, such as lamb's wool, mohair, and sheepskin. The fabric may be one of these or a blend.

Lamb's wool, mohair, and sheepskin are designed for use with solvent-based formulations while synthetics are for use with latex. Lamb's wool will have an adverse reaction, just as a natural bristle brush, if used with latex; that is, it will swell and go limp.

Synthetic nap sleeves can be used with solvent-based finishes, but some alkyds contain strong solvents. It is best to read the label to see if it is okay to use these nap sleeves.

Nap Thickness.   Sleeves also come in various nap or pile thicknesses as well as qualities (Fig. 1-1). Nap thickness runs from $\frac{3}{16}$ to $1\frac{1}{2}$ in; $\frac{3}{16}$- and $\frac{1}{4}$-in thicknesses are classified as short-nap covers, $\frac{3}{8}$- to $\frac{3}{4}$-in as medium, and $\frac{3}{4}$- to $1\frac{1}{2}$-in as deep.

The mohair sleeve may have a $\frac{3}{16}$- or $\frac{1}{4}$-in pile (Fig.1-1*a*). It is used for applying gloss and semigloss paints. It produces a so-called orange peel finish, which is not perfectly smooth but which most users find acceptable. A brush or pad yields a smoother finish.

These rollers work best where the surface is perfectly smooth. If there are indentations or ridges or rises of any sort or depressions or cavities, they do not work well because the nap is not thick enough to penetrate.

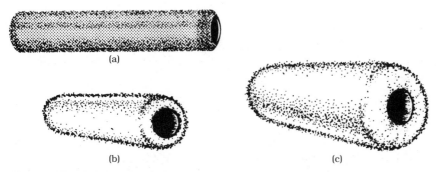

Figure 1-1. Roller sleeve naps. (*a*) Mohair nap. (*b*) Half-in nap. (*c*) Heavy (1½-in) nap. (*Courtesy of Purdy*)

However, although commonly used and designed for use with shiny paint, the short-nap roller, as mentioned, does not produce a glass-smooth finish. Rather, if it is examined closely, the finish produced resembles the skin of an orange and, in fact, is called by painters an *orange skin* or *orange peel* finish. For a glass-smooth finish, either a high-quality brush or paint pad must be used, as explained later.

For the application of flat and satin flat, that is, eggshell finish paint, the standard roller used is a ⅜-in nap. This roller can also be used to apply gloss or semigloss paint, and it has the advantage of having a nap that is deep enough to cover various imperfections in the wall or ceiling that a ³⁄₁₆- or ¼-in sleeve might miss.

A ½-in roller (Fig. 1-1*b*) is also used to apply flat and satin flat paint, but not gloss or semigloss because it does not smooth out the paint as well. The ½-in roller brings more paint, as you might expect, to the wall and can be useful if there is a question of whether the paint will cover. The more paint brought to the surface, the better the coverage.

Rollers with ½-in naps are commonly used on concrete and other semirough surfaces. They are also a good choice where a wall is a bit rough and the application of more, rather than less, paint is needed. For smooth walls, most painters favor the ⅜-in roller.

For this latter situation, some painters will use a ¾-in nap roller even on smooth walls. Painters say that this speeds the job and that by the time it is rolled out, the paint film is only the thickness of paint applied with a ½-in roller.

Some painters, particularly on the west coast, use a ¾-in lamb's-wool cover just because it holds more paint than the synthetic version. When it mats up, so be it: It is worth it, they say.

Rougher Surfaces.   The rougher the surface, the heavier or thicker the nap should be.

The ¾-in nap is commonly used on masonry surfaces, which may be too rough for the ½-in nap, although the latter is commonly the choice for concrete floors which are rougher than plaster or Sheetrock walls but which ordinarily do not require a $\frac{3}{4}$-in nap.

As mentioned, the rougher the surface, the heavier the nap. The reason is that as the nap becomes saturated with paint, it slops—the paint-saturated fibers slop into all the grooves, nooks, and crevices.

Interior work normally does not require a roller heavier than $\frac{3}{4}$-in. But some walls and ceilings are coated with textured paint or have a tooled or "worked" surface which requires the thicker naps.

On the latter, no definitive specific recommendations can be given because the degree of roughness of the surface will vary. The best idea is to start with the shortest nap that you think will work and then graduate to heavier naps as needed.

Heavier Naps Used Outside.   Exterior work commonly requires the heavier-nap rollers. They are used on concrete work—foundations—and sometimes are used on various kinds of siding. This is a very important point: Rollers are much faster for painting than brushes, outside as well as inside, and knowing this fact can make the job a lot easier.

For example, asbestos cement shingles can be painted with a $\frac{3}{4}$-in nap quite easily, thereby eliminating having to cut in with a brush where shingles overlap. It is a real time saver.

The $\frac{3}{4}$-in nap sleeve can also be used on flat wood shingles, say, cedar shingles, and on some vertical sidings.

The $1\frac{1}{2}$-in nap (Fig. 1-1c) is the thickest-nap roller. It is designed to paint rough surfaces, but it also works very well on chain-link fence. Some painters use it on siding, such as asbestos cement, because it applies so much paint that it makes cutting in unnecessary. But backrolling—going over the surface with an undipped roller—is recommended to eliminate the textured look of the extra paint applied. To paint the individual wire strands that compose the fence with a brush is a time-consuming operation. But if the heavy-nap ($1\frac{1}{2}$-in) roller is saturated with paint and drawn across the wire, it will virtually paint both sides at the same time because the paint-saturated fibers wrap around the wires; a light pass on the opposite side will finish the job.

I once was involved in a group effort—the painting of a 5-mi-long chain-link fence around a hospital in St. Alban's, Queens, New York, and it went amazingly fast with heavy-nap ($1\frac{1}{2}$-in) rollers. (Paint also floated onto parked cars, and required a cleanup which was not so fast!)

If you are in doubt about selecting a roller sleeve, there is another fail-safe system: Select by brand name. Three good ones are Purdy, Wooster, and Liebco. But note that most manufacturers have a good, better, and best line, and you should get the best. Just ask the dealer which is best.

Sleeve Quality.   To determine general quality, first look at the nap. Is it thick and substantial, or thin? To make a comparison, hold low-cost and high-cost covers side by side. The thicknesses of the material will be evident. If you can see seams, reject the sleeve. Those seams not only indicate poor quality, but they also can leave marks on the surface.

Squeeze the roller and release. Does it pop back in shape or does it keep its squeezed shape? If it does not regain its shape when it is dry, it certainly will not do so when it is soaked with paint.

Roller Handles

Roller handles come in a variety of qualities and sizes (Fig. 1-2). The standard size is 9 in, meaning that the cage or barrel part that holds the roller is 9 in long. But there are handles 7 in long and ones that are 3 and 4 in long. There is also an 18-in-wide roller for quicker wall painting.

Handles may be made of plastic or wood. Wood handles are normally an indication of top quality. The advantage of wood is that paint dribbles are absorbed into it; in plastic handles, however, paint dribbles rest on the surface, making it slippery and perhaps more difficult to hold.

Better-quality wood or plastic handles are configured for gripping by fingers. Poorer-quality handles are not shaped.

Handles, also called *roller frames,* come in three separate constructions: (1) a solid cylinder, which can be made of metal or plastic, (2) an open style with floating end caps, and (3) a spring cage frame with four or five thick wires (Fig. 1-2*a*). The cage type allows roller sleeves to be slipped on and off more easily.

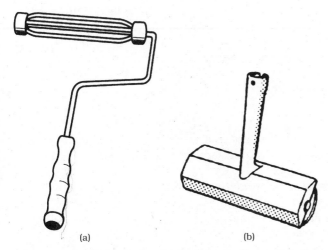

    (a)   (b)

Figure 1-2. Roller handles. (*a*) Spring cage frame. (*b*) Roller with spatter guard. (*Courtesy of Padco*)

The five-wire spring cage frame works best. It gives solid support to the roller cover along its entire length, and this translates to a more even application of the coating.

Handles with caps are poor-quality tools because there is no interior support for the roller. Solid-cylinder handles are not as commonly available as the other types, and the fact is that the cage type will suffice.

Before you purchase the handle, spin the frame to verify that it spins freely. To test the quality of roller handles, simply heft the various types. The good roller handles will be made of thicker, heavier materials which contribute to tool stability.

Here, too, Liebco, Wooster, and Purdy make good handles.

Rollers with Shields. Rollers are also available with built-in shields, trough-like sections designed to reduce dripping and spattering, in some cases by 90 percent (Fig. 1-2b). Rollers with these guards are very effective but they have to be rolled slowly, which can thwart a painter's need for speed.

Extra-Wide Rollers. For painting long, flat areas such as halls in a school, there are 18-in-wide rollers and handles. The handle has a yoke on it which can accept and hold the roller tightly. As you might expect, such a roller—double the usual 9-in size—can feel heavy after a day's painting.

Other Rollers. Rollers are also available in other sizes, such as 3 and 4 in wide, and 7 in, usually in a $\frac{3}{8}$-in nap. Such rollers are used to apply paint in tight situations, such as inside cabinets, or between areas, such as shelves, where it would be difficult to fit a 9-in roller. These smaller rollers can also be useful in painting siding and exterior trim, such as fascia boards and narrow eaves, where they can be readily drawn along the board but a 9-in roller would prove unwieldy. Some rollers, such as the one in Fig. 1-3a from Padco, can be a boon in painting some types of siding. The roller is light and easy to handle, and this type has a nap at the end so that it tends to catch the butt end of the siding sections. Long-handled versions of this roller allow the painter to reach into relatively inaccessible areas.

Another type of roller available is the texture type, or carpet roller. It is designed to work with sand paint. The carpet roller is available separately in 9-in lengths built into a 7-in part of an assembly which includes the handle and shield.

Texture rollers are made of a netted material (Fig. 1-3b). It is a dense, interwoven material. First the paint or joint compound is applied to the substrate with another tool, such as a regular roller with a $\frac{1}{2}$-in nap or a trowel, and then the texture roller is run back and forth across the surface in order to give it texture.

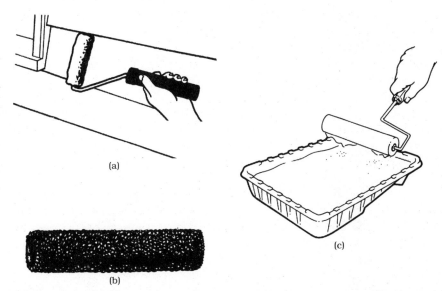

Figure 1-3. (*a*) Narrow roller. (*Courtesy of Padco*) (*b*) Texture roller. (*c*) Foam roller. (*Courtesy of Purdy*)

Another specialty roller is the pipe roller. It consists of a handle and a series of small rollers in an assembly that follows a half-circle configuration; when this roller is used, it follows the contour of the pipe. In other words, more roller surface is in contact with the pipe than would be if an ordinary roller were used.

Foam Rollers.   A number of foam rollers are available (Fig. 1-3*c*). One is the standard 9-in length. These work fairly well in a pinch, doing a good job of applying glossy paints smoothly, but they do not last a long time.

Another roller is the corner roller. This is a round piece of foam with a wedge-shaped edge built onto it as a handle. As the name suggests, this roller is designed to paint corners. The roller is drawn down the corner, and that is it. How this would beat using a brush is a mystery to me.

Another roller, made by Padco, is 4 in wide and consists of a dense foam that is designed for applying polyurethane and enamel paints smoothly. It does a good job, but the finish is the orange skin type mentioned above; glasslike smoothness is not possible.

Most roller handles are threaded to accept correspondingly threaded poles, so painting high areas is not a problem. Indeed, with appropriately sized poles, the painter can probably paint 90 percent of many houses, such as ranches, from the ground—no ladders or scaffolding is required.

Figure 1-4. Power roller. (*Courtesy of Graco*)

Power Rollers. Rollers, such as those made by Wagner, also come powered. There are various kinds, but they all work essentially the same way (Fig. 1-4). The roller is lined with a series of tiny holes. It is slipped onto the roller frame which is attached by tube, in turn, to a power unit containing a paint supply. When the power is turned on, the paint is sucked up through the hose into the roller and flows out the holes. The operator can turn the flow on and off as needed. Power rollers come as complete units and as an attachment to an airless paint sprayer.

Another type made by a number of manufacturers is the telescopic roller. Wagner's, for example, converts any standard airless pump spray (see Chap. 17) that is compatible with 1000 lb/in^2 or less; the unit can roll up to 2 gal of paint in 10 min. A trigger is squeezed—or not squeezed—to control the paint flow through a handle 55 in long, enabling the user to paint floors and standard-height ceilings as well as walls without using a ladder; 36-in extensions are also available.

The unit uses a 12-in-wide roller with an optional 9-in frame. It can be used with latex, oil, stains, and other coatings.

One type, which is highly portable, is powered by D cell batteries.

Trays

Roller trays are made of either plastic or metal (Fig. 1-5) and are commonly of a width to accommodate a 9-in-wide roller.

One main consideration in buying is to get a tray that is deep enough to hold the paint well. Both metal and plastic trays come in various depths, and those that are shallow do not hold a lot of paint—refilling often is required—and there is a greater chance that paint will slop over the edges. The metal tray in Fig. 1-5a does not hold much paint, a sure sign of inferior quality. The type of roller shown can also accept a shallow roller liner, which does not hold much either, of course.

Thin plastic tray liners are available, but it is not a good idea to use them. They are too shallow; when they are placed in a deep tray, they make the tray, in effect, shallow, too. (In a pinch a tray can be lined with heavy-duty—not light-duty, which can tear—aluminum foil.)

Trays may be made of thin to fairly thick plastic. The thin plastic is not good because it is bendable. This can be a real liability when the painter must move a tray that is half-filled with paint from one spot to another without spilling (Fig. 1-5b).

Trays may or may not have ladder-lock feet on them; these enable the tray to be locked securely onto a step of a stepladder.

(a)   (b)

Figure 1-5. Roller trays. (a) Metal tray. (b) Plastic tray.

Trays also come 18 in wide and are intended for use with the 18-in roller mentioned above. Some have a spout for filling the tray with water, stabilizing the tray so that it cannot tip and spill the 5 gal of paint that it can hold.

Grids

Professional painters commonly use a paint grid (Fig. 1-6) rather than a roller when applying the same color in a large area or a few rooms. The grid has hooks attached to it, and it hangs at a slant in a 5-gal bucket. The bucket is kept half filled with paint, which allows the painter, usually with the roller on a stick, to dip the roller into the paint and roll off any excess onto the grid. Paint can be reloaded onto the roller quickly, and the bucket can be moved along as the painting progresses.

Also, metal grids are available for use in 2-gal cans and plastic grids for use in 1-gal paint cans (Fig. 1-7). They are simply leaned against the inside of the can, and a small roller is used for painting.

Figure 1-6. Paint grid. (*Courtesy of Commercial Painters Supply Corp.*)

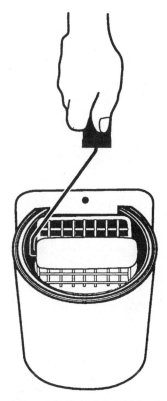

Figure 1-7. Paint grid for 1-gal cans.
(*Courtesy of Padco*)

Pads

The paint roller was a major advance in paint applicators, because it made it possible to apply paint evenly, quickly, smoothly, and easily, something that was not always possible with a brush. There, experience in using the tool was important.

The paint pad (Figs. 1-8 and 1-9), while not creating a revolution, has nevertheless proved its worth in a variety of situations. It has uses both inside and outside the house. The rougher the nap, the rougher the surface on which it can be used (Fig. 1-8a). One of its advantages as a painting tool is that there is no overspray, as there may be with a roller. Also, you can paint faster than with a brush, and paint and polyurethane can be applied smoothly.

Paint pads are used with a tray. The pad is drawn across the roller in the tray that removes and picks up paint, which is then transferred to the pad (Fig. 1-8b). Usually it is best to wipe on the coating with the back of the pad slightly raised. Another name for these is shingle pads (Fig. 1-8c), and some painters swear by them. In addition, edger pads are simple pads (Fig. 1-8d) with nibs on the edges

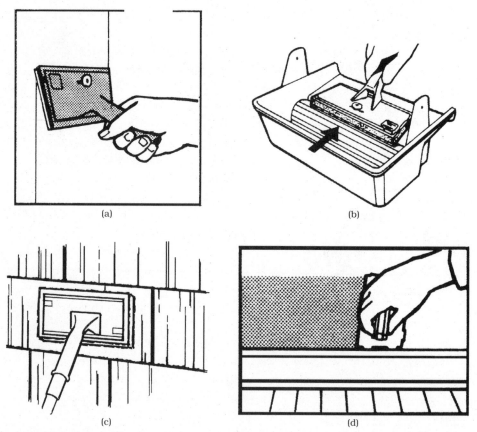

(a)   (b)

(c)   (d)

Figure 1-8. Paint pads: (*a*) Basic pad. (*b*) Pad used with a tray. (*c*) Paint pad in action. (*d*) Edger pad. (*Courtesy of Padco*)

to help guide the edger. Some have tiny projecting wheels that perform this function. Most painters do not use them.

Paint pads come in a variety of configurations, but the basic pad is 6, 8, or 10 in wide. Thousands of tiny fibers are mounted on a foam backing.

One type of pad has short fibers and is designed for applying paint or polyurethane on smooth surfaces. The material is wiped on gently.

Another pad has rougher fibers and is designed for painting cement block, concrete, stucco, and rough wood. Unlike with paint pads which wipe on the paint, a light scrubbing action is used to drive the paint into all cracks and crevices.

Manufacturers say paint pads require that only a certain amount of paint be applied, and to this end special applicator trays have been designed. The paint pad is pulled over a ridged, rotating roller in the tray and picks up the proper amount of paint. The tray can simply be set on the floor, but there are also hooks on it so that it can be suspended from a rung-type ladder.

Pads can be useful for painting shingles, depending on the type. The smooth pad is normally narrow enough to slip under shingles whose butts are slightly raised. Thus, the paint can be applied in one sweep, rather than forcing the painter to cut in the butts with a brush.

Pads for Decks.   The best way to apply stains or clear finishes to a deck is usually by brush because the material is worked into the wood by the pressure created by brush strokes.

But a second-best applicator is the stain pad. This is a regular size pad, but it has a fluffy yet strong nap perhaps 1 in thick. The pad is dipped into the coating material and then, in effect, wiped on—and in. The stain pad is the next best thing to a brush because it lets the painter drive the stain or other coating into the wood as a brush does (Fig. 1-9).

Figure 1-9. Stain pad. (*Courtesy of Padco*)

Edgers.   There are also a couple of paint pads which are used as edgers to apply the paint in close quarters. One of these is a pad with wheels projecting out just a bit from one end. The pad is dipped in paint, and then the paint is wiped on with the wheels riding against an adjacent parallel surface, such as a molding or a ceiling. The other type of edger pad has no wheels, but is simply a rectangular pad (see Fig. 1-8*d*).

Most pads, like roller handles, can accept threaded poles, although these are usually force-fit—there are no threads.

Brushes

Brushes come in a variety of sizes, and there exist some special-purpose brushes that work quite well (Figs. 1-10 and 1-11).

Generally, brushes are available in widths from 1 to 5 in. The sizes are 1, 1½, 2, 2½, 3, 4, and 5 in. These brushes are available with square-cut or angled ends, the latter for trim work. The chisel trim brush, with its slanted bristles, produces a good, straight line for cutting in (Fig. 1-10*c*). The square trim brush—the ends

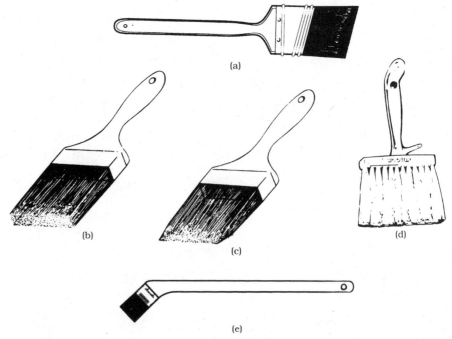

(a)

(b)

(c)

(d)

(e)

Figure 1-10. Paint brush types. (*a*) Angled. (*b*) Square trim. (*c*) Chisel trim. (*d*) Tampico. (*e*) Radiator. (*a, b, c courtesy of Wooster Brush Co.; e courtesy of Purdy*)

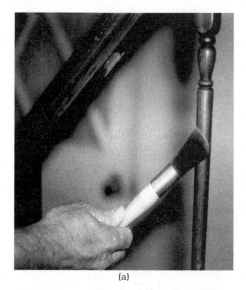 

(a)   (b)

Figure 1-11. (*a*) Round brush. (*b*) Staining brush.

of the bristles are cut square—is used primarily to apply coatings over flat areas (Fig. 1-10*b*). The angled brushes make it easier to paint windows in particular because their bristles are cut so that they do not suffer stress when paint is applied and thus last longer (Fig. 1-10*a*).

The tampico brush is designed for applying thick waterproofing paints as well as roof coatings (Fig. 1-10*d*). It has a pistol-grip handle and a clip to allow the brush to rest on the edge of the bucket. Such brushes work, but sometimes rollers work equally well—and more quickly. The radiator brush is angled to enable it to get paint behind and between radiator vanes (Fig. 1-10*e*).

The round brush has bristles arranged in a circle, and when the brush is applied to a surface, it tends to wrap itself around the surface (Fig. 1-11*a*). Its bristle design also prevents it from *fingering,* or clumping up into separate parts. The staining brush is 5 in wide and thick and has many fine bristles (Fig. 1-11*b*). The bristles are fine because stain is much thinner than paint and it works better. This brush has a removable handle; a stick can be screwed into the brush and the brush used like a broom to coat a deck.

Buy the best-quality brush possible. Wooster, Liebco, and Purdy are good brands, but be sure to get the top of the line. Good brushes hold more paint and apply it more evenly and smoothly. They make the job look better—and they save a lot of time. It is estimated that it can take a painter 25 percent longer to paint with a second-line brush than with a good one; a poor-quality brush can make the job up to 80 percent longer. To translate that into real time, if a job took 4 h with a good brush, it would take an extra 3 h or so with a low-quality brush, and the job would not look that good.

Most pros buy the best and then take care of them, for they are the tools of their livelihood. Some painters have had brushes for decades.

Just what sizes you select will be more or less arbitrary—within reason. But figure a 2-in angled brush for trim such as windows and a 3-in brush for baseboards and application of glossy paints to doors and cabinets. If large, flat areas of wall are to be brush-painted, a 4- or 5-in brush should be used.

Natural and Synthetic Bristles. In selecting high-quality brushes, the main factor is what the bristles are made of. It is a cardinal rule in painting that natural or animal hair brushes must be used with oil-based paint and synthetic bristles with water-based paint.

Prior to World War II, all brushes were made of animal hair rather than synthetic materials. Indeed, synthetic materials were not needed because most of the paint being used was oil-based.

Natural Bristles. The best natural brushes were made with bristles from Russian and Chinese hogs. The hogs, or wild boars, developed thick hair in response to harsh winters, and the natural vegetation nourished them. They were—and still are—the best natural bristles available today for several reasons.

First, hog bristles are long. The bristles will wear down even faster than synthetic bristles, but it will still take time and because of their length it takes a while before the hog bristle brush becomes useless.

Second, they are thinner and tapered at the ends, which tends to allow more control in applying the paint.

Third, the ends are "flagged," or split (Fig. 1-12). Flagged ends hold paint better and spread it more evenly than unsplit ends. Flagged ends are characteristic of animal hair used for brushes, such as hog's hair. Manufacturers of synthetic brushes make them flagged.

In the industry *natural bristle* does not have to mean hog hair. Today hair from other animals is used including horsehair from tails and manes, bear, beaver, skunk, and squirrel tail (often called *camel's hair,* which seems a stretch). But they are not terribly well suited for house painting, although they have other uses. (Sable, badger, and camel's hair are not as big in diameter and as stiff as hog hair and are used as artist's brushes or, when mixed with other bristles, such as badger, are preferred for fine glazing and graining, while horsehair is used for dusting brushes.)

Natural bristle brushes (also called *China bristle* because of their origins) should, as mentioned, only be used with oil-based paints. If they are used with water-based paints, the natural hollowness of the bristles absorbs moisture—

Figure 1-12. Unsplit (*left*) versus flagged (*right*) brush tips. (*Courtesy of Wooster Brush Co.*)

up to 40 percent of their weight. Hence, they swell and become soft and limp, just as human hair does, when wet.

Synthetic Bristles.   Brushes made with synthetic bristles, which have no natural hair in them, are best for water-based paint because they do not absorb that much water. One major synthetic material is nylon, and this absorbs only 4 percent of its own weight. Polyester, the other major synthetic material, does not absorb any water at all.

While there is no question that synthetic materials should only be used for water-based paint, the question is, Which is the best choice?

Pure nylon bristle brushes are more flexible than polyester and provide a smoother coat. Also they are more abrasion-resistant than polyester and last longer, particularly when used on a rough surface.

On the positive side for polyester, it holds its shape better when heat is intense. For example, at 100°F nylon will go soft while polyester will not (though it makes one wonder who would be painting in such heat), and nylon is also sensitive to certain chemicals, such as ketones.

Many brushes are blends of nylon and polyester, with the idea being to combine the best qualities of each type of material while keeping the negative characteristics out.

Bristle ends may be either square cut or tapered or "chisel cut" (also called *chisel-edged* or *level*); the bristles on the outside of the brush are longer than those on the inside, or level. The tapered brushes allow a sharper paint line to be made, facilitating cutting in.

With level or flat brushes, all the bristles are the same length. Such brushes are not used when precision is wanted, but for doing broad, flat areas.

Synthetic brushes made of nylon or a blend of nylon and polyester are chisel-cut and can have ends that are cut so the bristle tips are flagged. But there exist synthetic flat brushes of lower quality made of many different *filaments* (which is the technical term for bristles) which are cut flat such as vinyl, styrene, and polyolefin.

Construction.   A high-quality brush is well made. For one thing, the butt ends of the bristles will be firmly anchored inside the ferrule—the metal band that runs around the brush and holds the bristle assembly to the handle. The bristles may be attached by vulcanized rubber or an epoxy glue that is resistant to water, oil, and solvents. Such brushes will not shed their bristles. The ferrule may be made of stainless steel, nickel, or brass.

High-quality brushes also have plugs inside the ferrule made of wood, aluminum, plastic, or a specially treated cardboard. First, the plugs help ensure a tight bond of the bristles in the ferrule. Second, they add taper to the brush, making it thicker at the base of the bristles and narrower at the ends, allowing for a sharper line. Third, they provide "wells" inside the bristles, which allows more paint to be loaded without dripping and keeps the center of the brush somewhat open for easier cleaning. Some brushes also have an insert—a narrow metal band inside the ferrule.

Brush Handles.   Handles may be made of plastic or wood. Wood tends not to slip out of one's grasp whereas plastic does. However, wood can crack and split if it is left in cleaning solutions for prolonged periods.

The handle should counterbalance the weight of the bristles. Handles come in various shapes, and the painter should handle them, much as one would try on a pair of shoes, before purchasing.

Quality Testing.   A brush can be tested for quality. Every new brush will shed a few bristles. But when you fan the bristles a few times and they continue to fall out, the brush's quality is suspect.

When pressed against a surface, the bristles should bend one-third to one-half in relation to the tips. Also, when pressed against a dry surface, the bristles should not divide into clumps, or "finger." If they do, they will also finger when wet, and uneven application will result. Finally, the bristles should snap back into position after this dry bending.

Other Brushes.   In addition to angle, sash, and wall brushes, there are a number of other useful ones.

The *stencil brush* has a short handle and bristles mounted as in a shaving brush. As the name suggests, it is usually used with a stencil; that is, the stencil is put in place, and the paint is dabbed on. It is also very good for coating carved moldings.

The *round brush* also resembles a shaving brush, but it has a round, long, tapered handle (Fig. 1-11*a*). It is good for painting narrow, round objects, such as pipes. When the brush is drawn along the pipe, the bristles tend to wrap around it.

Varnish and enamel brushes are 2 to 3 in wide and are designed for applying thick, glossy coatings. They are made of fine animal fibers. Some may have an oval shape, may be almost flat, and may be thicker midway across the ferrule.

The *staining brush* has very fine bristles and is 5 in wide (Fig. 1-11*b*). This brush is designed to apply exterior stains. It is able to be loaded with stain and minimize dripping of this wafer-thin material.

The *stippling brush* looks like a scrub brush with a handle made of aluminum or wood and $3\frac{1}{2}$ to 9 in long. The bristles are dipped into the paint and then dabbed on the surface. This brush is used to create special effects, as detailed in Chap. 7.

Stucco and masonry brushes have wide, thick bristles. Some look like stipple brushes; others look like flat wall brushes (Fig. 1-10*d*). The bristles are usually made of nylon. This brush is used to apply cement paint, paste, or other thick coatings to rough surfaces. (*Note:* A heavy-nap roller is usually much easier to use.)

Roofing brushes are triple-headed brushes about $3\frac{1}{2}$ to 7 in wide and are designed for painting shingle roofs. They work like scrub brushes.

The *radiator brush* has a long, thin handle and angled bristles so that it can paint behind and between radiator sections (Fig. 1-10*c*).

Artist's brushes are slim brushes which sometimes come in handy for painting very delicate, narrow lines.

Paint Mitts

The paint mitt is for painting metal where using a brush or other applicator would take a long time because of the intricate shape of the item. For example, the paint mitt would be good to use on a fire escape or wrought-iron fence with a number of thin railings and fancy ironwork. The mitt is just dipped into the

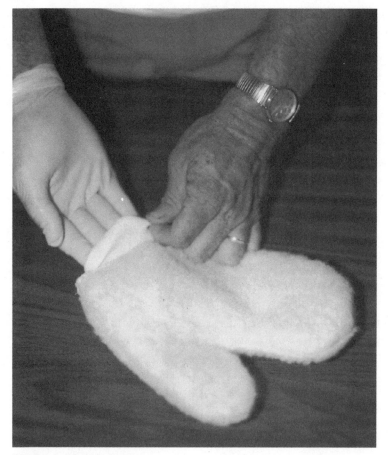

Figure 1-13. Paint mitt.

paint; then the part is grasped, and the mitt is run down its length, painting all sides at the same time. And you can paint anything that your fingers can snake into.

Paint mitts (Fig. 1-13) are available in various qualities. If you look at good- and poor-quality ones, you'll know right away which is best. When saturated with paint, the mitt is an excellent tool for painting intricate surfaces. It is best to wear a vinyl glove under it to protect against paint seeping through.

Brush and Roller Accessories

One of the most difficult situations I ever faced in painting a house was an eave of a roof which was about 10 ft above another roof. There was no safe way to set up a ladder, so I ended up using a brush holder—an accessory that can be screwed onto the end of a pole and which, in turn, has clamps for holding the brush (Fig. 1-14). The handle of a brush or scraper or wire brush is slipped into a clamp and tightened in place by turning down nuts. The holder can be rotated and locked at various angles, allowing places to be worked on that would be hard to reach with other tools. I remember carefully dipping the brush in the stain and then raising the brush to the eave and swabbing it home.

(In a pinch I could have used duct tape to attach the handle of the brush to the pole, but this felt a bit more secure.)

This is but one of a number of useful accessories to be aware of that can make jobs easier, faster, and safer.

Paint poles are one such accessory. These are made in a variety of materials and lengths from 1-ft-long multipiece units that can be used individually or screwed together to create a pole 4 ft or so long on up to telescoping poles which extend 20 ft or more.

Poles are made of wood, plastic, or fiberglass. The wood poles are 4 ft long. Some have a wood thread cut into the end, but these are not the kind to get. The threads can become misshapen, and will not fit the roller well. If this occurs, the pole can be salvaged by a device which has threads on it and can be clamped onto the end of the pole.

Wood poles that have metal threads (Fig. 1-15) are better. These will not become misshapen. Some poles are secured by force friction fitting them into the roller handle (or brush holder), such as when they are used with the line of Padco paint applicators.

Plastic poles are also threaded at the end. Plastic poles are 4 ft or longer. To use the longer types, the telescoping part is pulled out and then locked in place at the desired length by twisting it.

Figure 1-14. Extension brush holder.
(*Courtesy of Commercial Painters Supply Corp.*)

Figure 1-15. Metal threading device for
wooden extension poles. (*Courtesy of
Commercial Painters Supply Corp.*)

Fiberglass poles are the sturdiest of all—and the heaviest. They are available
in telescoping sizes. Their disadvantage is their weight. The longer the pole, the
heavier it is and the more difficult it is to handle. Trying to paint the top of a
house with such a pole could be difficult. However, it could be just what you
need for painting a flagpole or other item that is very high.

Fiberglass poles do have the advantage over aluminum and wood of being
shockproof. We have all read stories about people being electrocuted when the
ladders they were standing on contacted an electric wire.

Scrapers and Joint and Putty Knives

Scrapers

The painter should have a variety of paint scrapers in his or her tool arsenal
(Fig. 1-16).

The standard scraper is 3 to $3\frac{1}{2}$ in wide, of rigid or flexible metal and angled.
For scraping, the rigid blade is recommended; the flexible blade, as suggested
below, is more for applying patching material.

Some scrapers can be threaded onto an extension pole (Fig. 1-16c). The result
is a tool where more pressure can be applied and which will also allow high-
up areas to be scraped from the ground.

For pure manual power in scraping, the hook scraper cannot be beat (Fig.
1-16a). It comes in various versions but essentially consists of a bent-over blade
that is pulled across areas where paint is peeling. When one edge on the blade
dulls, it can be reversed to bring a new edge into play.

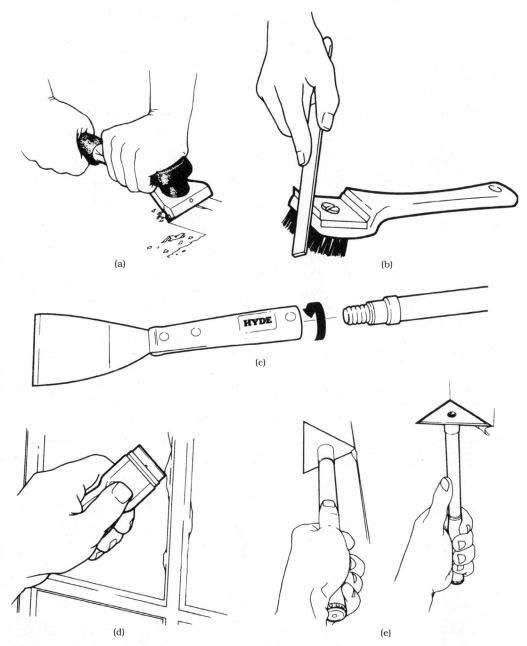

(a)

(b)

(c)

(d)

(e)

Figure 1-16. Scrapers. (*a*) Hook type. (*b*) Hook type with blade sharpener. (*c*) Rigid scraper. (*d*) Razor blade. (*e*) Triangular shape. (*Courtesy of Hyde Tools*)

Some hook-type scrapers have carbon-steel blades that can be sharpened with a file (Fig. 1-16b). Some also have a wire brush, handy for scraping dense peelings or rust.

The triangular scraper can be used to scrape flat surfaces as well as corners. Interchangeable tips allow rounded grooved surfaces to be scraped (Fig. 1-16e).

The razor-blade scraper is good for scraping paint off windows (Fig. 1-16d). The unit uses ordinary single-edge razor blades which are retractable.

Variation in Quality.   A standard scraper has its limits, but it can accomplish most scraping jobs inside and outside the house.

For jobs where there is a great deal of scraping to be done, a hook-type scraper is recommended. This comes in a couple of sizes but essentially consists of a long handle with a blade on the end; this blade is a flat piece of metal with two edges sharpened and bent over. The tool is used by pulling it across the area where paint is peeling. Its big asset is the pressure with which it can be applied.

When one edge of the blade wears down, a new edge can be used. A screw holding the blade to the handle is loosened, and then the blade is rotated to bring the new edge into play.

Even better, you can get the hook-type scraper (Fig. 1-16b) with a carbon-steel blade that can be sharpened with a file.

Wire brushes (which are discussed below) may also be used for removing peeling paint.

For Patching.   Standard-size scrapers ($3\frac{1}{2}$ in) are also used for applying plaster and spackling compound. Here, it is best to use a scraper with a flexible blade (Fig. 1-17a). A flexible-blade scraper simply is able to apply patchers smoothly because more of the surface is in contact with the material, therefore allowing better feathering of the material. A rigid scraper does not work as well except when applying patcher to very small holes.

Scrapers come in a variety of qualities with both plastic and wood handles. The wood-handled versions are usually better and are recommended.

Power scrapers are also available. These consist of regular scrapers that are driven by a small motor. Wagner is one manufacturer.

Joint Knives

A close cousin to the scraper is the *joint knife,* so called because it is mainly used for applying joint compound when taping the joints of drywall panels (Fig. 1-17b).

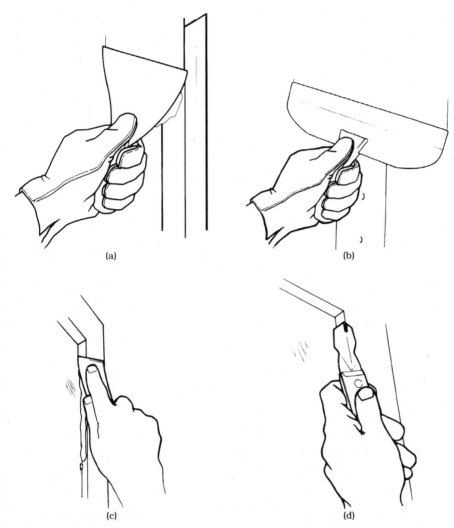

Figure 1-17. Various applicators. (*a*) Scraper with flexible blade.
(*b*) Joint knife. (*c*) Putty knife. (*d*) Putty knife with both flat and slanted blades.
(*Courtesy of Hyde Tools*)

These knives range from 6 to 12 in wide. The 6-in size can be used for light scraping, but its basic use is to apply joint compound. Its width and flexibility allow it to do a good job of smoothing other patching materials.

Joint knives come in different qualities. Handling and hefting them should quickly show which is best, and price will certainly be an indication of quality.

Putty Knives

A couple of putty knives, so called because their main job is to apply window putty (today more properly called *glazing compound*), are also essential (Fig. 1-17c). These come with plastic and wood handles. Again, manufacturers have good, better, and best lines. Get the best.

If you are not good at applying glazing compound in a neat bead, one tool that works well is the combination putty knife–applicator (Fig. 1-17d). With this the putty can be applied more easily than with a regular putty knife. It has a slotted blade that rides along the window frame as the putty is applied. The flat part is used to scrape out and apply dabs of glazing compound, and the slotted end is used to apply it. The slotted end makes getting a smooth bead easier for apprentices.

Sandpaper and Sandpaper Accessories

Sandpaper Accessories

Sandpaper can be bought by the sheet, folded over, and applied where needed. However, there are a number of accessories available that can make working with sandpaper easier.

One such is sanding blocks (Fig. 1-18). In a standard sanding block, paper is cut to the proper length, then the ends are clamped in place on a rubber sanding surface. A good way to save money here is to cut standard sandpaper sheets into block-sized pieces rather than buying them precut.

In a sanding block with a handle, paper is installed just as in a regular sanding block (Fig. 1-18b). It allows more pressure to be applied to the surface and has a larger sanding surface than that of the regular block. This type of block works the same way as the smaller one except it is bigger and can be used for sanding wide patches or joint compound.

A sanding stick accepts paper as other blocks do (Fig. 1-18c). The blocks, however, are made so they can swivel when screwed into the stick, so the surface of the block can stay flush with the substrate. Such blocks are made of plastic and metal; the metal one is better.

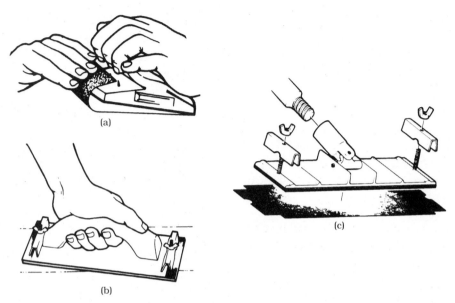

Figure 1-18. Sanding blocks. (*a*) Standard block. (*b*) Block with handle. (*c*) Sanding stick.

Sanding Stick

For sanding large areas, the sanding stick is the way to go (Fig. 1-19). A sanding pad is permanently attached to the end of a pole, but it is loosely joined so that the pad can conform to the surface being sanded. Its most common use is for sanding drywall joints. The eccentric head lies flat.

Sandpaper

Sandpaper is essentially an abrasive material bonded to a backing of paper or other material (Fig. 1-20). It is, of course, a vital tool for the painter in giving patches of various kinds their ultimate smoothness.

Sandpaper is classified by the type of abrasive or grit used, its weight, type of coating, and grit number. The back of the sandpaper describes what type of grit there is and the degree of fineness.

Four grit materials are commonly used: aluminum oxide, emery, garnet, and silicon carbide.

The grits come in various hardnesses and so are suitable for sanding certain materials. Garnet, which is a reddish-brown abrasive, is the softest of all and is used on wood almost exclusively. Emery, a black abrasive, is used on metal. Next up the scale of hardness is aluminum oxide, which is exceptionally hard and long-wearing and can be used on wood, painted surfaces, alloy steel, high-carbon steel, tough bronzes, and some hardwoods.

The hardest grit of all is silicon carbide, a bluish-black sandpaper which is good on aluminum, copper, cast iron, and plastic.

Grit comes in varying degrees of coarseness, varying from 12—which is very coarse—to 1200—which is superfine. (The higher the grit number, the smoother the material.) If sandpaper is being used in a machine, lower numbers are used than for corresponding hand sanding.

Sandpaper also comes in *open* and *closed coated* varieties. On closed-coat papers the grit particles cover all the paper. This leads to the paper's becoming clogged with the material, such as wood, being sanded. Open-coated papers have more space between grit particles and do not clog as quickly. Indeed, they can be cleaned and reused.

Figure 1-19. Sanding stick in action.
(*Courtesy of Wm. Zinsser & Co.*)

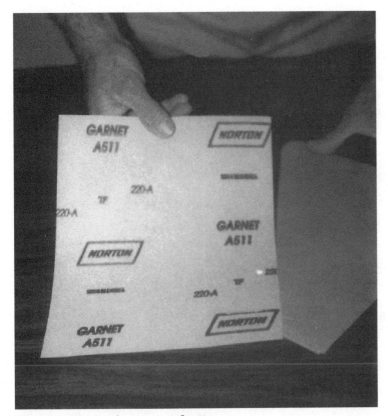

Figure 1-20. Sandpaper specifications.

Sandpapers also are fabricated for wet and dry sanding. The backing on wet sandpapers is made to resist water and may be dipped into water or a light lubricating oil to effect final polishing.

In general, for scuff-sanding a 220-grit paper is recommended. Sanding of plaster patches is normally done with medium or 100-grit paper. Specific sandpapers are suggested as various procedures are described in the book.

There is also available a screen type of sandpaper for sanding joint compound and plaster (Fig. 1-21). This looks like screening; as the surface is sanded, the dust particles escape through the holes, preventing clogging. A plus is that it lets you sand without having to stop frequently to change clogged sheet. These particular screens (Wetordy) are coated with a hard silicon carbide that lets both sides of the screen be used.

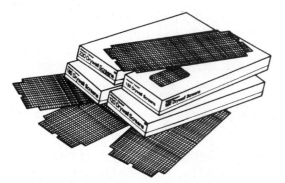

Figure 1-21. Drywall screening paper. (*Courtesy of Commercial Painters Supply Corp.*)

Ladders and Scaffolding

Ladders

The painter uses two kinds of ladder in everyday work: the stepladder and the extension ladder.

Stepladders.   As with anything else, the idea is to buy a high-quality stepladder. They come in three grades: type 3, or household grade; type 2, or commercial grade; and type 1, industrial grade. Type 1 is rated at 200 lb while type 2 is 225 lb and type 3 is 250 lb; but the weight tests are conducted at 4 times these values.

The painter should get the type 1 ladder. The standard length is 6 ft, but they are available in lengths from 2 to 16 ft. A 6-ft ladder is definitely a must, but one that is 8 or even 10 ft can come in handy, particularly for painting cathedral ceilings. As jobs progress, you'll be better able to determine what works best for you.

Ladders are made of wood, metal, or fiberglass. Fiberglass and wood are heavy while metal weighs perhaps half of what wood does. Although it is sturdy, aluminum can bend a little which might seem disconcerting. The best bet is go to the store and climb up and see how you like each kind.

Extension Ladders.   Extension ladders are available in sizes up to 40 ft, and, like stepladders, they are made of wood, aluminum, or fiberglass (Fig. 1-22). Aluminum is the lightest, but it does conduct electricity. Wood is heavy and can conduct also (when wet) while fiberglass does not.

They also come in various grades. The professional should get type 1, which is the strongest grade available. It does not necessarily mean, however, that the ladder is top-quality. Here, stick to good brands such as Werner and Keller, but get their top-of-the-line product. If an extension ladder accepts replacement parts, this is an indication of top quality.

Many painters prefer fiberglass ladders for the simple reason that they do not conduct electricity, unlike aluminum and wood, when wet. Every year people get killed while using aluminum stepladders.

Figure 1-22. Extension ladder. (*Courtesy of Commercial Painters Supply Corp.*)

Note, incidentally, that some power companies, if given enough notice, will disconnect incoming power lines where they connect with trim so the painter has free access to work without any risk of shock. The power company normally will provide alternate power so the occupants' lives are not disrupted while the regular power line is down.

Ladder Accessories.   There are many ladder accessories available, but by far the most common and popular with painters are ladder jacks, which hook onto rungs and across which an extension plank—or just a stout board—can be laid. These come in various versions but are inexpensive and efficient.

A standoff accessory that hooks onto the top of the ladder can also be useful, particularly when you are painting windows. It lets you paint the entire window from one ladder position.

Roof brackets are also handy. Here, shingles are lifted, and the brackets are secured beneath with nails driven into the decking. A board is then extended across them, providing a scaffold for the painter.

This setup is excellent for safe and easier painting of dormers. *Tip:* Only secure the brackets in the morning when roof shingles are not soft. If you lift them when soft, say, after a day in sunlight, they could tear. Some painters wet them down to cool them off before lifting them.

And there are many other accessories that you might find useful. A trip to a well-stocked paint store or home improvement center will be instructive.

Scaffolding

Most painters will not have need for scaffolding, but on some jobs, say, where there is a long, unobstructed section of wall to paint, or the job involves extensive repairs, scaffolding may be called for.

It can be rented, and the sections put together like an Erector set. Scaffolding also has wheels, so you can roll it along as you go.

Scaffolding does not take long to assemble.

Miscellaneous Equipment

Utility Knife

A utility knife is also an essential in the painter's tool arsenal. A variety of types are sold, but the standard one consists of a handle in which blades are mounted with more or less of the cutting edge exposed by manipulation of a button, which slides the blade forward or backward.

In the last few years, a new generation of utility knives with break-away blades have come on the scene. Here, the handle is loaded with a blade which is segmented into parts. As each part of the blade grows dull, it can be clipped off and a new, sharp section used. Such blades can be especially useful in hanging wall coverings where sharp blades make trimming the wall covering easier.

Wire Brushes

These are thought of as being for scraping peeling paint off metal, but wire brushes can also be used to scrape paint off wood. And they are particularly useful where the surface is ridged and does not readily allow a standard scraper to be used. Here, the wire brush can be pulled down along the ridged surface, and its stiff yet flexible wires do a good job of removing peeling paint.

Wire brushes come in a variety of configurations, from those shaped like scrub brushes to ones with long, curved handles to ones with wide handles (Fig. 1-23). The wire brush in Fig. 1-23b has a knuckle guard which protects fingers while allowing good force to be applied. Toothbrush-sized wire brushes let you wire brush areas which would be inaccessible to regular-sized brushes (Fig. 1-23c). For really tough brushing jobs, the straight-back wire brush design allows maximum pressure to be applied (Fig. 1-23d).

Some wire brushes also have a scraper blade mounted on the back for minor scraping.

Wire brushes come with the bristles made of a variety of materials. Stainless steel is recommended. The other types—steel, aluminum, and brass—will wear away while in use and can leave a metallic residue on the surface. This can change the surface texture and mar the job by reflecting sun improperly. Also, paint

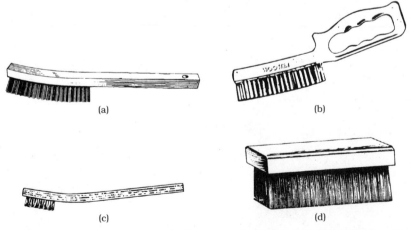

(a)

(b)

(c)

(d)

Figure 1-23. Wire brushes. (*a*) Classic style. (*b*) Wire brush with knuckle guard. (*c*) Detail brush. (*d*) Straight-back brush. (*Courtesy of Commercial Painters Supply Corp.*)

applied may look discolored, and steel residue may rust if water-based paint is used over it.

Caulking Gun

Caulk is available in two basic forms: tubes or cartridges. The cartridge type is standard and is dispensed with a cartridge gun (Fig. 1-24). Cartridge guns come in a couple of versions, and the byword again is *quality.*

Guns come in a number of hand-operated forms, including one that has a barrellike housing for the cartridge and another which has a framelike one.

To determine the quality of cartridge guns, pick them up and try them out. You should be able to see which is best, and price will certainly indicate quality. At least one manufacturer—Wagner—sells a powered caulking gun.

Caulking guns are normally thought of for outside use, but they can serve well inside, particularly for patching cracks in joints that keep reopening. Flexible caulk expands and contracts with house movement.

Mixing Accessories

Mixing of paint is ordinarily done by "boxing" it—pouring it back and forth between cans—or mixing with a stick.

A variety of accessories are available for power mixing as well (Fig. 1-25). Some are simple L-shaped metal sections designed to be chucked into a drill while others, also used with an electric drill, resemble eggbeaters in design.

Such mixing accessories can be useful for mixing joint compound and other patchers as well. In the heaviest versions, the accessories can be used for mixing concrete and joint compound.

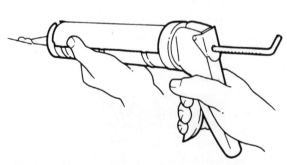

Figure 1-24. Caulking gun. (*Courtesy of Hyde Tools*)

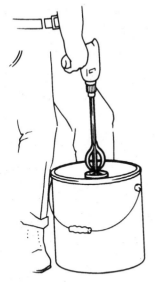

Figure 1-25. Paint mixer. (*Courtesy of Hyde Tools*)

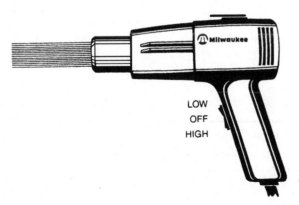

LOW
OFF
HIGH

Figure 1-26. Heat gun. (*Courtesy of Commercial Painters Supply Corp.*)

Heat Gun

For the painter, the heat gun, which is also known as the *paint stripper* and the *hot air gun*, has a number of uses other than removing paint (Fig. 1-26). It can be used to soften caulk or window putty to make it easier to scrape off; indeed, removing window putty can be a very annoying job. It can also be used to dry paint or patcher, when speed is essential. It has, of course, other uses around the home.

It is important to realize that a heat gun emits a tremendous amount of heat, being capable of operating at temperatures in excess of 1200°F. Such high temperatures can be hazardous in terms of both injury and fire. Chapter 12 on preparation gives tips on using the heat gun.

Cloths

Drop Cloths.   I once knew a painter who was so good, so neat, that he did not require drop cloths. I must say that the sight of him painting in a living room containing wall-to-wall carpeting, glass-top tables, and the like without protecting them was very unusual.

Most of us, however, are mere mortals, and we do need to use drop cloths. A variety are available, some of which are waterproof (or paintproof) while others are not.

Plastic drops come in various thicknesses and sizes, usually ranging from 1 to 6 mils thick. As the sheeting gets thicker, the overall size gets bigger. Hence, a 9- by 12-ft plastic drop cloth might be 1 or 2 mils thick while a 10- by 20-ft one might be 4 mils thick.

Plastic drops are usually recommended for use over furniture and the like where their waterproofness is a boon, but not on the floor. Plastic is slippery and can be hazardous underfoot. Note, too, that paint takes a long time to dry on plastic and could be transferred to other things. For floors, canvas drop cloths are good. These come in various weights; the 8-oz size, while not totally liquidproof, will prevent most spatters from seeping through.

Tack Cloth.   After wood is sanded, a certain amount of dust is left, and it is important to remove this. If an oil-based product is going to be used, the tack cloth can be used to wipe up the dust. The small square of cloth is sticky, and it is designed to take off more dust than mere dusting could accomplish.

If a water-based product is to be used, then a damp cloth is advisable; the tack cloth can leave a residue that can interfere with coating adhesion.

Burlap.   This is good for wiping away wood filler before applying a coating.

Other Equipment

Brush Comb.   This looks like a comb except the bristles are hard metal set fairly widely apart (in comparison to a comb) and mounted on a handle (Fig. 1-27). It is used to comb out brush bristles after use. As one paints, paint tends to build up in the heel of the brush. To clear a brush of this buildup, it is always a good

Figure 1-27. Brush comb. (*Courtesy of Hyde Tools*)

idea to comb out the bristles, starting from the ferrule. A buildup can prevent the bristles from moving freely.

Carpenter Square. When a large patch is made in Sheetrock, this can be essential to cut the patch squarely.

C Clamp. These C-shaped devices which are tightened down with a worm gear can be very useful to the housepainter. On more than a few occasions it is necessary to rig something for various purposes, and C clamps are invaluable for safety and security.

For example, the exterior of a house on very sloping terrain may need to be painted. When set in place, one leg of the ladder may not reach the ground while the ladder is kept level. To remedy this, a stout board can be attached by C clamp onto the bottom of the ladder rail, to make the leg as long as it has to be to level the ladder.

Another instance of the need for C clamps is found in creating scaffolding. This is often done by setting two stepladders a short distance from each other and parallel to a wall. A stout board is set on corresponding steps, and C clamps are used to make sure it stays solidly in position.

Cleaner Tool. This tool has teeth on one side for combing out brushes and a half-moon shape on the other. It is used to run along and squeeze paint out of a roller prior to washing.

Cold Chisel. This type of chisel, which comes in various sizes, has a tempered blade and is hard enough to cut through steel. But the painter can use it for chipping out plaster and concrete prior to making patches or chipping out broken shingles.

Circuit Tester. This is a device to ensure that the electricity is off. When there's a question, the circuit tester will resolve it.

Dust Brush. Any old brush will do (horsehair is best, though). It is used to dust moldings and the like before painting.

Electric Drill. A drill is required for a variety of jobs. Equipped with the right accessory, it can be used to strip rust or paint. One can also chuck a mixing bit in it, as mentioned before, to mix paint. Electric drills are available in corded and cordless models.

Files. Files come in various cuts, but a flat file or two in the mil cut will serve the painter well. Files can be used to resharpen the blades of hook-type scrapers or perhaps to remove rust.

Keyhole Saw. This tool, which gets its name from the fact that it can cut the hole for a lock mechanism, has a curved handle and toothed blade. It is good for cutting plasterboard, which is often needed to make patches.

Nail Set. Many times in painting wood or drywall, the painter will discover that nailheads are protruding slightly. For a neater job, these should be set below the surface, something the nail set achieves quite well. Then the depression is spackled over.

Razor-Blade Scraper. Occasionally, paint can spatter on hard, smooth surfaces, particularly glass. When dry, this paint is easy to remove with a razor-blade scraper. It consists of a flat handle and a retractable single edge. It readily peels the paint off the surface.

   If you wish, you can also use regular single-edge blades, but these are not as easy to manage as the blade mounted in the handle.

Spinner Tool. This is a good tool for cleaning brushes and rollers (Fig. 1-28). The brush or roller is mounted on the spinner, and pumping the handle, much as you would use an eggbeater, spins the brush or roller rapidly, driving off excess paint and solvent. It is best to do this inside a large box so that overspray does not stain nearby objects. It is also known as a *dry spinner.*

Caulks

As mentioned before, caulk is a sealant used to seal seams in the house. On the outside it is used wherever dissimilar materials meet, such as where windows

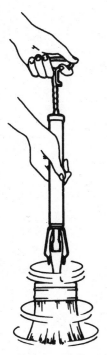

Figure 1-28. Spinning tool for cleaning brushes and rollers. (*Courtesy of Hyde Tools*)

meet siding, and on the inside to seal seams around the tub or where a kitchen counter meets a wall.

A wide variety of caulks are available. There are a couple of general distinctions to note. First, to be used inside the house, a caulk should state on the label that it is *mildew-resistant*. This means it contains a mildewcide that resists the formation of mildew. Exterior caulks do not necessarily contain a mildewcide. Many caulks make excellent adhesives. For example, silicone, which happens to be the Cadillac of caulks (because it can last so long), is a tenacious adhesive that can be used for a variety of jobs.

There are many caulks which seem to have distinct uses, such as sealing around a chimney or windows, but which have, in fact, the same ingredients. Only the color may vary. Check the label. Manufacturers like users to buy a different caulk for each job when just one would do the trick in a wide variety of applications.

- *Latex with acrylic.* This is available in a variety of colors, and it can be used for sealing around windows and doors as well as the tub and wall. Note that some caulks are labeled latex but contain no acrylic, which is an important ingredient.

- *Butyl rubber.* This comes in white or gray. It is an excellent caulk, because of its resilience, for use where masonry moves, such as between the house wall and a patio and driveway. It can also be used to repair cracks in sidewalks.

  Once applied, butyl rubber caulk, because it is so sticky, is better left alone. If you try to tool it, it will stick to the applicator.

- *Silicone.* This Cadillac of caulks comes in a variety of colors and clear. As mentioned, it is the best caulk available and is more expensive than others. It will stick to almost anything. Standard silicone caulk cannot be painted without the paint rolling off the caulk, but there are some types that can be painted.

- *Oil-based caulk.* This is the low end on the quality spectrum. While cheap, it dries hard and is not very durable.

- *Aerosol caulk.* This is dispensed from a spray can and expands as it is released. It dries hard and waterproof. As such, it is a good filler when great gaps exist in materials, such as where shingles meet the foundation.

- *Caulking cord.* This is a soft, segmented material that can serve as a caulk or as filler before caulking is applied (Fig. 1-29). As a caulk, it remains flexible

Figure 1-29. Caulking cord.

and can be stripped off as needed. The most common brand name is Mortite. This comes flat and segmented into six beads of various sizes. Beads are stripped off as needed. It has various uses (including use as a sealer around a sink drain). Caulking cord can be used inside or outside as a caulk, but it also makes an excellent filler caulk. On cracks that are particularly deep, the caulk is laid in place to fill, then other caulk is applied.

Miscellaneous Materials

A variety of materials will be required, some serving equally well for interior and exterior painting. Following is a roundup.

Acetone

This is nail polish remover. It is a highly volatile material: It has a zero *flash point*, meaning it will ignite when the temperature outside is 0°F or above. To understand that, consider that paint thinner will ignite only above 107°F.

Acetone is used as a thinner and cleaner. It cleans contact cement, lacquer, epoxy, as well as polyester and vinyl resin. Acetone can be used to remove dry latex paint. It evaporates very quickly.

As with any other chemical, test it first on a small section of the material to be treated, to make sure it has no adverse effect, such as leaching out the color.

Acoustic Patch

This patch is used to repair loose, damaged, or puffy acoustical ceiling materials. It comes in two colors to match tile, new white and old white. (There is also a special thin acoustic paint which will not interfere with soundproofing.)

Ammonia

The nonsudsing type of ammonia is very good for cleaning glossy surfaces prior to painting because it does not create a soapy film. Also, when mixed half and half with water, ammonia will take off shellac.

Bleach

This comes in various qualities. Clorox or something with similar strength (5% hypochlorite) is suggested. Bleach is the only thing available to the painter that can kill mildew, and it is the basis of a cleaning solution for both interior and exterior work.

Brush Cleaner

Occasionally, a paint brush is left out, and the paint in it hardens to the point where the brush cannot be cleaned by ordinary means and is useless. This is where the brush cleaner comes in. Hard brushes can be soaked in this potent blend of chemicals and become soft again, so that the paint can be washed away.

Brush cleaner is not expensive and can be well worth its cost, if it brings a brush back to life that costs 10 times as much. Brush cleaner commonly can be rinsed away with water, but it is also highly flammable.

Degreasers

These products are made to remove oil and grease from asphalt on concrete driveways. Check the label. Some are designed for concrete and others for asphalt. Basically, these are poured on and washed off.

Denatured Alcohol

This is alcohol which has been chemically modified. It is the prime thinner of shellac and, in fact, is used to make the various "cuts" of shellac. (See below.)

Glazing Compound

This used to be known as *putty,* but for some years now it has been called *glazing compound,* which is far more flexible than window putty. Glazing compound comes in two forms: oil-based and latex-based, which comes in a cartridge. Note that the oil-based version requires that an oil-based primer or paint be used on top of it, whereas latex-based compound can use both.

Isopropyl Alcohol

This is rubbing alcohol, the kind commonly available in drugstores. For the painter, it is a good cleaner of interior caulks.

Kerosene

There are at least two types of kerosene: fuel-grade and solvent-grade. The solvent grade, which evaporates slowly and has a weak odor, is the only one painters should use.

Kerosene is a good cleaner of tar and oil and also dissolves grease. Importantly, it can be used for deep-cleaning brushes that have been used with oil-based paint.

After the brushes are cleaned with paint thinner, immerse them in kerosene. This is always a good idea, but it is most important in hot weather, when any residue of paint left on bristles can dry hard quickly.

Lacquer Thinner

This is a principal material for thinning and cleaning up contact cement, but it is also an excellent cleaner, because it leaves very little residue. (It should not be used with shellac.)

Lacquer thinner contains methanol and toluol and is highly flammable. It also comes in a variety of grades. If you are using it to thin or clean up lacquer, stick with the brand of thinner made by the manufacturer.

Naphtha

This is used to thin and clean up oil-based paints. It used to be called benzene, but the spelling was too much like the toxic material benzine, so the name was dropped to avoid confusion.

Paint Thinner

Also commonly known as mineral spirits, paint thinner is the most common cleaner and thinner of oil-based coatings. It is relatively inexpensive and safe to use.

"Specs" paint thinner is of a higher quality than that ordinarily found in stores, and it has less odor. Mineral spirits are available in an odorless version, but there is some odor. Mineral spirits are available in various size containers, from 1 qt to 5-gal jugs.

Mineral spirits can ordinarily be used where turpentine is suggested and will cost far less.

Toluene

This is used in lacquer and paints used to make traffic marks. It is banned by many states but is still popular where sold because it thins the lacquer without weakening it, that is, dissolving its nitrocellulose resin.

TSP

This is trisodium phosphate. Because of environmental strictures, TSP is no longer available in all parts of the United States, but some places have TSP substitutes.

TSP is mixed with water, and it can remove gloss and grease from surfaces. It is a good cleaner, but it can promote the growth of algae because of the phosphate in it. Hence, on wood and concrete, which are porous, its use is questionable. On surfaces which are not porous and where the TSP can be washed away thoroughly, it is effective.

Patchers

Joint Compound

This comes in various tub sizes up to 5 gal, which contains 64 lb of material. It comes in standard as well as lightweight versions.

Joint compound, also known as *joint cement,* is used to seal the seams between drywall panels. It is applied with joint knives like a thin coat of butter over the seams: joint tape is embedded in the seam; and then, after drying, more coats are applied and feathered out so that when the job is finished, the joint is invisible.

As a material, joint cement's big advantage is that it can be feathered out to a paper-thin coating and still stick tenaciously. On the negative side, it shrinks, which is why multiple coats are required to fill an area properly.

Many painters use joint compound as an overall patcher of cracks and holes. Sometimes it is mixed with plaster to give it more filling ability and make it dry more quickly but still have a consistency that can be worked for a while.

Another use for joint compound is as a "skim" coat, applied with a large broad knife thinly to smooth over imperfections (cracks and holes and bumps) that may cover large areas of a wall or ceiling.

Joint Tape

This tape, which is used in conjunction, as mentioned, with joint compound to seal joints between drywall panels, comes in various forms. The standard is a paper tape with tiny perforations, but there is also tape with holes and the newest material, fiberglass.

Masking Tape

A sharp distinction must be made between regular masking tape and painter's masking tape (Fig. 1-30). The former really is not suited to paint jobs, because in masking off items it has tenacious sticking power, which grows as time goes by, and when removed, it can tear off paint or wall covering beneath.

Painter's masking tape has easy release and various time periods, depending on the tape, during which it can be peeled off without causing any damage. The tape roll is inserted in the dispenser, and it can be quickly rolled on and automatically clipped (Fig. 1-31). It is good when a lot of masking off needs to be done.

One complaint about these tapes is that paint can seep in under the edge of the tape, destroying the sharp line that the painter is trying to achieve. This may happen with some tapes, but high-quality tapes, such as those made by 3-M, do not allow seepage.

Wagner makes a masking product that works well. It is called Glass Mask. It is a soft, waxy material that is rubbed onto the glass, where it meets the muntins. It protects the glass from paint, and when painting is finished, it can be peeled off easily.

Plaster of Paris

Commonly known as *plaster*, this material is made from gypsum, a compound found in nature and first shipped to the United States at the turn of the century when a huge amount of it was discovered under and outside Paris, France.

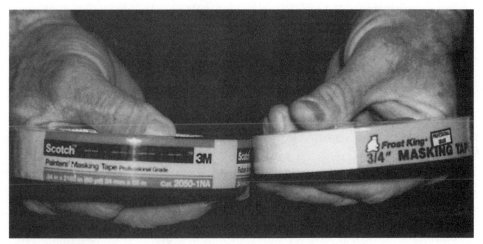

Figure 1-30. Painter's tape (*left*) and masking tape (*right*).

Figure 1-31. Tape dispenser. (*Courtesy of Commercial Painters Supply Corp.*)

Plaster has a number of advantages for the painter. First, it is cheap and dries quickly—in about 10 min it is rock-hard. It can be used as a base to fill large holes in plaster, then topped with spackling compound or joint cement; which is easier to work with.

Patching Plaster

This works somewhat as plaster does, but with an important distinction: While Plaster of Paris will dry in 10 min, patching plaster normally has an open time of one-half hour. It is much more forgiving.

Joint Compound

This is *the* material used to seal seams between drywall sheets or "boards." It is also a very good patch material, its big advantage being that it can be applied smoothly but very thinly and it sticks tenaciously. As such, it is a good material for smoothing out thin, rough areas such as where paint is missing.

It comes in lightweight and regular-weight forms (the lightweight is just that—lighter than the regular) and is very inexpensive. It is available in 5-gal and smaller containers, ready for use.

Spackling Compounds

A variety of these patch materials are available, and they are thought of as being for small holes and cracks and for use where a thin coating is needed.

They come both powdered and (the more expensive) premixed and in two basic forms which might be called heavy and light. A material such as MH Ready Patch, which is very good, is a heavy patcher, and there is a whole new family of lightweight patchers such as Fast 'n Final and Red Devil's One Time. Pick up the container, and you might think it is empty. It is just formulated like that—with tiny glass beads or bubbles in it.

The advantage of these lightweight patchers is their fast drying. Other patchers may take hours to dry (joint compound requires overnight), but the lightweight patchers take minutes, which can be a big advantage to a painter where time means money.

Care must be taken with any of these patchers to carefully read the label instructions to find out the depth to which they may be applied. Most must be applied $\frac{1}{4}$ in at a time, although Fast 'n Final can go $\frac{1}{2}$ in without cracking. Some painters prefer to use something like plaster for the deeper holes first, then use a spackling compound on top, which makes the job easier because of the latter's workability.

Most of the above compounds are designed for interior use, but there are some for exterior use. These are applied in the same way as the interior materials, but can take the rigors of weather. Such products are handy for filling in nail holes and the like as well as patching rough areas to give them a smoother look. MH Ready Patch can be used outside.

Other Fillers

Wood Putty

A variety of wood putties are available. It comes ready-made in a variety of colors, in a natural tannish color that can be tinted, and in powders.

It is used for small repairs to wood and to hide nail holes prior to staining and clear-coating. It also comes in sandable and nonsandable versions; the sandable types are generally more useful for the painter.

Wood Fillers

Wood fillers are wood-putty-like repair products for rotted wood. Minwax makes one, a two-part epoxy system that is applied with a putty knife. The same company also makes a hardener which can be injected or applied on soft or decaying wood, hardening it to make a more suitable base for the patcher. When dry, the patcher can be sanded and worked as regular wood.

Another company, Abatron, makes a two-part adhesive putty system consisting of resin and hardener. When blended, it can be molded by hand and applied by putty knife or trowel. The material hardens in 2 h at room temperature, and then it can be planed, sanded, chiseled, and sawed just as real wood. The product is called WoodEpox.

Water Putty

This plasterlike product can be used inside or outside the house (Fig. 1-32). The most commonly found brand is Durham's Rock Hard Wood Putty. It is mixed with water and dries rock-hard; then it is used like spackling compound.

Safety Equipment

Safety is not a fascinating subject, but it is something that the painter must be aware of. Getting hurt is one thing, but getting hurt also means that you cannot be involved in your livelihood. The following are tools and equipment that the

Figure 1-32. Water putty.

painter should be aware of and use as necessary. A variety of safety techniques are sprinkled throughout the book in appropriate chapters.

Gloves

A wide variety of gloves are available, but for ordinary painting most painters favor the soft, brown cotton gloves. They protect the hands while allowing an important "feel" of the brush—it can remain an extension of the hand, which it should be.

For cleaning, rubber gloves with long sleeves work well, but for stripping paint where aggressive chemicals such as methylene chloride are being used, neoprene gloves or gloves which specifically state that they are for stripping are a must. Methylene chloride will eat through plain rubber or plastic.

Also vinyl gloves are very cheap. Some painters like these for cleaning and painting.

Glasses

Many types are available, in plastic as well as hardened glass that is shatterproof. They can be bought in plain and prescription types.

It is a good idea to wear glasses when you are power washing or chipping something or sanding. Debris can fly off a surface—right into your eyes.

Goggles

These are large glasses with protective sidepieces. They are used mainly for protection against the errant splash of harmful chemicals, but some types are made to withstand impacts, which are unlikely to occur while housepainting.

Breathing Masks

A number of products on the market protect, to varying degrees, against harmful vapors and dust (Fig. 1-33). Before you purchase any breathing apparatus, make sure it is adequate for the task at hand. And any mask *must* fit tightly. An ill-fitting mask can leak and can be dangerous, only offering the illusion of protection.

Paper Mask

This is a cone-shaped, white paper mask with a rubber band to affix it to the wearer's face. It protects against dust but not vapors.

Figure 1-33. Paper mask. (*Courtesy of Commercial Painters Supply Corp.*)

Filter-Type Mask

Made of plastic and with a replaceable filter, this mask will do an adequate job of protecting the user against sanding dust, but not against vapor.

Cartridge Respirator

This resembles a military gas mask with two protruding filter cartridges and a heavy rubber strap to hold the mask on the head (Fig. 1-34). The cartridge-type respirator protects the wearer against paint spray, which can be atomized into very fine droplets. The painter should be very careful to select a respirator that can do what is needed. And it must always be worn airtight.

It comes in two models: one covers half the face, and the other is full-face. These are the ultimate in breathing mask protection, but check that the one you buy is designed to protect against the specific substance you will be working with or around. Look for the label that says the mask is government-approved against the particular vapor or substance. One mask, for example, might be approved for paint fumes but not for lead dust.

Saving on Paint and Other Products

As discussed in detail in Chap. 2, the best paint to buy for a variety of reasons—not the least of which is that it makes the job much easier and faster—is a particular manufacturer's best.

Most painters deal at one shop where they have credit. They can pick up whatever they need quickly and effortlessly before the job, or if there is a lot of paint involved, they can have it delivered.

Figure 1-34. Cartridge-type respirator.
(*Courtesy of Commercial Painters Supply Corp.*)

Companies will normally give a painter a 10 percent discount off retail, but it can be more. That is fine, but you can do even better by shopping around. Paint is always on sale somewhere, and the savings can be significant. Many times paint sales are held in the spring, but an even better time to shop is in January.

The job should be planned, of course, so that no quarts of paint have to be bought. Bought by the quart, paint costs double the gallon price. For example, 1 gal of paint might cost $20. But 4 qt of paint at $10 per quart makes $40 for the gallon!

Of course, the large economy sizes of paint are available, and these usually cost less—sometimes a lot less than the per-gallon price. The standard larger size is 5 gal, but 2-gal containers are available.

Interior and exterior stains are sold in small and large containers. Avoid quarts. You can buy interior stain in half-pints, quarts, and gallons. Exterior stains are usually available in quarts, gallons, and 5-gal containers.

Thinners

You can usually save on paint thinner by buying the larger sizes, like the 5-gal bucket. Keep the 5-gal can in the shop, and fill a 1-gal container as you need it.

Sandpaper

Sandpaper is sold by the package and by the sheet. Buy it by the sheet. You can save 10–15 percent of the cost of buying it by the package.

Plaster of Paris

This product is packaged from 1-lb boxes all the way to 25-lb bags. Guess which is cheaper. If you can use it all, you can save a lot by buying in quantity, but be very careful about its storage. Put it in a dry place. Plaster unintentionally mixed with moisture is ruined plaster.

Exterior Stains

Sales are periodically run on exterior stains, and the savings can be significant. The best months are usually October and November. Stain is composed of a pigment and vehicle or solvent; and if the cans sit on the shelves over the winter, the pigment will settle to the bottom and can be difficult to mix in the spring. Dealers want to unload it, thus the fall sales.

Buy it, then store it upside down, so the pigment on the bottom gets a chance to redistribute itself.

2
Paint

It is important for the painter to know not only how paint is made, but differences in types and why and how they perform as they do. Understanding these things helps the painter pick the best possible paint for the job, avoid problems, and be more knowledgeable about problems that are part and parcel of every painter's job.

What Is in Paint?

A variety of materials go into the making of paint, but it essentially consists of solids and liquids, with the solids suspended in the liquid portion, or vehicle. Solids are what stay on the surface after the liquid portion evaporates.

Solids are composed of a variety of ingredients, each designed to give the paint a specific property, but they are mainly made of pigment and binder (Fig. 2-1).

The pigment is solid grains of color—powder—which gives paint its color and much of its hiding power. Pigment is suspended in the liquid, or vehicle. This suspension is why it must be stirred before use.

Other components are binders, or resins, which hold the paint together, as it were, and additives which give the paint specific desirable properties. The thinner, or vehicle, evaporates when the paint dries, leaving the film.

Organic or Inorganic

Pigment may be organic or inorganic. Inorganic pigments are made from various metals while organic ones come from petroleum-based chemicals.

Pigment can be further broken down into prime pigment and extender pigment. Most paints contain both. The prime pigment gives paint its hiding ability

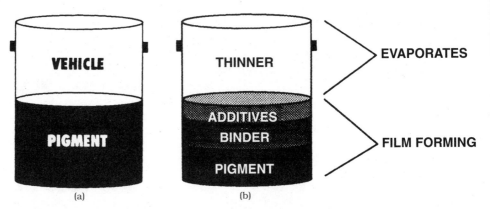

Figure 2-1. Paint composition. (*a*) Liquid, or vehicle, and pigment. (*b*) Other components. (*Courtesy of Behr Process*)

and color. In white or pastel bases, the major prime pigment is titanium dioxide, which has superior whiteness and hiding power. Titanium dioxide is not used in darker colors; here, the colorant added to the paint gives it its "hide."

Extender pigments, which include talc, silica, carbonates, and the like, reinforce and extend titanium dioxide. By themselves, however, they do not perform well as hiding agents.

Titanium dioxide is much more expensive than pigment extenders. At this writing titanium dioxide costs $1 per pound while extenders cost anywhere from a lowly $0.04 to $0.15 per pound.

To make a paint cheaper, of course, just cut back on the titanium dioxide and increase the extenders. And the price reflects this. In an example in *Painting and Wallcovering Contractor* (November–December 1995), it was stated that you can

> see the economics at work in the ProMar line of interior flats made by Sherwin Williams specifically for contractors. In top-of-the-line ProMar 200, priced at $14.99, titanium dioxide constitutes 13% of the paint by weight, while another 29% was taken by extenders…but with ProMar 700, at the more frugal price of $9.50, titanium dioxide drops to 6% while extenders have increased to 31%.

This does not mean that the paint will not cover well. Indeed, manufacturers can add other things, such as toners, that make for "dry hiding," which is like adding something cold to water that makes it translucent rather than transparent (Fig. 2-2). But while it covers, the surface is more porous, less scrubbable. This explains why bargain-basement paint is not washable. Note in Fig. 2-2 the content of binder and prime pigment in *a* versus *c*. In *b* the paint depends on extenders for hiding; but even though this will make the paint cover when dry, it loses washability and other qualities in the process.

While pigment essentially gives paint its color and hiding power, depending on the type, it can invest the paint with other properties. For example, some pigments are harder than others, some affect the gloss of the paint (smaller particles make for higher shine while larger make for a flatter one), and some are also mildewcides, able to kill mildew on the surface. Pigments also give paint texture.

Note that until the 1950s the main pigment used in paint was lead. As research later revealed, however, lead is a hazardous substance, and its use was gradually outlawed, being completely outlawed in the 1970s. Today lead is not used in consumer products, just as a drier in some commercial applications. (See also Chapter 5.)

Extenders Equal Less-White Whites

Extenders also make paint much less white than titanium dioxide does. If you want a very white paint, titanium dioxide is the only way to go. Paint with a lot of extenders is gray, and over time it will get grayer, and so will the colored paints it is added to.

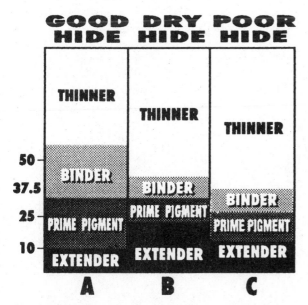

Figure 2-2. The elements that make a paint cover.
(*Courtesy of Behr Process*)

Another drawback of paint containing extenders is that it looks as if it is not hiding when applied. The painter who is not aware of "dry hide" often applies more paint than is necessary.

Binder

The binder part of the vehicle is just that—a binder. It "glues" together the pigment particles into a uniform paint film and makes the paint adhere to the surface. The particular type and quantity of binder, such as acrylic, also determine many of the paint's performance properties such as washability, scrubbability, color retention, and adhesion.

Binder also is the substance which keeps paint particles that do not dissolve in suspension in the can. Without it, they would collect at the bottom. Binders are made up of substances called *resins,* which may be natural or synthetic.

The more binders or resins in the paint, the better the paint and the greater the gloss and durability of the paint. It is no small wonder that binders constitute 25 percent of the weight of alkyd semiglosses. As the binder content decreases, the paint film becomes softer and less scrubbable.

When latex paints were first introduced in the 1940s, the binder was styrene-butadiene, but as time went by, this proved to be too sensitive to ultraviolet rays, and the paint would become yellow and brittle.

Polyvinyl acetate followed as the next binder, but this, too, had problems. Chiefly it was not being compatible with alkaline masonry surfaces.

In 1953 the painting industry started to use acrylic binders. These had better color retention and none of the problems associated with their predecessors. Acrylic is still considered to be the best binder, but today's paint may be acrylic or styrene, polyester, terpolymer, rubber, polyvinyl acetate, or a mixture of these. The more acrylic in the paint, the better the paint. If a can says 100 percent acrylic, then this is the only binder in it, and this is a mark of quality. Some manufacturers use acrylics for interior semigloss and exterior latex paints, but not flat; but others do. One manufacturer, Behr, uses 100 percent acrylic in all its paints.

Liquids

Paint requires a liquid portion, of course, or else the pigments, binders, and other solid materials in the paint will not flow. The liquid in paint is made up of a solvent and a diluent. A *solvent* is a liquid that is capable of dissolving another substance. Thus solvent dissolves the resins.

Most of the solvents are used in so-called oil-based paint, that is, those that use mineral spirits as a solvent. Water, although it does dissolve substances, is not considered a solvent for paint because it does not dissolve latex resins.

Latex paints have their own name for solvent, which is *diluent*, mentioned above, which comes from the word *dilute*. Both solvents and diluents are known as *thinners* because they are capable of thinning paint to its original consistency.

Additives

In addition to solvents and diluents, pigments, and binders, paint may contain one or more additives. These impart vital properties to the paint depending on the end use. Latex paints tend to contain more additives than alkyds because they are trying to imitate some alkyd properties, particularly the ability to flow.

These are some additives:

- *Thickeners.* These increase the viscosity of paint.
- *Drying agents.* They make the paint dry faster.
- *Preservatives and/or fungicides.* Some of these increase the shelf life in the can while others help retard or kill the growth of mildew on the dried paint film.
- *Ultraviolet inhibitors.* The damaging rays of the sun are the ultraviolet ones, and the inhibitors retard or block these, improving the life of the paint.
- *Antiskinning agent.* These prevent or reduce the formation of a paint skin on paint once the can has been opened.
- *Antifoaming agents.* These are used to minimize air bubbles and foaming.
- *Coalescing agents.* These are used to aid drying of latex paints.

It is the combination of the elements in a paint that makes it what it is, and this can and does vary depending on the area of the country where the paint is to be used. For example, if paint is going to be used in the southeast, where there is high humidity and, therefore, a potential mildew problem, a heavier concentration of mildewcide would be included and perhaps a preservative. In the northern section of the country, though, the paint may have more flexibility built in, so that it can better respond to the extremes of temperature.

But the quality of the paint depends on the kind of pigment used and the amount and type of binder. The more there is, the higher the quality of the paint.

Oil, Alkyd, and Latex

In most cases, the painter will be using latex paint and, as long as it is around, oil- or alkyd-based paint. True oil-based paints are in the minority today. Essentially, a true oil-based paint consists of a vegetable oil, such as soybean or linseed oil, binder, and mineral spirits. But less than 5 percent of all paints use this basic formula.

Much more common—well over 95 percent of the coatings—is alkyd, also a binder. Alkyd-based paint really consists of a modified vegetable oil, fish oil, tung oil, castor oil, or the like. The chemist will replace some of the molecules in the oil with a synthetic resin, thereby improving and strengthening it. Mineral spirits are still the solvent.

Latex paints contain only a tiny amount of solvent; the solvent or diluent is mostly water.

Gloss and Sheen

Gloss is the ability of a given paint to reflect light (Fig. 2-3). This can be measured by using a device called a *gloss meter,* a small box that aims light at the dried paint and then measures how much of the light is reflected. One of the standard measurements of gloss is taken at a 60° angle, the light being directed at the paint surface at this angle.

Depending on the paint's ability to reflect, it is characterized as any of a variety of sheens ranging from flat, which has no shine, to high gloss, which has the most light reflectance of all.

The gloss of a particular paint is a reflection of the ratio of the pigment to vehicle. The greater the amount of pigment, the flatter the paint; and this, in turn, relates to the distance between pigment particles in the paint. In glossy paint, where a greater surface area of the pigment particles is exposed because there is more space between them, more light is reflected. In flat paints, less surface area is exposed; hence less light is reflected.

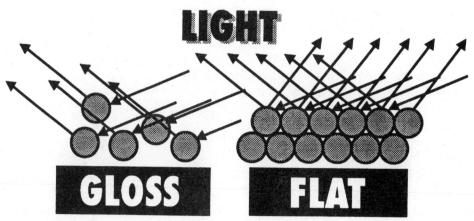

Figure 2-3. Paint particle surface for glossy and flat paints. (*Courtesy of Behr Process*)

The most common gloss range readings used by manufacturers are

Flat, 10 percent

Eggshell (it has the sheen of an egg), 10 to 40 percent

Semigloss, 40 to 60 percent

Gloss, 60 to 80 percent

High-gloss, 80 percent

Shine, as mentioned before, relates to the binders, or resins, in the paint. The greater the amount of resin, the glossier, the less porous, and the more scrubbable the paint.

Also note that different manufacturers have different definitions of what constitutes various shine levels. One's semigloss might be another's satin flat.

The best way to check—short or rushing out and buying paint samples—is to compare the color cards of various companies. Those cards contain actual paint chips—not photographic reproductions.

Interior and Exterior Paint

It seems elementary, but the most important thing to be aware of concerning paint is that some is formulated for interior use and other for exterior use. Each has different environmental problems to overcome. Some people use exterior paint indoors on the assumption that it is tougher. After all, it is used outside. In fact, some of the highest-grade exterior paints can be worse to use than a poor-quality interior paint.

Each type of paint, as mentioned, has different properties. Commonly, interior paint is formulated to be scrubbable and stain-resistant, to have hiding ability, to be splatter-resistant, and to be able to be touched up.

Exterior paint is formulated for color retention, resistance to fading, flexibility (to withstand expansion and contraction due to weather), mildew resistance, and resistance to tannin bleed, a chemical in some woods.

So, for example, an exterior paint could be used in the bathroom and achieve greater mildew resistance, but at the sacrifice of scrubbability and stain resistance.

How Paint Works

When paint is applied to a surface, the drying process begins. The vehicle portion of the paint starts to evaporate, leaving a film of paint behind. As mentioned, the film is composed of a binder, additives, and pigment.

Just how a paint dries is important. If it does not dry correctly, this can lead to cracking, peeling, and other maladies.

Paint dries in two different ways. *Solvent release* refers to the way oil-based paint dries, while *coalescence* is the name given to the way water-based paint dries. And it is the way in which the paints dry or "cure" that gives rise to their differences. As paint dries, the paint film becomes thinner—the volume taken up by the vehicle is gone—and begins to condense as the pigment, binder, and additives begin to pull close together.

As they dry, oil-based paint particles begin to connect and form new, longer particles in a process known as *chemical bonding.* In water-based paint, however, the pigment, binder, and additives do not chemically bond as the paint dries. Instead the particles move close together to fill the gaps left by the evaporating water particles, a phenomenon known as coalescence.

The result is paints that perform quite differently (Fig. 2-4). Oil-based paint is hard and brittle, while water-based paint is softer and more flexible. Hence, oil-based paint may crack when movement, say, expansion and contraction of wood siding, occurs whereas water-based paint, being more flexible, will not crack.

What Does It Mean?

All the above is fine to increase the painter's arsenal of knowledge, but what about consumers? What qualities are important to them?

Washability

A prime consumer concern is washability, and the glossier the paint, the more easily washed it is. But the shinier the paint, the more light is reflected, which can be annoying in some settings (such as a living room). And since the paint is thinner, it will show imperfections in a substrate more readily than flat paint. Still, washability is desired.

Based on the above, where a paint requires greater washability, the glossier paints are preferred. Such areas might include bathrooms, kitchens, and trim.

Hard and Brittle with No Place to Bend   **Soft and Flexible-Many Places to Bend**

OIL-BASED PAINT   **WATER-BASED PAINT**

Figure 2-4. Oil-based versus latex paint finishes. (*Courtesy of Behr Process*)

For bedrooms and living rooms, flat and satin flat, also known as *eggshell*, are preferred. Satin flat is considered washable, while flat paint generally is not—scrub it, and it will come off.

Some manufacturers say they make scrubbable flats, and this may well be true—in the laboratory. Scrubbing machines will remove soil without degrading the paint film. But the scrubbing process may leave what is known as a *burnish mark* or shiny mark on the surface which essentially mars it. In sum, we do not consider any flat paint scrubbable in a practical sense; those small marks may be removed with a damp cloth.

Paints of various manufacturers can differ to some degree even though they are described as the same. For example, one manufacturer's semigloss paint may be slightly glossier than another's. One way to detect differences is to compare color-chip cards, which accurately reflect the sheen levels.

On labels of most paint cans a number of features are listed. The painter should be well aware of what these mean.

Drying Time

Another important idea for a painter to understand is the drying or cure time. In fact, they are two different things. *Drying* refers to surface drying, but *curing* occurs when paint dries all the way through.

Drying times for alkyd- and latex-based paints can vary considerably according to the weather and temperature. When the humidity is high, paints can take far longer to dry than they ordinarily would, simply because the rate of evaporation is decreased. It is important to allow the paint to dry—not only to recoat it, but also to clean it. Some paint, for example, can be recoated in a matter of hours, but it may be weeks before it can be washed. That, essentially, is the difference between drying and curing.

Flammability

The key term when the painter is considering whether a paint can catch fire is *flash point*, or the point at which a paint could catch fire. Although there are variations, every alkyd-based product should be considered flammable, simply because some products ignite when touched with a spark and others do not. For safety's sake, it is best to assume that all can.

Odor

All paints have some sort of odor, but it is a matter of degree. Latex paints, for example, have an odor, but it is not strong and pungent, but mild, sort of like wet leather.

Alkyd-based paint has a strong odor that is really disliked by some people. Before using it, the painter should make sure the customer is aware of its smell. The odor lingers as well.

There are other odors which are even stronger than those of alkyd-based paint. For example, oil-based waterproofers such as Drylock have a very strong smell. (Fortunately, at least in the case of Drylock, a latex version is available.)

Alcohol-based products, such as BIN primer, also have a very strong odor, and it lingers.

Coverage

This is another item on the paint can label. Normally 1 gal of paint covers about 400 ft^2. There are so many variables in any paint job, however, that I think this ratio is unrealistic. For example, when a surface is rough, or absorbent, or very dry, or if there is a severe color change, then it is highly unlikely that 1 gal of paint will cover 400 ft^2. To cite an extreme example, to cover black paint with white paint will certainly take two coats of paint, and 1 gal will cover far less than 400 ft^2.

Also the applicator used makes a difference. A brush will apply paint sparingly, while a roller will apply it more heavily; and the heavier the roller, the more paint that is used. So, too, coverage is dependent on hiding power, discussed above. The better the paint, the better its hiding power.

In general, to calculate coverage, I believe that 325 to 350 ft^2/gal is realistic.

Lead-Based Paint

Lead-based paint was outlawed for use in residences in 1976, but it is still something the painter must understand and deal with because it still remains, as detailed below, on many homes.

Lead-based paint was extensively used in the United States until the early 1940s, and it was used particularly for the exterior portions of dwellings until 1976. In 1971, Congress passed the Lead-Based Paint Poisoning Prevention Act, and in 1976 the Consumer Product Safety Commission (CPSC) issued a ruling under this act that limited the lead content of paint used in residential dwellings, toys, and furniture to 0.06 percent.

Today, lead-based paint is still manufactured for purposes not covered by the CPSC ruling, such as for products made of steel.

In 1986 the Environmental Protection Agency (EPA) made a study of the prevalence of lead paint and concluded that some 42 million U.S. homes still had interior and/or exterior lead-based paint. When remodeling is done, just how to remove this lead-based material safely has become a big question.

Lead paint is a very nasty poison. Even ingesting minute amounts of it can lead to damage to the brain, blood cells, and kidneys and can contribute to high blood pressure. Ingest a little more, and it can lead to loss of hearing, impairment of mental development and IQ, growth retardation, inhibited metabolism of vitamin D, and disturbance in blood formation.

Because their bodies are small, children are particularly at risk. Indeed, the American Academy of Pediatrics regards lead as one of the main hazards to small children.

How lead is able to damage human beings must be understood in order to deal properly with the problem.

Outdoors, as moisture and UV rays from the sun bombard paint, it chalks, becoming a powder. This lead dust floats through the air and gets into the soil around the foundation of the house—and it can enter through gaps in the house.

Poor-quality lead-based paint on interior surfaces can also shed this powder, and it becomes a hazard when coatings are broken through during preparation for painting and remodeling or simply due to aging. The dust is not really removed by normal housecleaning methods.

There are a variety of ways to deal with the problem of lead-based paint, from removal to leaving it in place. Methods are suggested in Chapter 5, Preparation, chief of which is to leave it alone.

Oil- or Water-Based Paint?

The age-old question of painters is, Which is better, oil- or water-based paint? Years ago, this used to be fairly easy to answer, because each paint had its own advantages.

Oil-based paint, for example, was commonly used on trim and doors because it flowed and leveled much more easily than latex, dried harder, and was much less susceptible to peeling in wet environments such as bathrooms. In fact, once some alkyds could outperform latex paints by 50 percent. In other words, latex paint was only half as good as alkyd-based paint.

But since government has begun to regulate paints, manufacturers have taken to their research laboratories to try to come up with better latex paint products. And they have. Today's latex paints are comparable with oil-based paints in every way, and chances are they will get even better. The feeling of manufacturers seems to be that since latex paints have come along so well, why even worry about alkyd-based paints if you have a latex paint that can duplicate what alkyd-based paint can do and surpass it?

One thing is sure, however. Whatever type of paint is chosen, it should be the company's top-of-the-line paint, as detailed below.

How to Buy Paint

It would be great if manufacturers made it easy for the painter to compare the ingredients in paint. But they are not obligated to, so they do not. For example, one manufacturer might give the percentage of titanium dioxide in the paint, while another gives the number of pounds. There is simply no easy way to assess what is best.

One good way to buy paint is by price. The more expensive the paint within a particular brand line, the more likely it is a high-quality paint. And industry experts advise the painter (as well as the consumer) to get a particular company's top-of-the-line paint. Even good paint companies have varying grades of paint, and the farther you go down the line, the worse it is.

The great thing about top-of-the-line paint is quite simple: It will perform well. It will flow better, cover better, and look subtly but significantly better than bargain-basement or lower-quality paint. Callbacks will be fewer, touchups will be possible, and one's reputation will be that much more enhanced.

This is not to say that there is no place for lower-quality material. Sometimes, for example, a landlord will want a home painted more often than is needed because of a new tenant, or perhaps a customer is on a tight budget, or the like. Then a lower-quality paint may be called for.

Be aware, though, that using low-quality paint can add to the length of a job. Indeed, it is estimated that using a high-quality paint can cut the job time 30 percent compared to lower-quality paint.

Be aware, too, that high-quality paint is a better deal over time than a low-quality one. In data developed by *Home Mechanix Magazine* (now *Today's Homeowner*) which compared low- and high-quality paint, it was found that the average cost of high-quality paint was $6.75 per year versus an overall cost of $8.39 per year for low-quality paint.

Paint: A Short History

Paint goes back to at least 2000 B.C. It was used for both protection and decoration. Early Christian and Egyptian artisans used mixtures of drying oils, resins, and pigments to make inscriptions and for pictures in tombs and temples. Interestingly, those paints of yesteryear are very similar in composition and appearance to the more elementary kinds used today.

The need for paint grew as the world's population enlarged and people began to travel. The need for decorative and protective coatings increased. People at the time applied coatings to ships, weapons, utensils, and buildings.

Natural pigments were used. White pigments were lead and natural white earths such as clay, gypsum, and whiting. Blacks were charcoal, lampblack, coal, and graphite. Yellow pigments were ochres, gold powder, and litharge. Reds were iron oxide, red lead, cinnabar, and natural red dyes. Blue was also used—eastern blue, lapis lazuli, copper carbonate, and indigo. Greens included terre verte, malachite, and verdigris.

Binders back then were such things as beeswax, gelatin, pitch, shellac, animal fats, and tree sap. There was not much paint made by modern standards. The standard of living was low, so few people improved things, raw materials were scarce, and the paint-making process was slow.

But better manufacturing methods came into being. By 1500 the first modern varnishes were being made, these by "running" resin with sandarac in linseed oil. Such varnishes were mostly used for ion-coating crossbows and other weapons.

Up until 1800, the most popular resin used for both protection and decoration was amber, either alone or in combination with linseed oil. However, this material was scarce, and this led to a search for a replacement. In the 1800s replacements in the form of fossil and nonfossil gums such as gum Arabic coal and elastic gum were used.

The paint industry exploded in the twentieth century, with more progress made in the first 50 years of the century than in the thousands of years before. Something called *ester gum* was made, and synthetic resins were formulated that replaced natural binders.

Technology also produced a host of paint and paint-related products such as nitrocellulose, phenolics, urea-and-melamine formaldahydes, acrylics, vinyls, alkyds, terpenes, coumarones, indenes, epoxies, urethanes, latexes, and acrylics. The result was new pigments with greatly improved durability, strength, and brightness.

Today, paint technology is still advancing, spurred by the desire for better products and ones that will be environmentally acceptable yet will perform well.

Volatile Organic Compounds

All solvents, diluents, and thinners except for water are volatile organic compounds (VOCs). When the sun strikes them, they link with oxygen, chlorine, and nitrogen to form a gas known as *ozone*. At high altitudes, ozone protects us against the ultraviolet radiation of the sun. But at ground level it is harmful, a component in smog that is not good to breathe.

In recognition of this, a few years ago, the Clean Air Act started to mandate the amount of volatile organic compounds that paint and stain could contain. States also applied their own restrictions. The result, in essence, is the reduction of VOCs in such coatings.

Paints containing alkyds are chiefly the problem, so more and more manufacturers are changing formulations. The government has mandated that paints contain only a certain amount of VOCs, which are part of the solvents, so the response of companies has been to reduce the solids.

The overall requirement is that the solid portion of the total coating content be reduced, and companies have done this. At this writing, the typical alkyd-based paint contains about 53 percent solids as opposed to 40 percent in the past; the typical stain jumped from an average 22 to 68 percent, and clear coatings went from 42 percent solids to 64 percent.

Because the coatings are thicker than before, they may cover better and penetrate porous surfaces better, because they do not dry as rapidly with a lower solvent content. On the other hand, they are more difficult to apply and take longer to cure.

The fact that they contain more solids does not mean that the products are better. As stated above, there are three kinds of solids: binder, pigment, and additives. Some manufacturers are increasing the binders in the paint, which makes for a better paint, while others are adding pigment extenders, which can make the coating better or worse.

Making coatings thicker has also meant that in some instances manufacturers have had to solve the problem of making them flow better. In some cases, the alkyd resin has been modified. Typically these are what is known as long-chained and form a strong film. To make alkyds flow better, the molecules were shortened. The result is that the alkyd takes longer to dry, but is more flexible than the longer-molecule coating and does not crack or peel as readily. However, alkyd-based coatings fade and chalk more readily than long-molecule coatings.

Latex coatings contain such small amounts of VOCs that they have not posed a problem for manufacturers. Indeed, companies have recognized the value of water as a solvent and have been developing more and more water-based products, such as interior polyurethanes and stains. There is a clear recognition by companies that as concern for the environment increases, the day may come when alkyd-based paints are a thing of the past.

A Word about Enamel

If there is one word that is badly misused in the painting trade, it is *enamel*. Years ago, oil-based paint enjoyed great popularity, and latex was not available in high gloss: *enamel* referred very specifically to semigloss or high-gloss oil-based paint. The understanding then was that the word described a paint that was hard and shiny—tough-wearing.

Then as the years went by, the term gradually became *latex semigloss paint* (years ago no one made latex high-gloss paint); but it also started to turn up in strange places to describe other sheens of paint, such as satin enamel and flat enamel.

In truth, today the word *enamel* is used where it should not be—not according to the original definition. Indeed, it is safe to say that the average consumer thinks of enamel as highly washable paint, and not all enamels are. This should be made clear to the customer when the paint is selected. (*Note:* A paint coating chemist defines an enamel as a paint with a gloss rating higher than 50.)

Waterborne or Water-Based Paint?

As companies have developed paint, some confusion has arisen over the terms *waterborne, water-based,* and *water-reducible.* The first two mean that the paint is formulated with water, thinned with water, and cleaned up with water.

Water-reducible paints are something else. These are alkyds which contain emulsions and surfactants, which make them more user-friendly. While they perform like waterborne paints (or water-based paints), they are still essentially alkyds.

3
Primers

Paint primers are sometimes not appreciated for what they can do, so finish paints are used instead. But often the only time a primer on a surface is not needed is for repainting when the color change is not severe. Then a first coat of finish paint will be fine. In other situations, primers are really the way to go. They reduce the possibility of problems not only in the present but in the future, and they ensure the best possible job.

Primers, like paint, come in 1-qt, 1-gal, and 5-gal cans, for interior and exterior use. Some can be used both inside and outside.

There is not just one primer, or primer sealer as it is also known, but many. Some can do a wide variety of jobs while others are designed to do just a few. Following is a discussion of properties which primers have collectively.

Properties

Adhesion

One property that a number of primers share is the ability to stick to a surface. For example, a finish latex or oil-based paint would not be able to stick to plastic laminate or ceramic tile, but there are primers that will.

Holdout

Some surfaces are very absorbent, and they must be coated with a primer sealer so that the finish paint does not seep in and look mottled or create different sheen levels. For example, if two coats of finish paint are applied on raw wood paneling, the first coat only partially seals the surface and is absorbed more or less when applied. A primer prevents this.

Reconditioning of Surfaces

Some surfaces are in bad shape and need some reconditioning before the finish coat is applied. For example, exterior paint often chalks or sheds a powder. If finish paint is applied over this surface, it will not stick well. But there are primers that can stick quite well as long as conditions are not too severe.

Hiding Power

Primers can also provide hiding power. For even better hiding power, tint the primer—all are white—as detailed later.

Tooth

Primers also provide more "tooth" for the finish paint—paint will adhere better to a primer than a finish paint.

Stain Blocking

Blocking a wide variety of stains is one of the prime functions of some primers (Fig. 3-1). For example, certain primers (particularly shellac-based ones) are excellent for blocking water stains from bleeding through the finish coat. If a finish paint is used as a blocker, it simply will not work because each application will resolubilize the water stain, creating, in effect, a fresh stain on the surface. Primer will not resolubilize it.

BIN is a white shellac-based primer that has myriad uses for the painter. It is basically a stain blocker, and as such, it sets up a hard film over tobacco stains, Magic Marker, water, crayon, etc., so they do not bleed through. It can also be used outside the house to block knots which can bleed, although it is too hard to be a whole-house exterior primer (expansion and contraction could crack it). BIN dries in about 15 min.

A sharp distinction should be made between the regular primer and the stain-blocking type; they are really two different products. While the stain-blocking type can perform the functions of the standard primer, the reverse is not true.

The house in Fig. 3-2 has been battered by weather, is bleeding tannin extracts, and has patches of mildew. Most of these primers are oil-based paint, but the manufacturer says Bull's Eye 123 works well. The house should first be washed with a bleach-based solution of some sort to kill mildew. It would also be possible, with power washing, to bring this back to the original color.

Various Primers

Following is an overview of primers and what they can do.

Latex Primer

Latex primers are formulated for both interior and exterior use on a variety of surfaces. For years, it was believed that the only coating that should be used on raw wood was an oil-based primer, because it penetrated better given that its molecules are smaller. But, in fact, acrylic latex primer will do fine in a wide

Figure 3-1. BIN in action. (*Courtesy of Wm. Zinsser & Co.*)

Figure 3-2. Cedar shingles needing stain blocking primer if painted or solid stained.

variety of situations, including use on woods that can "bleed," such as cedar and redwood, once strictly thought of as needing oil-based primer. Specific uses for oil-based primers are discussed in detail below.

Latex primers can also be used on raw drywall and plaster surfaces and on vertical masonry surfaces, such as brick and block walls. They are applied just as finish paint would be, with brush or roller. Latex, of course, has the advantage of being water-soluble, making cleanup a lot easier.

One type of primer included among latexes is PVA (polyvinyl acetate) primer. This is designed for use on new drywall only, and it is generally cheaper than other latexes. In my view, the other latexes work better.

First Coat

A particularly good primer for raw drywall is First Coat. This is a paint with a high solids content that is excellent when the painter wants to minimize surface defects without giving the area a skim coat (see Chapter 5). It hides all surface defects and readies the area for painting. The product comes dry for mixing with water and ready-made. Like paint, it can be applied with brush, roller, or spray.

Tint Primer

If the topcoat is not white, then primer (which is always white) should be tinted with about half the colorant used to tint the finish paint. This will make covering easier. If this is not done, the finish paint has to cover what is, in effect, a white paint, something that may be difficult in darker colors.

Like finish paint, standard oil-based primer thins and cleans up with mineral spirits. Like other primers, it is available for exterior and interior use. It can be used on wood and masonry, but I do not see any particular advantage to it. Indeed, it takes much longer to dry than latex (overnight) and is more difficult to work with.

It does have some uses, however, that latex does not. If a wall covering is to be primed, a latex is not recommended because it has a water base. Wallpaper paste is water-soluble; if the water in the latex seeps through and gets at the paste, that can resolubilize it, causing the paper to fall off and/or creating an environment favorable to mildew. Oil-based primer will not affect the glue.

Bleeding Woods

Oil-based primer is also good for the so-called bleeding woods. Cedar, for example, contains *tannins*—chemicals in the wood which are soluble in water. Oil-based primer will not resolubilize them. Neither, as suggested, will acrylic latex primers, designed for the job.

Oil-based primers are also good for use with metal (Fig. 3-3), where latex should not be used unless specifically allowed by the manufacturer, as detailed on the label. (The water in the latex can contact bare metal, and rust will result.) There are, of course, oil-based primers for interior and exterior metal.

Oil-based primer is useful where there is water vapor movement and where there is old, chalky or dirty paint. Oil-based primer seems to work better than latex here; but no matter what is used, preparation is crucial.

Shellac-Based Primers

Shellac is made from the resinous secretions of the lac beetle cut with denatured alcohol. The finish that results is very hard (for years clear shellac was the main material used on floors). And shellac has been found to be an excellent stain-blocking primer that dries quickly (15 min) and can block out just about everything. BIN is the most well-known brand of shellac-based primer.

Shellac-based primers can be used anywhere inside the home, but are not recommended for use in the bathroom without the use of an oil-based primer as a topcoat. To me, this seems like wasted effort. Why not just use something like oil-based Kilz (which dries in 1 h, unlike other oil-based primers) or a standard oil-based primer to begin with?

Figure 3-3. Oil-based primer used on metal railing.

Metal Primers

Another category of primers enables the painter to deal with rust without taking it off. For example, Rust-Oleum makes a product called Clean Metal Primer which allows light rust to remain on a surface. The flaking rust is knocked off, and the product is applied. Its ingredients make the rust inert. The product comes in a white and a sort of khaki color for use under darker paints.

Rust-Oleum also makes a product called Rusty Metal Primer which is for heavily rusted surfaces. This is applied to the rusted areas only, and the fish oil in the product drives the water out of the rust and renders it inert. The product is deep red.

Extend is another product. It comes in a spray which is black and brush-applied material which is tannish. However, they work as Rust-Oleum products do, rendering rust inert.

Making Primers Work Better

To make a primer more effective, it should be tinted to a paler shade of the color being applied. Some manufacturers have formulas for tinting primers; if not, use about half the amount of colorant used to create the color of the finish paint.

Universal colorants are available for doing this, but the store where you deal can do it as well. All primers, no matter what their base, can be tinted.

Although one property of primers is that they stick tenaciously, a light sanding with fine sandpaper (220 grit) will help guarantee good adhesion. I recommend it.

Chapter 6, Painting, reviews jobs and recommended primers.

4
Color

The professional painter should keep in mind a number of factors when selecting paint for a job, but perhaps the most important rule is to *never* choose paint for the client. Let the client do it, and carefully explain how different forces affect the final color of paint.

This rule should be ironclad. Many a frustration has resulted from the painter's picking the paint color. People simply have different tastes. In essence, a paint as perceived on the color swatch or chip will hardly ever look the same when it is on the house.

The procedure, normally, when a paint is mixed, is to dab a little of the mixed paint on the color chip and then dry it. The chips used to match are paint, so they will likely be very close. Note, though, that if a chip has a flat or eggshell sheen, the dried dab will appear different, and sometimes dramatically so because of the way it reflects light (Fig. 4-1).

Paint is chameleonlike. It will change color depending on the amount of light in the room. In the room, shown in Fig. 4-1 for example, the paint would seem darker than that in a room with a skylight or picture window.

Factors Affecting Paint Color

Paint can look really different—much darker or much lighter or even a slightly different color than that seen in the store. Those factors that affect paint color are surface porosity, the light reflectance of the paint itself, the amount of light in the room, and the reflectance of colors from adjacent objects.

Figure 4-1. Light affecting paint color. (*Courtesy of Dutch Boy Paints*)

Surface Porosity

Just how the surface absorbs paint affects how it will finally look. For example, a surface will absorb flat paint better than semigloss or high-gloss paint. And a primed surface will hold out the finish paint better than an unprimed one. This will affect the color somewhat.

The paint itself will reflect light. Flat paint reflects little or no light, while glossy paints reflect a lot. This also alters the color a little.

The light in the room affects the color. For example, in a room in the back of the house that has a virtual wall of glass, lots of light will come in, and this tends to make the paint on the wall look lighter. If there are only one or two windows, however, the effect will still be noticeable and the paint will look darker.

The amount and kind of light affect color. For example, if the light in a room comes from fluorescent tubes, this will be a colder light than incandescent.

The objects in the room also reflect color. Red objects reflect red color, green objects reflect green, and so forth.

Collectively, all these factors have an impact on the final color.

Safest Way to Proceed

To ensure that the color is correct, have a small sample made and try it on the wall. A quart is enough. Incidentally, never pick colors by the color of any paint in the can. Colors always dry darker than they appear in the can.

Picking Colors

Ultimately, picking colors for the inside or outside of a house is subjective. What is good for one person will be poison for another. But the painter should know some basics in order to give a client some input on what might be best and how color works.

Color Affects Mood

Color has an effect on mood—both positive and negative.

There is a story about a police precinct in New York City that decided to spruce up its holding tank, a small jail that held prisoners until they were transported to a larger prison.

The cell was painted pink, and the cops noticed that this had a very calming effect on the prisoners—at first. But as the hours in the cell wore on, the soft pink color produced the opposite effect—the prisoners became almost riotous. The precinct was forced to go back to the bile green color it was before.

It is generally accepted that cool colors such as blue and green tend to be calming while reds, yellows, and other warm colors tend to excite. Neutral colors such as beige and off-white are also calming.

Color Hints

Here are some helpful hints for a customer selecting a color:

- Colors in one room should complement those in other rooms. For example, it would not be a good idea to paint five rooms five different colors. The effect would be chaotic. The best idea is to use complementary colors, even the same colors. This rule was brought home to me when I was hired to paint a posh apartment in New York City. The client hired an interior decorator to select the colors, and as I remember it, almost all the rooms were a light blue with a darker blue as an accent color on trim, and they looked quite good. Think of what that apartment would have looked like if all the rooms were different colors!

- Coordinating colors should be selected at the same time as wallpaper, flooring, and furniture are chosen if these are new or are being changed. Colors are often chosen from colors in wallpaper or a rug.

- A customer may have no idea what colors to pick. Here, suggest that he or she choose a favorite color from a piece of clothing. This might be a starting point for picking something the customer likes.

- A favorite painting or rug may contain pleasing color combinations or at least serve as a starting point.

- When a room contains multiple colors, the general rule is that the main color is used in two-thirds of the room and other colors are used in one-third. This usually happens automatically because the walls, which contain the greatest area, are painted first.

- In a room, the ceiling is usually the lightest color (often but not always white), walls are darker, and floors are the darkest element of all (Fig. 4-2). Room ceilings are often white. To lower the ceiling in Fig. 4-2, it should be painted the same color as the walls.

- Bold or bright, warm colors make a room seem smaller. So do darker colors.

- Light, pastel colors make a room seem larger.

- If a room is too sunny, use blues and greens as a moderating effect.

- Unequal amounts of color in a room are visually interesting. The main color should be used in one-half to two-thirds of the room.

Color to Cure Architectural Flaws

Color can also be used to correct architectural flaws, fooling the eye so that they are not so noticeable. The following are some situations in which paint can help.

- *Low ceiling.* Some ceilings are very low and create a claustrophobic feeling. The basement is one such. To "raise" the ceiling, paint the ceiling a lighter color than the walls.

Figure 4-2. Room ceiling painted white appears higher. (*Courtesy of Dutch Boy Paints*)

- *High ceiling.* There are a couple of ways to "lower" it. Apply a medium or darker color to the walls and ceilings, or use a darker color on the ceiling than on the walls.

- *Undersized room.* If a room is very small, use light, pastel colors.

- *Narrow rooms.* Here, paint the short walls at each end a darker color than that of the longer walls.

- *Irregular angles.* If a room contains irregularities such as chimneys jutting into a room, paint everything the same color. This tends to reemphasize such things.

Exteriors

Just as one would try to make the interior of a building work, so the exterior should be thought of the same way. To this end, there are a number of color rules to keep in mind.

- Colors must work together, and on the exterior of a home one is required to work with a number of given colors, that is, the roof, the masonry materials such as brick or concrete, and the landscaping. All should blend together and yet have some contrast.

- A number of color experts subscribe to the idea of having three colors on the outside: one main color and two other colors for the trim. In this scenario, the siding is one color, a little on the conservative side. The front door (as well as the rear one) and the windows are one color which complements the siding color. The shutters, lamp post, mailbox, and house numbers might be another color. The colors, again, are different but complementary.

- In designing the color scheme, avoid having the trim or any other color that is different from the siding stand alone from the other colors (Fig. 4-3). For example, a beige house with bright violet doors and windows and yellow shutters could look chaotic. Colors must work together.

- Consider the direction the house faces in designing a color scheme. A house that faces east and has no shade may be too bright and need a cool color. On the other hand, a house which faces west and is in the sun may need a cool color.

- Do not draw attention to downspouts, gutters, electrical conduit, meters, air conditioner units, and vents by painting them. These should be the same color as the siding or trim so they will not be noticeable.

- Do not draw attention to an attached garage by painting it a boldly different color. It should be the same color as the siding or a softer shade of it.

- For chimney and foundations, use a deeper shade of the body color; this tends to make them seem more solidly mounted.

- As with the inside, consider color values for a home and what they can do for it. Medium to dark colors usually make a house appear smaller, and light to neutral colors make it look strong.

- If the goal is to make a tall house seem shorter, paint the top a deeper tone than the bottom. This also works when the lot on which the house sits is small and it is desired to reduce the house size, and for new homes where the landscaping has not grown in and the house appears stark and overwhelming in size.

Figure 4-3. Trim color should complement the siding color. (*Courtesy of Dutch Boy Paints*)

- Using a dark color to outline windows and trim will make a house look smaller. A lighter color on the trim will make a house look larger. In other words, dark outline colors tend to pull the size of a house in while light ones expand it.

- Color ideas can come from a variety of places. Consider using a color a client likes from the inside of a home, or pick up a color from stonework outside or perhaps flowers or a plant. Color ideas can also come from checking color schemes of similar-style homes in the neighborhood.

- Victorian and other period houses were painted specific colors. If the client has a house of this type and wants to know what the colors were, check in

Figure 4-4. Exterior colors appear darker in the shade and brighter in sunlight.
(*Courtesy of Dutch Boy Paints*)

the library. At least one company (at this writing) has a "Preservation Palette" color card which shows original colors of period houses.

- Obtain color cards of manufacturers at paint stores and home centers. A number of these show homes painted with various combinations of colors.

- To test how combinations of colors work, draw a picture of a home and shade various areas with colored pencils. Or take a photograph of the house then photocopy, enlarge, and color it. The colors will not be accurate, but they will give the client the sense of how the colors will work.

- As with colors on the interior of the house, exterior colors will look different in different lights (Fig. 4-4). Hence, it is best to buy quarts of colors, apply them to an area, and observe how they look overall and in various lights, to make sure they work for the customer.

PART 2
Interior Painting

5
Preparation

It is an old adage and cliché that preparation makes the job, and it is a cliché because it is true. Preparation *does* make the job. Preparation on the exterior of the home is estimated by some painters to constitute some 80 percent—other painters put it at 90 percent—of the job's labor. While the percentage is lower on interior work, it is still significant. Another cliché in the trade is that it is not the paint that fails (if it does), it is that the preparation was not done well enough.

Removing—and Moving

Before you do any work, remove or stack furniture in the room(s) where you will be painting. The ideal situation is an empty room. But if this is not possible, group all the furniture at the center of the room—close enough so that you can reach the middle of the ceiling from your ladder.

Good-quality drop cloths should be draped over furniture. Some painters like to put a layer of plastic on first, followed by drop cloths.

Floors, of course, must also be covered. Here, no plastic should be used, simply because it is too slippery underfoot. Also paint stays wet on plastic for quite awhile and can be inadvertently tracked to unprotected areas. Cloth works better.

A convenient, out-of-the-way work area should be set up. It is important that drop cloths or other coverings be laid between the work area and the area being painted. Here, again, it is far too easy for shoes to pick up paint spatters from drop cloths and track it into other, unprotected areas.

Good drop cloths should be periodically cleaned. Dust builds up in the fabric and at some point leaves a residue wherever it is laid.

To Mask or Not to Mask?

The average job requires much cutting in with a brush, and most painters have a sure and steady hand and can do this quite readily. However, some painters prefer to remove doorknobs, switchplates, and the like—or tape them up.

In most cases, I don't feel taping is necessary. Just carry a rag, and wipe up spatters or spills while they are wet.

Taping may be required where there is some intricate work to be done. If this is the case, or if any masking is to be done, it is best to use painter's tape, as mentioned in Chap. 1. Its big advantage is that it can be peeled from a surface without accidentally stripping off paint or the wall covering facing. Masking tape is simply too aggressive.

Tapes are available in a variety of lengths, widths, and qualities. 3-M makes a number of good ones. Also available is tape that is partially coated with adhesive. These also come in narrow and wide rolls.

Cleaning Surfaces

At some point when it is convenient—either before or after drop cloths are put in place—surfaces must be cleaned. What you do depends on what you are cleaning, but in general cleaning is a very important step that can get short shrift. Jim Ochs, technical director for the William Zinsser Company, says that many problems that occur relate to the fact that people do not clean surfaces, and "You can't expect a paint to stick on a surface that is contaminated. The adhesion of the paint applied depends to a large degree on the cleanliness of the surface: Few paints can adhere themselves, for example, to a greasy wall."

The overall idea in cleaning is to do as little as you have to, but do what needs to be done. In some cases, the client will do it. In others, it will be left to the painter. As a general rule, though, kitchen and baths need a washdown and so does trim, even though it is not obviously soiled. (Sometimes feeling the surface will reveal a greasy, oily surface where mere looking does not.)

Some walls, such as in the living room or bedroom, just have to be dusted. A dust brush (Fig. 5-1) or small feather duster works well here. Something as simple as dusting can be crucial to the success of a paint job. Paint may not adhere to dust. Be sure to dust off the tops of ceiling moldings. You could always wipe the dust off as you go, but it is better and quicker to do it beforehand.

If walls have to be washed, a mild laundry detergent and water will do fine for removing most soil. But in some cases, such as in the kitchen, there may be a buildup of grease that must be removed. Here, TSP (trisodium phosphate, Soilax, or the like) will do a good job of cutting through the grease and cleaning it. You can also use Top Job or any other detergent.

Figure 5-1. Dust brush. (*Courtesy of Commercial Painters Supply Corp.*)

When the washdown is done, use clear water to wipe the walls and remove any soap residue. This residue can interfere with paint adhesion, working as a chalk or powder does.

When you wash a wall, work from the bottom up. This prevents dirty streaks of water from running into uncleaned areas which are difficult to clean.

Be particularly careful when you clean paneling prior to painting. As Ochs points out, "A woman will use Pledge or Liquid Gold on her paneling every Saturday for years, and you can't expect a paint to stick to this." He advises a thorough cleaning with a good-quality detergent. And if it looks as if the wax is not coming off, use mineral spirits to cut through it.

Some of the primers today can cover virtually any mars or marks on a surface; but you should at least clean the mar or mark if it is very noticeable, to make the job easier for the primer. Use a scrub brush and a strong detergent to clean the stains and a putty knife if there is a buildup of material such as crayon or wax.

Mildew

Mildew is a spore which thrives in a damp, dark environment where soil tends to accumulate (Fig. 5-2). The bathroom is just such an environment. Mildew usually shows up in the form of clusters of black dots, but it can be green, brown, yellow, and other colors.

Mildew must be removed completely. If it is not, it will eventually eat through any paint applied to it and create unsightly stains. Bleach—sodium hypochlorite—is the only commonly available material that will remove mildew. Sometimes,

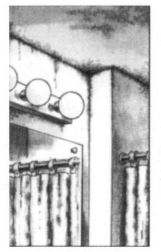  

Figure 5-2. Mildew thrives in a damp, dark environment.

it is hard to tell whether a blotch is mildew. To test, dab straight bleach on the blotch. If it lightens, then it is mildew. Bleach will have no effect on plain dirt.

A wide variety of products are available for removing mildew. Some products, such as Mil Klean by W.M. Barr Company, are just sprayed on and rinsed off 10 minutes later. Others are wiped on.

If you use any products containing bleach, it is a good idea to wear gloves and goggles. Bleach is a caustic material, and if it contacts skin, it can burn. Final treatment of the area should be a rinse with clear water.

Mildew usually grows where ventilation is inadequate, there is no exhaust fan, or the fan is undersized for the volume of moisture it has to remove. If a proper exhaust fan is not going to be installed, a product called *Damp Rid* works well. This is simply a small container of crystals which draw moisture from the air. It lasts about 6 weeks before the crystals must be replaced. (This product also works well in the basement.)

Marks

If a wall is marked in some way, say, by felt-tip pen, tobacco stains, pencil, or other permanent marks other than grease, you need not spend a great deal of time trying to get them off. The best bet is to spot-prime them and then paint. If a wall is heavily marked, just prime the whole area, because the primed spots might bleed through the finish coat. This could happen with a single mark, too, but sometimes it does not, depending on how well the finish coat occurs. If it does not cover well, the spots could bleed through.

Peeling

Walls or ceilings may have areas of peeling paint, and it is necessary to remove all that is actually peeling and any paint that might peel. The finish paint will adhere only as well as the paint below it has adhered.

To test whether the paint is sound in various areas, use a utility knife to cut a small X in the paint film. Apply a piece of transparent tape or the tape part of a Band-Aid to the cut area, and then pull it off sharply (Fig. 5-3). If the paint sticks to the tape, the paint has to be removed. Try this in several areas.

If just one or two layers of paint are missing, simply remove what's loose with a stiff-bladed 3-in scraper, and then use a block and sandpaper (or a machine) to sand down the paint to remove any roughness.

If there is a buildup of paint film and the scraping action causes cratering of the surface where the paint is missing, paint alone will not form a film thick enough to fill these cavities. For a better job, you can "float" the edges: Apply compound along the edges, feathering them to nothingness toward the inner part of each crater, and then sand lightly.

Figure 5-3. Testing the old paint surface to see if the new paint will adhere.

A 6-in-wide —or more—joint compound knife can be used for this job, as well as joint compound. Joint compound shrinks as it dries, but it can be applied in very thin layers and will do a good job of hiding the edges of these cavities.

For an even better job, you can float the entire cavity, in effect skim coating (see below).

Heavy Peeling

If your scratch test has revealed that much of or all the paint must be removed, if paint is heavily peeling, or if there is an indication that the only viable way to do this is by machine, then a belt sander works well. Small models are available— a fact that will be well appreciated if it is the ceiling that is to be done.

It is advisable to wear a mask during this operation, because a considerable amount of dust will be kicked up. Plastic sheeting should be hung over openings to prevent the dust from migrating to other areas.

Sanding

The big idea about sanding is not to have to sand—to apply the material so smoothly that little or no sanding is required. In fact, if heavy sanding is required, it will be very difficult to end up with an area that is smooth enough to be painted. The key, as mentioned in Chap. 1, to achieving smoothness in applying the patcher is to use a scraper or joint compound knife with a flexible blade.

Wall Liners

In some cases, you may have large, sanded areas and large areas where the wall is fairly rough, and no amount of patching will make it perfectly smooth. One way to get a smooth wall is with a wall liner, which essentially covers the wall with a smooth, thin material that is paintable and can have wall covering installed over it. There are three kinds of liner: canvas, polyester, and fiberglass.

Canvas

Canvas by Wall-Tex comes in 54-in-wide rolls and can be used when a wall is in pretty good shape. It is made with 80 percent cotton and 20 percent polyester. A close cousin is Sanitas lining, a fabric-backed vinyl that looks like the primed canvas of an artist.

If the wall is textured, masonry block or heavily patched or coated with sand paint or stippled, it is not a good idea to use it—it will show through. But for the wall that is only moderately bad, patched or with paint missing and some extensive but not very bad patches, canvas wall liner will work quite well. The material can be painted or have wall covering installed over it.

Polyester

This is a sheet material made of polyester and cellulose. It comes in various weights and is an excellent choice when the job is particularly tough, as in sandy surfaces or poor walls. It bridges gaps very well.

You have to ensure that the edges of this material stay clean and intact, because they butt together and should be seamless. Manufacturers suggest that this liner be installed horizontally because there are fewer seams, but in a pinch it can be installed vertically. Unlike canvas, it does not come primed.

Fiberglass

Of the three materials available, fiberglass is the most difficult to hang. It comes in 36-in-wide fiberglass rolls and is capable of heavy-duty wear—it will actually close up if slightly punctured—but it is essentially applied to a coat of wet paint, and there are fibers to be watchful of.

It comes in light- and heavy-duty versions. The light-duty one is for use when the wall is smooth, and the heavy-duty one for when it is rough. Fiberglass can be either painted or papered.

Wall Preparation

Preparation of the walls for liner is essentially to make it tight and sound; you do not want loose materials on it. You can follow the methods described above to achieve this if just patching is to be done. If there is wall covering, this should be removed. The reason is that the liner is installed with paste which has water in it, and this could resolubilize the paste, loosen it, and therefore loosen the liner. For removal methods, see Chap. 20.

After the walls have been patched and are clean, they should be sized. This, too, is discussed in detail in Chap. 19. Such sizing provides tooth for the liner and good surface which prevents the paint from being absorbed too quickly. It also permits you to more easily slide the liner around for positioning.

Hanging Canvas or Polyester Liners

To hang canvas or polyester liner, a prepared vinyl premixed paste will work fine. You can get it in various sizes from 1 to 5 gal. A roller can be used to apply the paste.

If you are installing canvas, apply the paste to the wall. Apply it to the entire area of a particular strip plus 2 in or so overlapping the next strip.

If you are installing polyester, apply the paste to the back of the strip, as you would wall covering, then "book it" as you would wallpaper—let it fold in on itself and rest for 5 or 10 min.

The methods for installing canvas or polyester are essentially the same. If you are installing it vertically, start at the top and smooth it, working downward. If you are installing it horizontally, put it in place and smooth it out.

As you smooth, you may encounter some depressions, cracks, etc. Although every square inch of the liner should adhere, do not force it down into the depressions. The idea is to hide them. Just as you would with wall covering, use a joint compound knife to press the liner in the joint at the ceiling and baseboard molding.

If you are hanging polyester, simply butt the seams as you would wall covering. Hang the next strip as you would wall covering. Trim around outlets as you go.

If you are hanging canvas, the procedure is slightly different (Fig. 5-4). The canvas is laid up in the wall and smoothed out, but then the seam is double-cut. Using a long straightedge and utility or other razor knife, hold the straightedges on the seams and cut straight down through the overlap.

Cut it as you would glass—in one sweep with no hesitation. When you have cut all the way down, peel back the sheet which still has a selvage on it and trim this off. Use a small seam roller to roll the pieces butt and flat; then use a sponge to wash away any excess paste from both the liner and the ceiling and baseboards. Paste left on new paint can affect its adhesion.

Hanging Fiberglass Liners

The procedure for fiberglass differs quite a bit from installing other types. As mentioned, the fiberglass strips adhere directly to the vapor-retarder paint while it is still wet. The material is smoothed and cut in the same way, and the seams are double-cut. Following this, another coat of paint is applied to seal the mat. Wait at least 2 days before painting or papering.

Textured Wall Liners

If you have very rough areas to go over or paneling or even concrete block, you can use textured wall liners that are extra-thick. They are installed as wall coverings are, and they can be painted; they do a particularly good job of hiding problem walls.

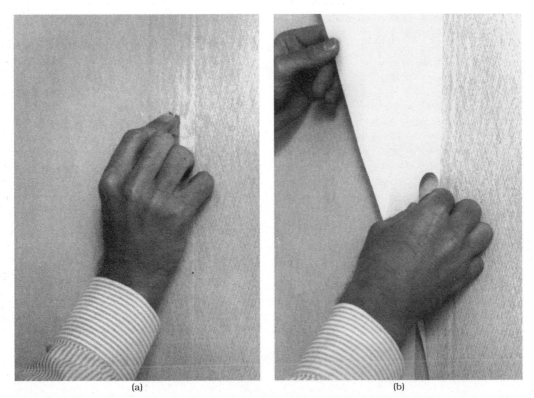

(a)   (b)

Figure 5-4. Installing canvas wall liner. (*a*) Seam is overlapped and then double-cut with a razor blade. (*b*) Excess is removed. (*Courtesy of Wm. Zinsser & Co.*)

Skim Coating

When plaster walls are in particularly bad shape, or when there is a textured finish of some sort that you want to smooth, or when a drywall job shows streaks, then skim coating is often the solution (Fig. 5-5). Doing this means applying a thin coating of joint compound over the entire wall surface, troweling it smooth. It is best to use a 10- or 12-in broad knife, spreading the compound on tightly and thinly (Fig. 5-5*a*). After it has dried, check for gaps, fill them in, and sand lightly. An inside-corner knife (Fig. 5-5*b*) can make the job go more easily.

Cracks

Walls and ceilings may develop cracks, particularly plaster walls, due to house movement. As time goes by, a house naturally settles, and if the movement is

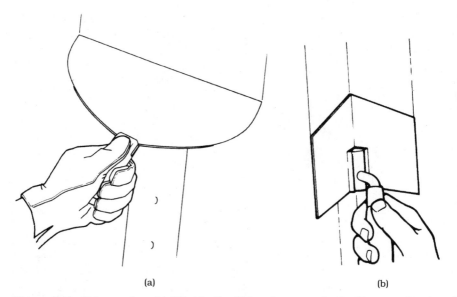

(a)   (b)

Figure 5-5. Skim coating. (*a*) Joint knife. (*b*) Inside-corner knife. (*Courtesy of Hyde Tools*)

great enough, the wall or ceiling material cannot take the pressure and cracks. The problem for painters is to fill these cracks in such a way that they do not return.

The most common place where Sheetrock cracks is at the seams. One way to handle this is to simply skim coat the cracked area. Sheetrock panels normally do not crack on the faces themselves.

Cracking is a quite common problem with plaster. Unlike Sheetrock, which is bonded firmly together with a tough paper skin front and back, plaster walls or ceilings are homogeneous masses with only the plaster to resist the stress from movement.

To patch a crack in plaster, first use a can opener or other tool (Fig. 5-6) to dig out the crack to a width of at least $\frac{1}{4}$ in. Brush away all loose material with a brush, then apply the patcher. Straight Plaster of Paris, which dries in about 10 minutes, or spackling compound of some sort may be used. A variety are available (I favor MH Ready patch). The key is the depth to which the patcher can be applied without danger of cracking. Many patchers can only go $\frac{1}{4}$ in deep, although a few can be applied up to $\frac{1}{2}$ in. If you are using the former, apply it in one or more applications no more than $\frac{1}{4}$ in deep. Whatever you do, it is important to force the compound into the crack so it fills completely (there are no air gaps). Slightly overfill it, then draw the scraper or joint compound knife along the crack to remove any excess. When it is dry, sand it.

If you are patching a crack that recurs between a wall and ceiling surface and molding, to prevent its recurrence, use caulk as a filler material (Fig. 5-7). Caulk has good sticking power, and it is flexible. Latex caulk works well, as does silicone. Most silicone caulks are not paintable—paint will not stick. If you want to paint it, buy the paintable kind. In lieu of this, you can get other types of caulks, such as Phenoseal, which are paintable.

For recurring cracks, a product called Tuff Kote Krack Kote works well. It contains a patcher and fiberglass material that goes over it. When the wall expands, which is the cause of the problem, the fiberglass expands with it and stays intact.

Holes

Holes that occur in Sheetrock normally result from something having hit the wall, such as a doorknob. Sheetrock is normally only $\frac{3}{8}$ or $\frac{1}{2}$ in thick and does not take a direct impact well.

Figure 5-6. Preparing to patch a crack in plaster.

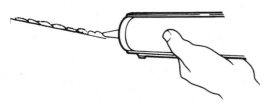

Figure 5-7. Using caulk to patch a crack.

There are various ways to patch a hole in Sheetrock, including using adhesive-backed fiberglass (Fig. 5-8) and ready-made patches. A number of these are available. One type consists of a square of sheet metal mounted on a piece of mesh which has adhesive on it (Fig. 5-9). A paper backing is peeled off, exposing the adhesive, and then the patch is placed over the hole and compound applied over it.

For holes that are bigger than such a patch can cover, there are other alternatives. One method is to cut a piece of metal screen that is 1 in or so larger all around than the hole. Thread a piece of string through the screen; holding the ends of the string, push the patch through the hole; and then pull the string out, so that the patch fills the hole and its edges overlap. On the outside, tie the string to a small stick that overlaps the hole and holds the screen backing in place. Apply a coat of patching plaster around the edge of the patch. When the plaster is hard, remove the string, and apply additional coats of patcher. Patching plaster (it dries in 30 min) or plaster of Paris (it dries in 10 min) works well for filling the hole. Use joint compound or spackling compound.

Another way to fix a larger hole is to use patch with clips (Fig. 5-10). First, the drywall is squared off, and clips are slipped over the edges. Screws are driven through the drywall into the clips, and the exterior portions of the clips are removed.

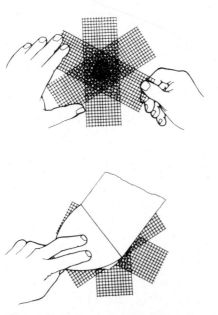

Figure 5-8. Repairing small holes in plasterboard with adhesive-backed fiberglass tape and compound. (*Courtesy of Hyde Tools*)

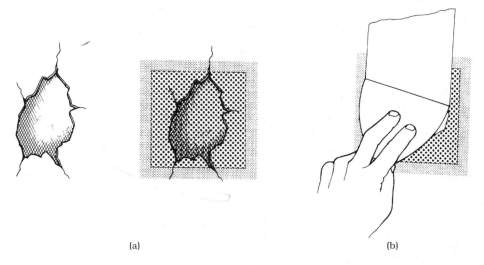

Figure 5-9. (*a*) Applying a self-adhesive patch. (*b*) Covering with compound. (*Courtesy of Hyde Tools.*)

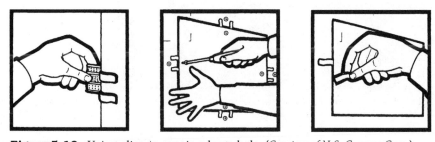

Figure 5-10. Using clips to repair a large hole. (*Courtesy of U.S. Gypsum Corp.*)

Another way, and one that I favor, is to use a piece of Sheetrock to make the complete patch (Fig. 5-11). First, use a utility knife to trim the edges of the hole, squaring it off as much as possible. Measure the hole; then cut a piece of Sheetrock that is the size of the hole plus 1 in all around. Use the utility knife to trim the Sheetrock to the size of the hole, but leave the paper covering in place.

Butter the Edges

Use spackling compound to butter around the perimeter of the hole a couple of inches. Then place the patch in the hole, embedding the paper flap in the compound. Use a joint knife to flatten the flap and to remove the excess compound.

Figure 5-11. A Sheetrock patch.

When the compound is dry, apply another coat, feathering it so the patch does not show. Run the knife across the compound in crisscross strokes.

Bigger Patches

If a large section of Sheetrock has been damaged, cut out a section to the framing members. You can do this with a utility knife (Fig. 5-12), cutting out a squarish patch along the top and bottom and cutting enough Sheetrock off the studs (or ceiling framing members) that the patch can be nailed in place. A saw may also come in handy (Fig. 5-13).

Cut a section of Sheetrock to fit into the hole, using a square to keep the edges straight (Fig. 5-14). Place the section in the hole, then use drywall nails to nail it at the edges to the framing members.

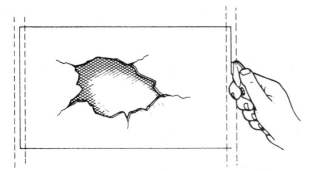

Figure 5-12. Cutting sheetrock to studs to repair a large hole.

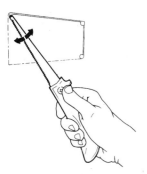

Figure 5-13. Using a saw to cut sheeetrock.

Next, seal the raw edges with drywall tape and compound (Fig. 5-15). Apply a 3-in-wide bead of joint compound to the cut edges, then embed pieces of tape in it, flattening the tape by drawing a joint compound knife across it. Feather the compound. When this is dry, lightly sand it.

To avoid using drywall tape, there is a product available known as *tapeless compound*. This comes ready-made in 1-gal cans. It can be applied to the wall without the use of tape, yet it seals and covers well.

Holes in Plaster

Plaster or wet wall is made by first securing a base of some sort, such as wood lath or metal mesh or gypsum boards with holes in them; then a brown or scratch coat of plaster is applied followed by two finish coats of white plaster.

Figure 5-14. Using a T-square to cut Sheetrock. (*Courtesy of Hyde Tools*)

Holes in plaster may be little or large. For small holes—a few inches in diameter—patching plaster works well.

If the hole is fairly shallow—up to 1 in deep—you can use patching plaster. First, wet the hole so that the drywall material does not suck water from the patcher, weakening it; then fill the hole halfway with the patcher. When this is hard and dry, apply additional compound. Slightly overfill the hole, then smooth and feather it with the joint knife.

Sometimes the hole is so deep that some filler material must be applied before the patcher. This can simply be crumpled-up newspapers stuffed into the hole, or steel wool. Once it is in place, apply successive coats (about ½ in deep) of compound until you smooth the material flush with the surrounding surface.

Sometimes plaster holes will be large enough to cut back to the studs. You can use a piece of Sheetrock as a base here. Just cut it to fit into the hole, and nail it in place with drywall nails.

If plaster is bulging or sagging, it means that the plaster has pulled away from the lath. There are a couple of ways to make the repair. First, use a cold chisel to cut away any of the plaster that is crumbling or loose. If the lath is in bad shape, take this out, too. Second, cut a piece of paper-backed diamond mesh lath that is big enough to fill the hole. Use galvanized nails to nail this to the studs, placing a nail every 5 in. Third, apply plaster—a scratch coat, followed by a brown coat and then a putty coat. New plaster and old plaster do not stick to each other very well. So before you do any plastering, coat the edges of the existing plaster with a product called *Plaster Weld* for better adhesion.

New Drywall

If walls are in such poor shape that skim coating or otherwise covering them does not work, then hang new drywall. This should be ¼ in thick. It will cover everything and will not entail (usually) having to modify molding in any way.

Other Preparation

There are a variety of other preparation jobs that the painter may encounter. One is painting paneling.

The paneling that is usually to be painted is the light to dark wood grain, grooved panels of 15 or 20 years ago or more. First, wash them down, as indicated earlier. This is to remove any built-up soil or dirt. However, if the paneling is waxed, that wax must also be removed. When the wax, soil, or dirt is removed, the panels are ready for priming.

A variety of primers are available. A favorite of many painters is BIN (see Chap. 3), and Kilz oil-based primer, which work very well, as do latex-based primers, such as ones that Behr makes. But any stain-blocking primer will do the job.

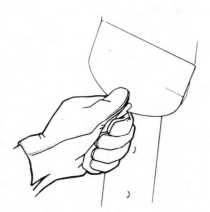

Figure 5-15. Tape and compound used to finish edges of patch.

Even though primers have tenacious sticking properties, it is suggested that you first scuff-sand the panels to provide even more tooth. Then wipe them down with a damp rag. Apply the primer with a ⅜-in-nap roller if the panels have no grooves and ½-in if they do have grooves; the extra thickness will make getting paint in the grooves easier. As mentioned earlier, primer should be tinted, as suggested on the can.

Formica, Tile, and Glass

These surfaces are highly nonporous, but any of the primers suggested above— oil-based, shellac-based, or water-based—may be used. But do *not* use BIN or any other shellac-based primer in the bathroom because it can crack. The manufacturer of BIN suggests that it have a top coat of an alkyd finish. But this seems like taking an extra step when none is needed—just use oil-based or water-based primers.

Concrete

Interior masonry, particularly on floors but sometimes on walls, is subject to cracking (Fig. 5-16). To handle this, use a cold chisel and a hammer to deepen and widen the crack, "V-ing it out," as painters say. Chip it out so that it is wide

Figure 5-16. A concrete patch. (*Courtesy of UGL*)

at the top and then wider at the bottom. Then the patcher can be packed in, and the shape of the cavity is designed to hold the patcher in place.

For dry cracks, ordinary concrete patcher may be used. This comes as a powder that is mixed with water. Sakrete and Quik-Crete are two brands.

If the crack is wet from running water, hydraulic cement must be used. This is actually cement that hardens in a few minutes—even when a crack is wet or has water flowing in it.

Wall Joint

Wall cracks and cracks at the floor-wall juncture may be effectively repaired. So can floor cracks that are not wet. However, if a floor crack is wet or if water migrates through it every now and then (particularly during rainstorms), probably the patch will eventually come loose. Water leaking through a floor ultimately cannot be stopped without using a sump pump or working to change the drainage or the like. If painted or sealed, the coating will eventually be driven off. There is no such thing as a waterproofer for a floor.

Efflorescence

Efflorescence is a white powder that commonly appears on masonry walls (Fig. 5-17). It is actually salts or calcium deposits that leach out of the masonry; when they hit the surface, the moisture evaporates and the deposits are left.

Efflorescence must be removed; paint will not stick to a powder (Fig. 5-18). To do this, scrub the deposits off with a brush. Follow by cleaning with concrete etch or a solution composed of 5% muriatic acid and 95% water. Mix it outdoors and wear gloves. Pour the acid into the water. Scrub off the efflorescence. Allow it to dry completely before painting.

There are masonry primers and paints available for concrete walls. But for uncoated masonry walls I believe that an interior latex-based primer will work quite well followed, when dry, by one or two coats of latex.

Kitchen Cabinets

One of the main things that the painter will be called upon to paint, and which will be scrutinized when the job is done, is kitchen cabinets. If the cabinets are wood, have been painted before, and are in relatively good condition, they can be painted again. If they are stained and varnished wood, they can also be painted.

First, remove the knobs and cabinet handles. For an easier job you can take down the doors; this will allow you to better control paint application. If you are

Figure 5-17. Efflorescence. (*Courtesy of UGL*)

painting the inside of the cabinets, this will also make things easier. You might suggest that the client consider getting new hardware; it can add just the right touch to a job.

Wash the cabinets thoroughly, as suggested above; then scuff-sand them, to provide a base with greater tooth for the finish coat and to remove any minor imperfections. If you wish, you can use liquid sandpaper, which will clean the wood as it cuts into it to make for better tooth. However, if you use this, you must paint within a specified time, usually 1 h, or repeat the procedure. Liquid sandpaper only has about 1 h open time.

Next apply a primer. One of the most common primers for cabinets is BIN or Kilz Oil. Both readily accept a finish coat and block out the cabinet substrate quite well.

Trim

This can be handled in the same way as kitchen cabinets. Clean, scuff-sand, and apply primer or a first coat of paint, as needed. If there are nail holes or gaps in the trim, they can be handled with spackle. If a clear coating were being applied, then wood putty would have to be used.

Dealing with Lead-Based Paint

The main problem that the painter must be aware of concerning lead-based paint is that it is not the particles of paint that contain lead, but the dust. If lead dust is raised (or if it falls), even the most scrupulously cleanup-conscious painter can miss some. It takes special care.

Today, experts feel that the best way to handle lead-based paint is to leave it alone as much as possible. Hence, if the paint is in good condition, just prime and paint as needed.

The following are some tips on how to paint a room that has lead-based paint. First, use heavy plastic drop cloths on the floor, and move furniture out of the room or wrap it in heavy plastic. To keep dust from migrating to adjacent rooms, tape plastic over doorways.

Before you sand anything, wet it down with water applied with a spray bottle. Then use wet or dry sandpaper to sand the area. If there are semi-

(a)   (b)

Figure 5-18. Removing efflorescence (*a*) with a wire brush followed by (*b*) scrubbing. (*Courtesy of UGL*)

gloss or high-gloss areas to be scuff-sanded, use a "presand," wiping the surface down with a terry cloth. This scuffs the surface without cutting it, releasing dust.

If the surface is in very poor condition and heavy paint removal rather than mere sanding is required, a chemical stripper may be used. Also, one of the wall liners may be appropriate as well as the paintables or wall covering.

When the preparation is finished, any chips or scrapings should be encapsulated by rolling up the plastic, then wrapping it in more plastic, and sealing it.

Any dust must be picked up. An ordinary vacuum does not work. Rather, a high-efficiency particle-arresting (HEPA) vacuum must be used. It is capable of picking up micrometer-size particles. Two passes of the vacuum should remove any dust that remains.

Read the Instructions

According to conversations with technical representatives of a variety of companies, one of the main reasons that people, including professionals, have problems with painting is that they fail to read the instructions on the back of the can.

It is a must, because the label contains information not only on how to apply the product, but also where and how it may *not* be used. Such details often spell the difference between success and failure in a job.

6
Painting

Preparing surfaces for paint may not be regarded as fun, but for many painters, if any aspect of the job qualifies as fun, it is the application of paint, where all the efforts expended in preparing surfaces pay off—in terms of finishing the job, getting any monies due from the client, and having the satisfaction of a job well done. The following are some hints to ensure that the job turns out well.

Mixing

All paint, regardless of the size of the can, must be thoroughly mixed before use. Before leaving the store where you buy it, ask the dealer to shake it in the machine; and before the job starts, this should also be done.

As mentioned in Chap. 1, there are accessories available for chucking into a drill for mixing paint; and, of course, you can also do it by hand. The best way to mix is to "box" the paint—pour it back and forth between containers. If you are using a 5-gal container, you can use two 5-gal buckets to make the boxing operation easier. Just pour off about one-third of the paint into each bucket and box among the three containers. A 5-gal can of paint weighs over 40 lb, and this can be taxing. *Tip:* When you pour paint from a 5-gal bucket, pour so that the paint flows past the farthest edge from the opening rather than the nearest. This gives you better paint control.

Paint can also be mixed by stick. Gallon and 5-gal mixing sticks are available at dealers. Just dip it in and move the stick through the paint in a figure 8 motion.

Mixing is particularly important when the paint is oil-based. Oil-based paint tends to separate into solids and solvents, and thorough mixing is required prior to use.

A 5-gal Jug with Grid

The easiest, most efficient way to paint manually is, as mentioned earlier, from a 5-gal container with a grid inside. Just screw the roller onto a stick, and work right out of the bucket.

If you are using different-color paints, you could also use a 5-gal container with a grid, but this would entail your emptying out and cleaning the bucket for each new color.

In these instances I prefer a tray and, as noted, a deep tray.

Some people use tray liners, but they can be more trouble than they are worth. My main objection is that they are not very deep and will not fit a good-sized tray, which is what should be used, very well. If you prefer not to clean when changing from color to color, you can line the tray with one continuous sheet of heavy-duty aluminum foil; avoid the thinner gauges—they can tear and defeat the purpose.

I would also suggest a wide-mouth can for working out of if you are using a brush. The paint is easy to get at when you are using a 2½- or 3-in brush.

Opener

The best opener I have come across for paint in the plastic 5-gal jugs with a lip on the side is the plastic hook-type opener (Fig. 6-1*a*). Sometimes, relief cuts must be made in the lid to free it. Metal containers work differently. They usually have a cap which must be unscrewed, sometimes with large water pump pliers; or to take off the entire lid, pry up tabs with a screwdriver or the like. (*Note:* If you have a choice between plastic and metal containers, pick the plastic; it is much less susceptible to damage and easier to handle.)

For opening 1-gal paint cans, nothing beats the little key with a hooked-over edge (Fig. 6-1*b*). It is the cheapest opener you can get and, in my view, the best. It hooks under the lid and pries it open.

Painting Sequence

Most of the time the ceiling is painted first, because any paint that drips down on the wall can be wiped off; any paint drip that is left on the wall will be painted over.

In general, it is best to paint against the light source. You can see light reflected off the wet sheen on the paint, and it is easier to see if you leave any *holidays* (missed spots). As much as possible, that light should be natural light—coming from a window or windows. It is the brightest light there is. I have found painting in artificial light, however bright, to be tricky. On more than one occasion I painted

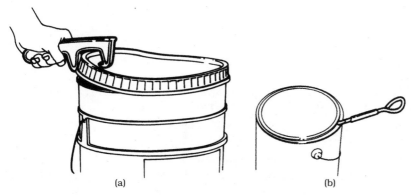

Figure 6-1. Paint can openers. (*a*) Plastic hook type. (*b*) Bottle opener type. (*Courtesy of Hyde Tools*)

at night and swore that I had covered everything, only to see some holidays in the cruel light of day.

It is a good idea to precondition any roller or brushes if they are new. To do this, just wash them in the solvent you are using, then squeeze them "dry." This removes any lint and gets the fabric ready to accept the paint well.

The job can be done from a 6-ft ladder or by using a stick while standing on the floor (Fig. 6-2). I like working with a stick, but some painters like to work from a ladder.

Power rollers are good if you have large, unobstructed areas to paint (Fig. 6-3). The bugaboo of power rollers—and spray equipment—is that they must be cleaned very thoroughly after use, which can be time-consuming.

Work small areas at a time, say, 3 ft by 3 ft. Apply the paint one way, then another. Do two or so adjacent 3-ft-square sections; then come back and roll out the entire area with a "dry" roller. This technique lets you catch any missed spots.

For speed, the painter should concentrate on going into the maximum dry area (within the 3-ft square) with each roll, or stroke, rather than rerolling previously painted areas (Fig. 6-4).

Use Enough Paint

And one of the keys to doing a good job is to use enough paint. Get in the habit of going to the bucket frequently: You let the paint, not you, do the work—lay it on, roll it off.

When exactly you cut in the juncture between the wall and the ceiling will depend on whether you use a stick or work from a ladder. If you use a stick, it is more convenient to cut in before you roll the ceiling.

Figure 6-2. Stick and roller. (*Courtesy of Wm. Zinsser & Co.*)

The brush line should be only 1 in or so wide, just enough that you can overlap with the roller without touching the adjacent wall. The thinness of the line is needed to avoid a different look that results when paint is applied by brush rather than roller, or vice versa.

If you do not have confidence in your ability to cut in a perfect straight line, use painter's tape, as noted earlier.

Note: A standard question posed by customers is, What is the difference between ceiling paint and wall paint? There are two differences. Ceiling paint is not washable while wall paint can be, and ceiling paint reflects light more evenly than wall paint.

Walls

When the ceiling is done, the walls can be painted. The walls are painted in strips about 3 to 4 ft wide. Start with an upward stroke. Again, use plenty of paint, go into the maximum dry area with each stroke, and paint 3- to 4-ft squares. Paint an adjacent strip; then come back with a relatively dry roller, and run it from floor to ceiling to make the strip smooth.

Trim is done last. You can do the windows and doors and then the base molding. Here, again, do not be afraid to use paint—not so much that it runs, but enough that you do not have to repaint each area. A tried-and-true technique is what painters call painting *from the dry into the wet*. Dip about one-third or one-half of the bristles into the paint; then skip ahead of the end of the previous

Figure 6-3. Power roller in action. (*Courtesy of Graco*)

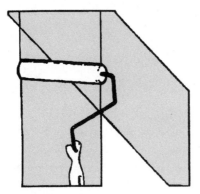

Figure 6-4. Achieving maximum coverage with roller. (*Courtesy of Padco*)

brush stroke by a couple of feet, and paint back into the wet paint. Brush it out as you go.

Painting window muntins can be easier if you use an angled sash brush. Position your body to the left or right a bit. This will let you see more of the wood than if you stood directly in front of the window.

When you paint windows, first, open, as shown, and paint what you can (left), then reposition windows (right) (Fig. 6-5). Some windows may be stuck with paint. The tool shown in Fig. 6-6, made by Hyde, is thin and has serrated edges for cutting through paint buildup.

Paint windows from the inside out—the muntins, the frames, and then the overall framework. Use enough paint, but watch out for sagging.

If you are using semigloss or gloss paint in the kitchen or bath, the procedure will depend on what you are using to paint with. If you are using a mohair or short-nap roller, use it in the same way as you would use a $\frac{3}{8}$- or $\frac{1}{2}$-in nap. As mentioned in Chap. 1, using such a roller will result in an orange peel finish—not perfectly smooth, but quite good looking.

If you want a perfectly smooth finish, use a high-quality brush designed for the paint you are using. Apply paint in strokes going across the grain, and finish with downward strokes.

Painting Glossy Surfaces

For better adhesion, any surface that already has a gloss or semigloss paint on it needs to be scuff-sanded before any more paint is applied. If this is not done, wet paint will be applied to a dense, shiny surface, and may not stick. After sanding, the surface should be wiped with a damp cloth to remove dust if a water-based paint is being applied or a sackcloth—an oil-impregnated rag—if an oil-based paint is being used. Any "powder" left on the surface will interfere with adhesion.

If you wish, you can use one of the no-sand products such as Kleanstrip makes. This is applied with a terry cloth, and it cleans the whole surface, making it tacky. Read the label for application instructions. Paint must be applied within 1 h at most for these products, or else they are not effective.

Painting Kitchen Cabinets

Kitchen cabinets can be given a spiffy new look. Follow the procedure given below regardless of whether the cabinets are painted or stained and varnished; the latter is the case in many older kitchens.

Figure 6-5. Painting windows. (*Left*) First position. (*Right*) Reposition. (*Courtesy of Padco*)

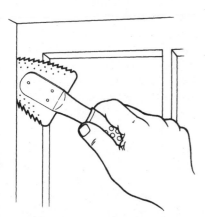

Figure 6-6. Removing paint from painted-shut window. (*Courtesy of Hyde*)

Preparing the Surfaces

First, clean the cabinets. There are a variety of products available, but here I recommend ammonia and water, whether the cabinets are painted or stained and varnished. If there is a wax on the cabinet, remove it with a wax stripper.

For maximum control in painting the doors, remove them from the hinges and lay them flat across sawhorses. Replacing the hardware is a good idea. You do not have to paint around it, and, it adds a nice touch to the cabinets.

Kilz Oil primer or BIN works well on cabinets. Both dry flat white, but they can be tinted—and should be—to the approximate finish color.

Paint the inside of the cabinets first, then the outside. If you are using a brush, apply the paint in light, crisscross strokes; finish with downward strokes. Two light coats are better than one heavy coat. For even greater smoothness, sand between coats with 220 grit sandpaper.

Only Two Coats Are Needed

In many cases you will not need to prime cabinets. If the color being applied is close to the existing color, then just a topcoat needs to be applied. If there is a severe color change, say, going from a dark green to white, then a primer is recommended.

Painting Paneling

Years ago, paneling with a wood-grain finish was popular, but today many people want to have these painted. The job is simple, as mentioned in Chap. 5 on interior preparation. First you must check to see if a wax has been used on the surface. If so, use a stripper or wash the wall with TSP. No paint or primer will stick to a waxy surface.

A primer is required on such panels. In any room but the bathroom, you can use a shellac-based primer. Just apply it as you would paint; as mentioned in Chap. 3, it dries very quickly. You can also use one of the oil-based primers, such as Kilz, or a water-based primer. The only requirement is that it be a stain-blocking primer. If the panel has grooves, use a $\frac{1}{2}$-in rather than a $\frac{3}{8}$-in roller. Once the primer is dry, a topcoat can be applied.

Painting Other Surfaces

New or Bare Wood

Here, a primer is essential because, as mentioned earlier, a primer will do a better job than a finish paint of sealing a surface and providing good adhesion. For this job you can use a variety of primers including straight oil, stain-blocking oil (Kilz oil-based), BIN (except in the bathroom), and latex.

New Drywall

Here, polyvinyl acetate (PVA) primer for drywall or a straight latex primer is okay. Apply this primer just as you would paint.

Aluminum

Raw aluminum is best primed with a latex primer, followed by any topcoat you wish.

Wallpaper

A stain-blocking primer such as Kilz oil-based primer to seal the wall covering in place is followed by a sizer/primer such as Muralo Adhesium.

Ferrous Metal

Raw metal should be primed with an oil-based primer, then topcoated after suitable drying time.

Textured Surfaces

If you are painting textured surfaces or masonry, such as concrete floors or walls in the basement, the only viable tool is a roller with a heavy nap. The same applies to walls with a textured-paint or masonry finish. Heavier-nap rollers have longer fibers and can more easily slop into the valleys in a textured surface.

For normal, smooth masonry walls, the $\frac{1}{2}$-in nap should be fine. For block with masonry grooves, the $\frac{3}{4}$-in nap works well. For heavier textured surfaces, the 1-in nap works well.

Note that to paint textured surfaces requires more paint than to paint smooth or semismooth surfaces, so this fact should be taken into account in your calculations.

Masonry walls should be coated with a latex primer, as noted in Chap. 5, followed by a latex finish coat. Latexes are much better able to resist the alkalinity that may still exist in masonry.

Masonry Floors

Interior floors may also be painted. A wide variety of paints are available, ranging from flat latexes and satin flat latexes to high-gloss oil-based paints. Which you choose will depend on the end use. If the area is in the basement and is being used as a shop, then a high-gloss oil-based paint is appropriate, simply because it cleans more easily. But if the floor is going to be used as a play area, the client may prefer a flatter surface so that kids will not slip, such as when the floor gets wet.

You can paint floors with a roller. First, sweep and clean the floor thoroughly, removing any grease or oil stains with one of the products suggested in Chap. 1. Screw the roller—a ½-in nap works well for masonry—onto a stick and apply a coat, being sure not to work yourself into a corner. When this is completely dry (check the paint can for times), apply a second coat. In other words, the first coat is used as a primer for the topcoat applied.

The above assumes that the floor is raw masonry. If it is painted and some is peeling, the floor must be stripped of peeling paint—a wire brush works well—then spot-primed and a topcoat applied.

The same paint that is used on a basement floor can be used on a garage floor if no car is stored there. If a car is housed there, the paint must be special—special in the sense that it can stand up to the heat of tires. Tires get very hot—400°F—and if a car with hot tires is driven onto the floor, the paint will lift up unless it is formulated to take the heat.

Epoxy paint, such as Litex makes, is one type that is normally used, but it must specify that it can be used for floors. United Gilsonite Laboratories (UGL) also makes a floor paint that is relatively cheap (and about $17 per gallon in a local home center). The manufacturer suggests putting a coat of paste wax in the garage where the tires will rest, but this is not required.

Concrete stain may also be used on floors, both inside and outside. It works just as wood stain does, penetrating the concrete. Also the concrete normally must have been installed at least 3 months earlier and be acid-etched before the stain is applied.

Painting Closets

The average interior paint job will require painting closets, and there is no mystery to it. Essentially, paint each as if it were a small room, starting with the ceiling, then doing the walls.

Most people use cheap flat paint in closets, and there is no apparent reason to get fancy.

Safety

While safety might be considered a boring subject, it certainly must be addressed. Your life can depend on safe painting practices.

The following paragraphs cover some safe practices to observe and some equipment that can be helpful.

Do Not Overreach

This rule is more applicable for painting outdoors, but it is applicable indoors. Only paint what you can easily see and reach. Reaching far from a ladder can lead to a nasty fall.

Be Aware of Electricity

Switches and receptacles in a house are live all the time, and you do not want to get wet paint in them. Notice where the electricity is and avoid it.

Ventilate

Whenever possible, crack some windows to provide ventilation. Breathing paint fumes—particularly oil-based paint fumes—is not considered good for the lungs. Breathing fumes all day is also not good for your equilibrium. By all means, take a break every now and then. Get some fresh air into your lungs, and clear your head.

Fumes can also be explosive. Ventilation is important for this reason. Although it is not likely to happen, mineral spirits, the prime ingredient in oil-based paint, have a very high flash point and can ignite.

Of course, some other solvents, such as lacquer thinner, have much lower flash points. Indeed, we consider acetone, which has a zero flash point, as an open invitation to disaster. Indeed, a woman was once using acetone to clean fiberglass in her bathroom. The phone rang, creating a spark—and the bathroom blew apart.

Running Out of Paint

Situations may arise on occasion in which you risk running out of paint. (It happens to the best painters.) This is no problem as long as you have enough to paint to a natural break in a room, such as the end of a wall. Then, if you mix a fresh batch of paint and continue painting from that wall, there will be no problem of a color change—there will not be any. It is a good idea, though, to paint right down the cornerline, overlapping new, unpainted wall as little as possible.

If you do not have enough paint to reach the wall, it is suggested that you buy enough paint to repaint the entire wall and the rest of the area. Even though you double-coated part of the room, it should not be noticeable.

Disposal of Paint and Other Materials

Paint

The best way to dispose of paint is to use it. This, of course, relates to proper estimating of the job, and today this is easier than ever in mixing custom colors, because of computer color matching. The match is generally quite good, so if more paint is needed in a particular color, there is rarely a problem getting it. If the estimate is correct, then there will be no paint to dispose of, other than a small supply you might leave with the customer for touchup or perhaps to paint a table or chair or other item.

In addition, various groups such as schools, churches, recreation departments, and local government antigrafitti campaigns are grateful for such paint.

Whatever paint is left and stored should be clearly labeled.

If the paint is going to be discarded, call local government to see where to do it. Do not dump it down the toilet or somewhere similar. This just adds to pollution and is likely illegal.

Rags

Of particular concern are rags used with solvent-based products. Throwing these in a paper bag or letting them lie around in a clump is an invitation to disaster. They can catch fire by spontaneous combustion, and they have been responsible for many deaths. Check with your local government on the best means of disposal. One good way is to fill a metal bucket half full with water, put the rags in it, then fasten the lid securely. Check with local authorities on how to dispose of the bucket.

One-Coat Coverage?

From time to time claims of one-coat coverage are made by manufacturers. Personally I have seen many paints cover in one coat, but only if the color combination is right, in other words, covering a light color with a light color. I do not know of any paint that will cover in one coat in all situations. To cite an extreme example, I would like to see the white paint that can cover a black wall in one coat. It is simply not going to happen, so the painter should not believe these claims.

How Much Paint Is Needed?

There are various ways to figure how much paint will be needed on a job, but the average I use is 325 ft²/gal. Most rooms take from 1 to 2 gal or less on walls (trim included) and 1 gal of ceiling paint.

   If you buy only gallons of paint, in reality, paint for a room often means 2 gal of wall paint and 1 gal of trim (semigloss or high-gloss) and a lot of paint left over. But paint always can be used by a painter, and it is better to have too much than too little.

7
Specialty Finishes

In addition to what could be characterized as standard painting, the professional painter should become familiar with and adept at a variety of specialty finishes and *faux* (pronounced "foe") finishes, the latter referring to finishes which imitate the look of some other material such as marble, granite, or wood at a fraction of the cost. Materials used are paint and glaze. Such finishes can enhance the look of surfaces and in some cases can solve problems.

Texture Paint

Texture paint is available ready-mixed and in powder form that is mixed with water. The ready-mixed versions, which I recommend, are available in water-based as well as oil-based formulations.

Texture paint comes in varying thicknesses, from material that has little more than a sandy texture to others that dry to what appears to be a field of stalactites or very rough stucco.

Despite variations in the paint, of one thing you can be sure: It will not cover nearly the same area as standard paint, simply because it is thick and so there is less liquid. For example, Dutch Boy sells (at this writing) a 2-gal bucket of texture paint with a coverage rate of 160 ft^2 per container. Two gallons of standard paint could reasonably be expected to cover from 600 to 700 ft^2.

Texture paint, as mentioned, is good for covering minor imperfections on walls or ceilings. The thick, rough film it leaves will hide hairline cracks, bumps, gouges, a rough drywall job, and assorted dings and leave a seamless, though textured, surface.

It must be applied according to the manufacturer's instructions. But it is safe to say that it can be done with a brush as well as a roller, and the heavier the nap of the roller you use, the thicker and rougher the film will be. Texture paint can also be applied and then worked with a putty knife, plasterer's trowel, whisk-broom, wallpaper brush, or crumpled paper to create various effects (Fig. 7-1).

You can also roll the surface with a textured roller, which is a network of plastic filaments in roller form that gives texture paint an even look (Fig. 7-2).

Sand Paint

In general, sand paint dries to about the roughness of a masonry wall or ceiling, considerably different from texture paint. It is normally used on ceilings.

Sand paint is available ready-mixed or loose. The loose material comes in bags which are mixed into the paint. I much prefer the ready-mixed material. During the job the sand stays in suspension easily. When it is loose material, constant stirring is required.

Sand paint may be applied by brush or roller. Use a 4-in brush with stiff bristles, applying paint in overlapping half-moon strokes. It does not look as good if it is applied with straight strokes.

If you apply it with a roller, as you would apply ceiling paint, a ½-in nap works well.

Note that manufacturers of sand and texture paint have material with slightly different finishes, sometimes quite different. What is sand paint to one may be more like texture paint to another. Salespeople in the store should have a display or be able to show you illustrated matter that compares finishes.

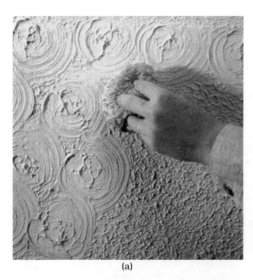
(a)

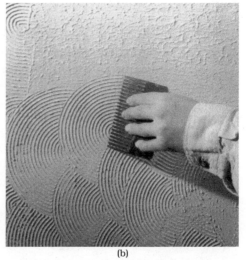
(b)

Figure 7-1. Texture paint applied with (a) a sponge and (b) a comb. (*Courtesy of Wm. Zinsser & Co.*)

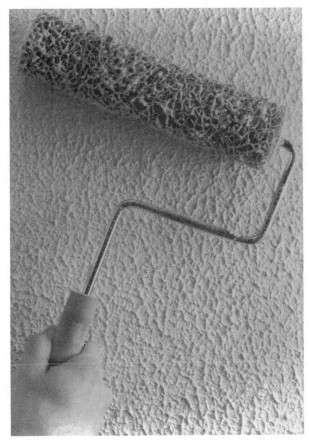

Figure 7-2. Working texture paint with a loop roller.
(*Courtesy of Wm. Zinsser & Co.*)

Other Specialty Finishes

Many of the finishes that today's customers like can be mastered by even the neo-
phyte painter rather quickly, although there are a few techniques which will require
more practice. As with other aspects of painting, there are different ways to achieve
what is essentially the same result. The following are some common ones.

In general, paint and/or glaze is used. Paint may be oil-based or latex,
depending on the open time needed.

Glaze is a clear liquid to which color is added to produce a translucent
coating with depth. It comes in various forms, but is essentially as stated. It
can be either acrylic- or oil-based; the latter is good when more open time is
needed on a project.

Sponging

A random two-tone pattern of paint can be achieved by dipping a sponge into paint and applying it to a base coat. In addition to giving a distinctive look, sponging is good for areas where the surface is not smooth or in bad condition. Sponging hides it effectively, as wallpaper would.

The basic tool required is a sea sponge, which is a flat or round sponge with an irregularly fissured surface (Fig. 7-3). A sea sponge has many more fissures and irregularities than a regular sponge. These sponges are readily available at paint stores today. They may be round or flat. They are also available from mail-order houses and in health food stores and the cosmetics sections of drug stores; these sources will be more costly than paint stores or similar outlets. As a last resort, although it should not come to that, a common flat household sponge can be used. Just use a razor or similar to cut sections from the sponge's surface so that it applies paint in an irregular pattern.

Colors.   Just as colors should be harmonious on the interior and exterior of the house, they should blend following sponging. The base coat and sponged-on coat

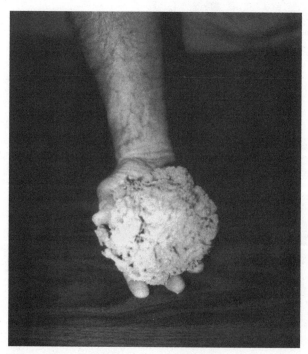

Figure 7-3. Sea sponge for applying paint.

must go together. If the base coat is dramatically different from the sponged-on coat, the result can be chaotic. Hence, it is a good idea to test colors on separate material before you begin. Mask off areas that are not being sponged with painter's tape (see Chap. 1). Latex or oil-based paint can be used.

First, apply a base coat of satin latex. Let it dry completely, then start the sponging process. Immerse the sponge in water, and squeeze out the water. Pour the paint into a roller tray. Dip the sponge lightly into the paint, then wipe it off in a rotary motion on the ribbed portion of the tray. If there is too much paint on it, it will be blotchy and drippy. To ensure that you have just enough, try it on paper.

Apply the paint, holding the sponge lightly (do not squeeze) and dabbing it on lightly. As you lift your hand off the surface, occasionally shift your hand from side to side to vary the look.

If you make a mistake—say, the paint is wiped rather than dabbbed on—have a clean rag handy to wipe off the paint so you can try again.

Variations.   The sponging coat can be done with glaze if you wish. Here, two parts acrylic medium to one part water, a transparent gellike substance found in various colors in art supply stores. As mentioned, applying glaze leaves a distinctive, translucent look with depth.

Different manufacturers also sell glaze. Zinsser, for example, sells a product called *Blend & Glaze* to which you can add latex or oil-based paint for greater open time. Universal colors may also be used.

Note that the open time is very important when you are using these techniques. For example, Blend & Glaze starts setting up in 10 or 15 min, so you have to move at a steady pace. Check the open time of any product you use.

Multiple Coats.   While standard sponging is done with one color, two or even three colors can be used. Each is allowed to dry before another coat is applied. For good looks it is usually best to use a light base coat and darker variations of this for the coats above. For example, a dark blue might be used, followed by a lighter blue and the lightest blue on top. Experts say that the color you want to see the most should be the top one.

When you are sponging anything, work 1 yd^2 at a time, and occasionally stand back to view the area being sponged. If certain areas do not look that good, you can touch them up.

If you have to sponge small areas, you can cut off a piece of sponge as needed.

Incidentally, in some sponging techniques the paint or glaze is taken off the surface—this is known as a *subtractive* technique—but it essentially involves applying the glaze coat to a base and then removing some of the glaze with a sponge. Your local library probably has a number of books which describe the technique.

Cloth Distressing

This technique, also known as *ragging,* is like sponging, except that you use a rag instead of a sponge to apply (or remove) a paint or colored glaze. Like sponging, cloth distressing is particularly good for use on surfaces which are in relatively poor condition, because the technique tends to hide, as wall covering hides blemishes.

Although the technique is generally known as *cloth* distressing, a cloth need not be used. A section of rug, a piece of plastic film, canvas, burlap, and more can be used. Experiment to see what looks best. It is heartily suggested that the customer be shown just what it will look like before you proceed.

Applying a Base Coat.   The base coat for the cloth distressing technique can be a latex satin flat or an alkyd satin flat or a semigloss.

The cloths that can be used include cheesecloth, old T shirts, and sheets. T shirts and sheets should be washed before being used to eliminate any lint, and they should be cut into 2-ft-square pieces.

Pour a portion of the base coat paint into a roller pan. Soak the rag in the glaze mix, then wring it out (Fig. 7-4a). Fluff out the rag and then let it drop softly into your painting hands, creating as many edges as possible. Bunch the rag up, and then, holding it lightly so that it keeps its shape, blot the wall lightly with it (Fig. 7-4b).

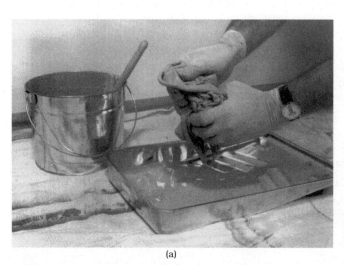

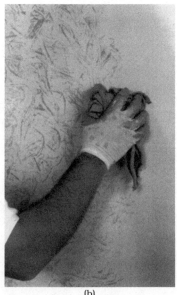

(a)   (b)

Figure 7-4. Cloth-distressing technique. (*a*) Preparing rag. (*b*) Blotting. (*Courtesy of Wm. Zinsser & Co.*)

Continue until the rag starts to lose glaze or paint, then dip it again. Continue as before, but as you do, shift the rag in your hand, but continue to hold it lightly to avoid repeating the design you are creating.

It is good to work in 1-yd^2 strips; every now and then, you should stand back to view your handiwork and to see if touchup is required.

As mentioned, you can also use plastic, a piece of a rug, canvas, burlap, and other materials for ragging on the paint.

Achieving Two-Tone Effect.   As with sponging, you can create a two-tone effect by using two coats of glaze. The first coat should be darker than the second, and you must allow the first coat to dry before applying the second.

There are also subtractive techniques employed with ragging. Here, the base coat is applied, followed by the glaze coat, which is then removed by blotting with a rag to the degree desired to create the finish.

Rag Rolling.   This cloth-distressing technique starts with a base coat (satin) of paint. Then a 2-ft-square rag is immersed in the glaze, which is poured into the roller pan. When the rag is thoroughly soaked, squeeze it out so there is no excess to drip. Fold the rag in half, then roll it into a sort of loose cigar.

Starting at the top of the wall, the rag, held on one end by one hand is rolled down using the flat of the other hand, thus distributing the glaze or paint.

When the rag starts to unroll, it is rerolled or dipped again, rolled, and more glaze is applied. The wall is done like this; you work in 2-ft strips and slightly overlap them.

Rag rolling may also be done by using a subtractive technique. Here the glaze is applied in a crisscross fashion by a brush or a roller; then the rag is rolled up and, from top to bottom, is used to roll some of the glaze off.

Stippling

This process leaves a subtle, aged look on a wall that is richer than anything that can be achieved with brush or roller. Essentially, a base coat is applied, then a colored glaze and a stippling brush are used to dab the glaze and create the effect.

If you intend to use this technique with any frequency, buy a stippling brush. It looks like a shoe brush and is expensive, costing up to $150. But it makes sense for the professional if the technique is in demand. Other brushes, including a shore brush and stainer's brush, could be used, but they do not achieve the same effect.

Technique.   It is best to use an oil-based glaze to ensure more open time. After a satin or semigloss base coat has been applied and is thoroughly dry (check the glaze manufacturer to see whether an oil-based or latex base coat should be used), apply the colored glaze. You can use a brush, applying the glaze in crisscross fashion from the top to the bottom of the 2-ft strip. However, it is best to do it with a roller for a large area, such as a room. Also a roller puts on glaze very evenly, which is important because while other techniques (sponging, rolling on) can hide imperfections in the wall, stippling will reveal them. (For this reason it is also important to use this technique only on walls in good condition.)

Use a Paint Tray. Work out of a paint tray, dipping the stipple brush in and dabbing on with light strokes. As you go, turn your wrist this way and that so that the glaze is not applied in a repetitive pattern.

Do the wall in 2-ft-wide strips. The use of an oil glaze should give you all the time you need to work, but if you believe you can work very fast, you could use an acrylic glaze.

Color Streaking

This is also called *stria* (Fig. 7-5). It is a technique created by dragging any variety of tools through wet glaze to create uniform streaks.

First, apply the base coat, then mask off areas not to be treated. Hang a plumb line about 3 ft from the corner of the room, as you would for hanging wall covering.

Roll on the colored glaze, then use a dry wallpaper brush to remove the glaze in long, continuous strokes, using the plumb line as a guide to keep your strokes straight. Leave an unbrushed area of glaze about 2 in wide at the end of the first strip, then repeat the procedure of applying more glaze and "subtracting" it with the brush. The 2-in-wide strip of glaze will ensure that there are no overlap marks where wet glaze is being applied over dry.

Open time on glaze is limited, however, so it is a good idea to have two people working on this technique, one to put the glaze on and the other to drag it off.

Marbleizing

Marbleizing, as the name suggests, is a technique for making ordinary materials look like marble. First, apply a base color to the item (say, a mantle). Dab on a colored glaze with a sea sponge, allowing the base color to show through. When the base color is dry, apply a second glaze color with a sea sponge. Let it dry. It should have a mottled look. Use white glaze or whatever color imitates a vein color well; then use an artist's brush to drag and push glaze across the surface. Use a small artist's brush or a feather to make very thin veining marks. Allow the surface to dry.

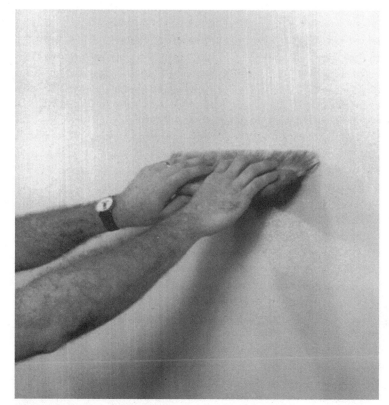

Figure 7-5. Stria technique. (*Courtesy of Wm. Zinsser & Co.*)

Other Techniques

There are a number of other techniques which essentially rely on glaze. The line of Ralph Lauren paints, for example, contains instructions for a number of techniques, including making a surface look like a denim fabric and a wall covering tea- or tobacco-stained (it looks better than it sounds), achieving duchesse satin finishes and imitating leather.

No Finish Required

The techniques which use paint are themselves finishes and do not require further coating. However some painters like to give added protection by applying either a water-based or an oil-based polyurethane, which is discussed in Chap. 11. But read the label to see which type is allowed for the product you use.

Graining

There are a number of products on the market that will mimic a stain without being true stains, in the sense that they do not penetrate. They are more films than penetrants, which gives them some advantages. In sum, the technique can give ordinary dull or painted wood or metal a beautiful wood-grained look. It is particularly useful on doors and trim. Zinsser's Blend & Glaze is good for this.

On a paneled door, start by applying a base coat, then use painter's tape to mask off one paneled section from the other. Apply wood-color glaze to one panel section. Allow the glaze to set for 1 min; then drag a comb or graining tool through it, making several gentle arcs. Next, drag the comb through the panel vertically, to create a wavier effect (Fig. 7-6).

Proceed to the next panel and repeat the procedure.

(a)   (b)

Figure 7-6. Simulating wood grain. (*a*) Subtracting glaze with a comb. (*b*) Finished door. (*Courtesy of Wm. Zinsser & Co.*)

Remove the tape, exposing horizontal rails. Apply the glaze, and drag the comb through it at an offset angle (11 or 1 o'clock), then drag it through again.

Take the tape off the stiles. Apply the glaze, then drag the comb, with cheese-cloth over the teeth, through it. Then remove the cheesecloth, and drag the comb through again.

Gel Stain

Another product which will give impermeable materials a wood-grained look is gel stain, which comes in a variety of wood colors and, as the name suggests, is a heavy-bodied gellike material.

It is oil-based. Brush it on the surface, then wipe it off with cheesecloth or a staining pad, creating a grained look in the process. Two or more coats can be used to make the color darker or lighter as needed.

Gel stain must be protected with a clear coating of some sort, either water-based or oil-based polyurethane. Read the label to determine which is allowed.

Staining with Artist's Oil

Painted woodwork, doors, and the like can also be stained with artist's oil, which creates a rich, grained appearance. The artist's colors are available in tubes in art supply stores and many paint stores. Using artist's oils on fiberglass doors (and other solid-surface, impermeable doors) can produce a variety of lovely wood colors, although it is labor-intensive. For example, burnt umber will give a rich, reddish brown color resembling dark oak or walnut; raw umber will give a cooler, woody look similar to English walnut or teak; raw sienna will produce a yellowish, light oak look; burnt sienna will give a strong reddish color like cedar; Prussian blue or Venetian red will create a weathered look.

Mix Colors

If you wish, you can mix colors. For example, a bit of burnt sienna mixed with burnt umber will give a handsome cherry look. To mix colors, squeeze out beads of color one next to the other, mix with your fingers (wear rubber gloves) and spread them out with a cheesecloth rolled up into a ball. If you do not like the color, you can remove it with mineral spirits. If the color has gotten into the grooved "grain," use a small stiff brush to wipe it out. Since the stain does not penetrate, it is very forgiving.

To better manage the operation, take the door off its hinges. You can stretch it across a pair of sawhorses, as shown in Fig. 7-7a. Before you apply stain, clean the door with mineral spirits or denatured alcohol. When it is dry, apply the artist's oil.

(a)   (b)

Figure 7-7. Refinishing door. (*a*) Sawhorse for easier application. (*b*) Color applied
in circular motion. (*Courtesy of Pease Doors*)

Squeeze out a 2-in bead of oil in the middle of the door or panel. Using the
balled-up cloth, push the color into the grain with a circular motion (Fig. 7-7*b*).
If the color is too thick, dampen the cheesecloth with a bit of mineral spirits.

Tip: As you go, be sure to get the color into the corners and grain of the door.
A 4-in bristle brush can help you to jab the material in place.

Brush Off

Once the stain is applied, use a regular brushing stroke to lighten the color, or
keep the door as dark as you wish. To lighten, just wipe the stain off the bristles at the end of each brush stroke. To darken an area, use a downward stab-
bing motion.

Continue the process as needed, squeezing out a 1-in bead of color for every
10-in by 6-in area. Keep rubbing with a circular motion, and use long strokes of
the brush to avoid brush marks.

When the color is all brushed out, stand the door up and look at it; then modify
as necessary with the brush, lightening it by brushing off material and darkening
it as suggested.

Let the door dry completely; then do the other side and the edges.

Apply a clear coat for protection.

Oil Stain

Another way to mimic wood grain is with the line of oil wood stains put out by
UGL. They come in a variety of wood colors and can be used on fiberglass,
Masonite, steels, and wood. When oil stain is used on an impermeable material,

such as steel, a wood-graining tool is employed (Fig. 7-8). The stain is wiped on, then the tool, which has a grain pattern imprinted on it, is run along the wet stain and rotated, to create the grain look.

Stain normally works by penetrating, but UGL says that its ZAR Wood Stain works because when it is wiped on, it produces an even film that adheres, unlike other oil stains that result in an uneven application.

The product must be applied in a certain way for best results. Toward that end, the company publishes an excellent how-to booklet with all the pertinent details. (The technique for fiberglass doors is shown in detail in Fig. 7-9.)

Once it is dry, a clear coat of ZAR exterior or interior polyurethane should be applied as needed. Follow the label directions carefully.

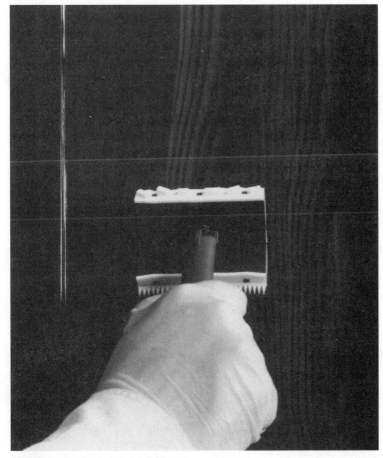

Figure 7-8. Graining tool. (*Courtesy of UGL*)

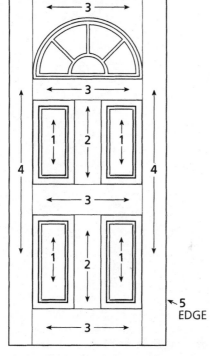

Figure 7-9. Steps for staining a fiberglass door. (*Courtesy of UGL*)

Paint with a Grain

Antiquing kits have pretty much gone by the wayside, but there is at least one
product left, called *One Stroke.* It is a goppy kind of paint which is brushed on
somewhat like a gel stain, but it has a sort of built-in grain. It comes in a variety
of colors. It is expensive, but it can be used inside and outside, and it might be
good for some applications, such as a door.

Clear Coats for Exterior
Use

A number of companies make clear coats for exterior use, but as suggested in
Chap. 15, these are not usually recommended (Zak says its clear will work)
because they do not last long under the stresses of weather and the sun, even
those with ultraviolet protectors against the sun. You can reasonably expect a
good, well-applied housepaint to last 7 years. A clear coating will last 1 to 3 years,
and this assumes that it has been applied thickly.

8

Waterproofing Walls

In the great majority of cases, the painter can help stop water problems in the basement. Manufacturers sell a variety of products for that purpose, and all, to one degree or another, work.

Before a waterproofer is applied, however, it is necessary to discover the source of the water. In some cases it may simply be due to condensation, which appears when warm, moisture-laden air contacts a cooler surface, such as a concrete foundation wall.

There are a number of ways to test for this. One is to tape a piece of aluminum foil to the wall and remove it after several days (Fig. 8-1a). If the room side of the foil is wet, the problem is condensation (Fig. 8-1b). To control this, one can cut down on such moisture-generating activities as showers and washing and drying, and cold water pipes can be insulated if they are sweating. Another way to remove moisture is with a dehumidifier, which does a very good job of reducing the amount of moisture in the air.

Seepage and Leaks

If condensation is not the problem, then seepage through masonry walls may be. Contrary to popular belief, masonry is not waterproof; water can and does seep through if masonry becomes saturated.

Saturation is the key term. Under normal conditions, water may penetrate masonry to some degree, but at one point—the point short of leakage—it will stop penetrating; when the weather clears, the moisture will evaporate.

Various factors cause seepage in walls. Probably most common is gutters. They get clogged, or leak, or are pitched incorrectly—or a combination of the three—so that the water is not routed away properly, as it should be. Water spills

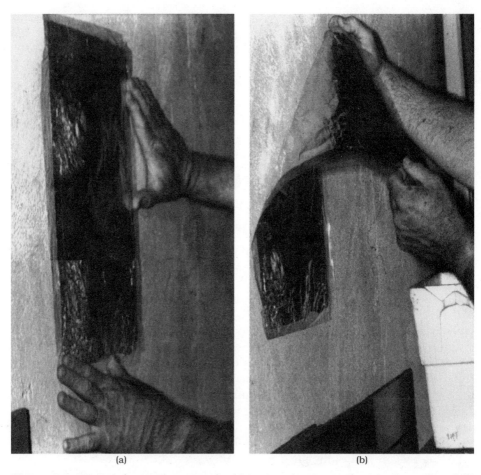

(a)   (b)

Figure 8-1. Testing for condensation by (*a*) taping aluminum sheet to the wall and (*b*) removing it.

onto the ground next to the foundation and saturates the soil, and eventually the water starts pushing into the relatively porous masonry (Fig. 8-2). As mentioned, if the saturation is sufficient, the water will eventually find its way into the basement.

Cracks

Aiding and abetting leakage in the basement are cracks in the foundation walls, which result from stresses on the house. The house moves and the foundation, which is fairly rigid, does not; thus a crack results. Cracks often form in masonry walls where the foundation meets the slab floor or other joists, but in solid walls they can form anywhere.

Before you apply any waterproofing material, these cracks must be fixed. The best material for repairing cracks in masonry walls is hydraulic cement. This differs from regular cement in that it will dry when wet. In fact, water can be actively leaking through a wall, and yet hydraulic cement will dry and stop the leak.

To make the repair first "vee" it out—make it wider at the bottom than at the top, so that there is enough surface area for the patcher to adhere. The V shape also makes it mechanically difficult for the patcher to fall out. To do this, you need a cold chisel and heavy hammer. Just peck away at the crack—wear goggles to protect your eyes against flying concrete chips—until small chips start to break free.

When all the concrete has been chipped out, use a stiff brush to remove any loose pieces. Wet the crack (it may be wet already); then mix the hydraulic cement powder with water, following the directions on the label. Pack it in place, and smooth it off with a small trowel. It should set up in minutes.

If the masonry has efflorescence on it, this should be removed as described in Chap. 5.

Figure 8-2. House with gutters. If these leak, the foundation may eventually also leak.

Waterproofers

There are a number of waterproofers on the market, including powdered and ready-mixed kinds. The powdered kinds are mixed with water to create the waterproofer. In general, the powdered types are cheaper than the prepared, as one would expect.

Although many brands are available, here I describe working with one brand, UGL (United Gilsonite Laboratories) Drylock, which I have used successfully.

Cement and Rubber Blend

Drylock is essentially a blend of cement and rubber, and it works by expanding and clinging to the pores of the concrete. If it is applied properly, the manufacturer guarantees it will withstand hydrostatic water pressure up to 4 lb/in^2— the force of water exerted by a column of water 9 ft high. In other words, the customer could have a lake outside the foundation wall, and the material would not yield.

Drylock may be used inside as well as outside the house on other above- and below-grade masonry surfaces such as retaining walls, cisterns, and swimming pools. When dry, the product is not toxic to people or animals. It may be used, for example, to coat a birdbath. It comes in white, gray, beige, and blue; and it can be tinted to light pastel shades. It can also be painted any color.

Three Forms of Drylock

Drylock comes in three different forms: oil-based ready-mixed, latex ready-mixed, and powder which you mix.

The oil-based material is cheaper than the ready-mixed, but its disadvantage is its strong chemical smell. Some people find this objectionable, and since the material takes about 24 h to dry, the odor lingers awhile.

The latex version, which is more expensive (about $3 more per gallon) than oil, dries in a few hours and does not have a strong solvent smell.

The powdered version works as well the others. It is available in white and in 1-lb boxes and 3½-gal reusable pails. It is mixed with water. It is, of course, cheaper than the prepared versions.

A key point to remember about any waterproofer is that it can only be applied to raw masonry. If the masonry has been painted, the manufacturer will not guarantee that the paint will stick. The reason is that it would be dependent for its ability to adhere to the wall to the paint film. If that went, the waterproofer would go with it. And, of course, a film of paint is not designed to stand up to the pressure of water.

Figure 8-3. Waterproofing raw masonry. (*Courtesy of UGL*)

Drylock can be applied with a brush or roller; two coats are required (Fig. 8-3). The first should be applied at the rate of 70 ft^2/gal, and the second coat at 125 ft^2/gal. The average can of Drylock can cover about 125 ft^2. Thus, 375 ft^2 of basement requires a little over 8 gal of material.

A sturdy brush may be used, but the job will be easier if done with a roller because of the rough surface. Most masonry can be painted with a roller with a $\frac{1}{2}$-in nap.

Drylock may be applied just as any paint. Roll it on as you would paint. There is really no need to use a brush—the job will be just as good with a roller.

Drylock may be applied even when the wall is wet—adhesion will not be affected.

In some cases, a third coat will be required. This is the case when pinholes appear in the coating.

9
Problems—and Solutions

There are a number of problems associated with painting interior surfaces. In many, perhaps most, instances, the solution is the same: Remove the existing paint by sanding, scraping, or other methods and paint.

Peeling

There can be many causes of peeling, but the essential problem is one of adhesion: When the paint peels, it is simply not adhering. Appreciating that single idea can go a long way to solving the problem.

It is important for the painter to try to diagnose the problem so that a solution can be devised that will work; or at least the customer can be advised of what the problem is and how to solve it. Some customers may not want to go to the expense, say, of sanding large areas of a room, to prevent a problem from recurring, so they should be made aware of the possibilities.

While there are many causes of peeling, the solution is usually the same: Sand and/or scrape off the peeling paint, and apply new paint. And often the problem can be prevented by proper preparation.

The causes of peeling, not necessarily in order of frequency, are as follows:

Dirt, Grease, and Grime

Some paints will stick to soiled surfaces, but most will not. A soiled surface is essentially a loose surface. When paint is applied, it goes directly on this loose, unstable surface, does not get a grip, and eventually falls off. All surfaces should be thoroughly cleaned prior to painting (see Chap. 5). This may be the problem if you can see the base coat intact beneath the peeling coat.

Calcimine, Whitewash, and Other Soft Finishes

Here, the peeling usually occurs on ceilings, where paints with a low binder content have built up over the years. When the fresh paint is applied, the roller agitates the surface and pulls the old paint loose, if it is not already loose.

The solution is to scrape and remove the existing paint. This can often be done by wetting the surface with hot water and scraping with a stiff-bladed scraper.

Poor Troweling of Plaster

Plaster consists of either two or three coats of material, with the final coat the "putty" or "white" coat. Sometimes this is not troweled properly, and the result is a chalk to which the paint does not adhere well. Paint will not stick to chalk.

The solution is to get the base coat off either by scraping or by using chemical removers and then applying an oil-based primer. Oil-based primers will wet any remaining chalk and adhere much better than latex.

Glue

When wallpaper is removed, a film of glue is left on the wall. This must be thoroughly removed, with a commercial glue remover such as DIF or a solution of vinegar and hot water. Glue makes an unstable surface to paint.

After you remove the glue, apply an oil-based primer to avoid the possibility of water in latex primer rewetting any traces of glue that may remain.

Uncured Concrete

If paint is applied to concrete that is uncured, it can peel, particularly if an alkyd is used. The concrete contains alkalies which combine with alkyd resins and cause what is known as *saponification,* the forming of a soap film on the floor. This leads to softening of the oil-based topcoat and poor adhesion.

Efflorescence

These are salts in the concrete that leach to the surface, either when the concrete is new or later. Efflorescence is a powder, and paint simply will not stick well to it. This is covered in detail in Chap. 6.

Moisture

Moisture can come up through a concrete floor and cause problems, particularly for alkyd paints. The moisture passes through the concrete, but when it contacts the paint film, the moisture pushes the paint up and off—it peels. Latex floor paints normally hold better on a concrete floor that has a moisture problem because they allow the moisture to bleed through to some degree rather than push the paint film off.

Moisture can also be a problem in a bathroom, where the constant assault of water vapor and actual water can take its toll on any but good-quality paints.

Also, if there is a break somewhere in the paint film, moisture can get behind it and drive off the paint.

Alligatoring

Here, paint pulls off the surface, cracks, and starts to resemble the hide of an alligator (Fig. 9-1). The reason is a lack of a bond between the surface and the paint; shiny surfaces simply do not provide a surface that topcoats can grip. It is always advisable, as mentioned in Chap. 5, to scuff-sand the glossy surface to be painted, even ones primers are going on. You do not have to sand hard for

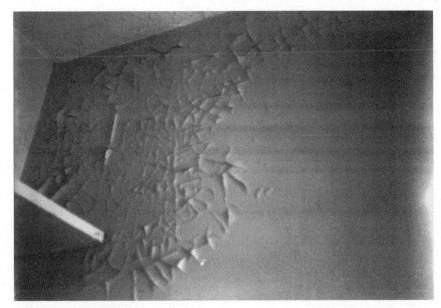

Figure 9-1. Alligatoring.

long, just "break the sheen," as some painters say. The procedure is not necessary on paints that do not have a gloss, such as flat and satin flat.

Another cause of alligatoring is that the base coat was not allowed to dry before the topcoat was applied. The topcoat does not get a good grip, and alligators ensue. Still another cause of alligatoring is the application of an extremely hard coating over a soft primer coat.

Flakes of paint adhere to the roller. One cause of this is low-grade paint. Poor-quality paint has poor qualities of adhesion and is ready to flake off—either by itself or when a roller is applied to it. The poor-quality paint gets wet, and the force of the roller passing across it pulls off the paint. As with alligatoring, the solution is to sand and scrape off all existing loose paint.

Paint Scratching

This usually happens with a latex topcoat. Latex needs an adequate time to cure, and before it cures, it is susceptible to being scratched.

Lack of Coverage

Paint may not cover for a variety of reasons. For one thing, the color contrast might be too great. The paint, however good, may not be good enough to cover.

Years ago, when paints were formulated differently, it could be said that dark-colored paints covered better than lighter ones, but that is no longer true. Titanium dioxide is the pigment in paint that covers; and to make dark-colored paint, this must be removed, lessening the covering power of the paint.

Another reason for poor coverage may be that not enough paint is being applied. Check the label to make sure that the coverage rates are being followed.

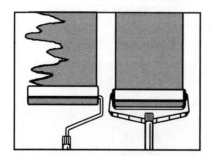

Figure 9-2. Poor versus good roller application. (*Courtesy of Padco*)

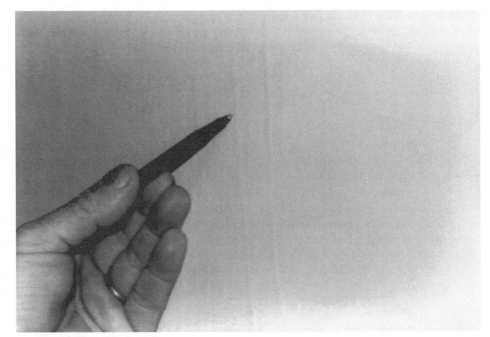

Figure 9-3. Paint sagging.

Poor-quality paint does not cover well and the only solution is to use good-quality paint. Also, if too much thinner has been added to the paint, coverage will be inadequate.

Another reason for lack of coverage is a poor-quality roller (Fig. 9-2). Poor-quality rollers have naps that are not good at holding paint, and so you have to frequently dip into the pan for more paint. Good-quality rollers (see Chap. 1) are a must on a job.

Sagging

This occurs when paint droops, taking on a curtainlike appearance (Fig. 9-3). Sagging can be caused by a variety of things. One thing may simply be that too much paint is applied, so it runs down.

Paint may sag because it is applied to a hard or glossy finish and is not gripping. Excessive thinning can make paint sag, and so will applying it to a detergent film. The solution is to sand the glossy surfaces and rinse off any detergent with water. It is always a good idea to check previously painted areas as you go for sagging, so you can brush or roll out the sags.

Make sure the paint is being applied at the recommended amount per square foot. Adjust the application as necessary. If you are applying paint and it still sags despite all remedies tried, apply it with upward strokes, wiping off the brush after each stroke.

Uneven Gloss

This is sometimes called *flashing*. One cause is that the porosity of the base coat varies. When the paint is applied, it is absorbed differently in different areas, with a resulting uneven look.

You can prevent the problem by priming properly. If the surface has not been primed, another coat of finish paint may solve the problem. If the surface is rough, though, you should expect some unevenness, though additional coats of paint can solve the problem.

Another reason for uneven gloss is that moisture has gotten into the paint film as it dries, and that makes it partially flat. The only solution is to apply another coat of paint.

Wrinkling

Here, the painted surface has the appearance of tin foil that has been crushed and then flattened out. The usual cause is that the topcoat dried before the base coat. As the base coat dries, it moves the topcoat and produces the wrinkles.

Other causes of wrinkling may be that a hard topcoat was applied over a soft base coat, too much paint was applied, or paint was applied to a glossy finish.

To solve the problem the wrinkled paint must be removed by scraping and sanding as necessary; then the surface must be primed.

Hatbanding

Here, a line of the applied paint appears darker than the rest of the painted surface (Fig. 9-4). Hatbanding can be caused by cutting in with a brush in the corner, creating a look different from the adjacent rolled surface, or by cutting in after a paint has dried, producing, in effect, a line that has two coats and adjacent areas that have one coat. In essence, the paint is a different thickness in different areas.

Figure 9-4. Hatbanding. (*Courtesy of Padco*)

The real solution is (1) to cut in around trim and at the ceiling juncture as narrowly as possible and (2) to use a dry brush to feather out the edges of the applied paint so that it will not be thicker than the roller-applied paint.

Cratering

This is caused by air bubbles trapped in the paint film or solvent, such as mineral spirits, shaking paint excessively (building up air bubbles), using a new roller without first wetting it thoroughly in the paint, or applying an oil-based paint too rapidly. The bubbles usually show up as the paint is being applied. Any paint that has been shaken should be allowed to sit for a couple of minutes so that any bubbles created can disappear.

Brush Marks

Most of the time this problem is due to low-quality brushes, and it can be solved by only using better-quality applicators. Brush marks may also be caused by a surface that is so porous that too much paint is absorbed. Excessive brushing can cause the problem, as can failure to allow enough drying time between coats or using the wrong type of thinner.

Yellowing

Paint can yellow from age, but it may also be due to fumes from ammonia products or to heat.

Crawling

Here, gaps appear in the paint film—it separates—shortly after application. The paint is not adhering because of deposits of grease or wax or because application is to a glossy surface.

The solution is to wash the paint off with a nonoily detergent, rinse thoroughly, and use sandpaper to take the shine off a surface, if necessary. Then reapply paint.

Burnishing

Here, part of the dried paint film has a polished appearance. It may be caused by the use of abrasive cleaners to wash the surface or by excessive washing. Besides not looking good, polished areas do not accept paint well.

To solve the problem, lightly scuff-sand polished areas and rinse; then repaint. To clean spots, use a soft, damp cloth. Fold the cloth into a pad, use a small amount of diluted household cleaner, and scrub only the affected area; then rinse clear. Do not use oily or abrasive cleaners.

Drywall Streaks

These occur when the texture of finished drywall looks different at the taped joints from the rest of the panels. It is also known among gypsum companies as *joint banding*. It is essentially caused by the differences in texture and porosity of the areas.

The problem can be worsened if spacklers oversand the joints. The roughened-up paper and compound absorb paint very differently from the rest of the panel.

The problem is greater or smaller depending on where the joints are located. In areas with very bright lighting, such as under skylights and atriums, drywall streaks can be quite noticeable. The lighting can be so good that a careful observer would even be able to distinguish a slight crowning at the taped joints.

If you, as a painter, have any input, have the boards installed, if possible, so that untaped areas fall where there is good lighting, and try to ensure that a high-quality job is done.

If there are definite drywall streaks, the best solution is to skim-coat the walls with joint compound as needed. As explained in Chap. 5, this provides an almost paper-thin coating that forgives all errors. If a customer does not want to pay for skim coating, the next best way to avoid streaks is to have the drywall primed, something that should be done anyhow. A good-quality non-polyvinyl acetate primer is recommended. Primer will tend to "homogenize" the surface, as one painter put it, making it all look the same.

Poorly Applied Paint

Although spacklers usually create the streaking problems, there are other causes, such as unskilled spraying of texture paints. In other words, some areas of the texture will have a different look or consistency than other areas. The problem can also manifest itself if two people are spraying. Each painter has her or his own "touch"—and it will show. To help guard against this, use primer. The drywall must be primed, the texture applied, and then the surface painted.

Paint can also have streaking problems as a result of uneven spraying or uneven rolling out of the paint. This usually is more common with semigloss and high-gloss paints; flat paint is much more forgiving.

PART 3
Interior Wood Finishing

10
Finishing Raw Wood

Paint is not the only finish the painter is called upon to apply. More than occasionally a customer will have raw wood to finish or perhaps trim that he or she wants refinished.

As with other finishes, it is important for the painter to make sure that the customer makes all selections relating to color. The painter never wants to be in the position of being responsible for a color or coating. This can be a road to disaster, particularly when it comes to stain: Stain, unlike wood, penetrates the wood rather than stays on top like a film, and wood cannot normally just be restained. Once a stain is in the wood and a color change is desired, the stain must be removed or a darker stain applied. Lighter colors do not work because they will not completely obscure the color beneath them, and the result is a two-tone effect.

Since it works by penetrating, stain can only be used over wood that is essentially raw or previously stained. If the wood is covered with a varnish, polyurethane, or other coating that is a film, the stain will not penetrate and will remain on the surface and peel.

Types of Wood

In the home, the main new wood the painter is required to coat is that used for trim, windows, and doors.

There are many types of wood, but they all can be broken down into softwood or hardwood. In fact, this classification relates to whether the tree is leaf-bearing or not and does not, strictly speaking, relate to the hardness of the wood. In the popular mind, softwood refers to wood that is relatively soft and hardwood to material that is relatively hard. For the painter, this breakdown—softwood is soft, hardwood is hard—will be fine.

Various Woods

A number of woods are commonly used inside the home. Far and away the most common softwood is pine, of which there are quite a few types, based on the kind of tree they come from. However, all pine can be treated as the same in terms of staining.

Probably the most common hardwood used is oak, but there is also birch, cherry, and other hardwoods.

It can be difficult, unless you are experienced, to identify the kind of wood you are dealing with; some pine, for example, looks a lot like oak. The important thing to know is whether it is a softwood or hardwood, because this relates to the way it accepts stains. Improperly prepared softwood can look blotchy.

There is a simple test to tell apart hardwoods and softwoods (Fig. 10-1). Press your fingernail into the wood. If it leaves a depression, that is softwood. Hardwood will not give.

Staining

To stain wood really means just to color it, because that is all that classic stain is—color. There are two basic kinds, oil-based and water-based stains. Oil-based

Figure 10-1. Testing for hardwood or softwood.

stain is the most common type of stain available. It is essentially oil colors suspended in mineral spirits. Minwax is one common brand name.

Oil-based stains are usually available in a variety of wood colors such as pine, oak, cherry, and ebony, as well as white.

Water-based stains are relative newcomers to the world of stains. These are colors suspended in water. Wood colors are available, as are pastel and other shades including green, gray, and purple. These stains dry in minutes, so only relatively small areas can be worked at one time. Behr is one manufacturer, but owing to the laws governing volatile organic compounds (VOCs), there are sure to be others coming on the market.

Preparation

Before you apply any color, however, you must prepare the wood properly. On most woods you do not have to do anything except a light sanding; but if a wood is nicked or gouged, it must be filled in with wood putty. So, too, must exposed nailheads. These must be countersunk—the heads driven slightly below flush— and then the depressions filled with putty.

There are a number of ways to do this, including mixing stain with a neutral-color wood putty and coloring a neutral-color patcher once it is on the wood. My personal favorite is simply to buy one of the wood putties (they come in various wood colors) in a color as close as possible to that of the wood being stained. In my view, there is no such thing as perfection when it comes to a patcher.

Whatever is bought, it should be sandable. Some putties are not—they are too soft.

Softwood

If the fingernail test reveals that the wood is a softwood, then a preconditioner is usually applied prior to staining. Preconditioners are available for both water- and oil-based stains. They make the stain go on more evenly on softwoods which have both hard and soft grain sections. Without the wood conditioner, the stain penetrates unevenly and looks blotchy.

You must read the instructions on the label, but stains commonly must be applied fairly quickly—within 1 h of application of the preconditioner. Indeed, with the Minwax brand preconditioner, you can apply the stain over the preconditioner while it is still wet.

Hardwood ordinarily does not require a preconditioner. The wood is consistently hard and will accept the stain more or less evenly over the entire surface.

Figure 10-2. Applying a wood conditioner.

Testing for Color

In looking for a particular stain color, it should be understood that any rela-
tionship between the color samples in a brochure or even pieces of wood on display in the store is "purely coincidental," as one painter put it once. Different
woods absorb stains in different ways, the lighting in the store varies from that
in a home, and the stain may have been applied more heavily—or lightly—than
you would apply it. The only thing a brochure or wood sample can do is to get
you in the color ballpark, as it were.

It is important, therefore, to test a stain color before you apply it (Fig. 10-3). Ideally,
you have a piece of the wood, say, molding, to be stained and could test that. If
not, you have to test a portion of the wood, say, under a window sill or in a remote
corner where the molding is located, to see how it looks in final position.

Some painters bring a piece of wood into the paint store, but even this is not
as accurate as it could be. Paint and other stores commonly use fluorescent
lighting, and this will not give a definite idea of what the color will look like
on site.

I suggest that you first decide which colors are close to what you want, and
then buy small containers to test them on site. Just open them carefully, and you
can return what does not work to the store for a refund.

Some companies provide small samples of stains so that you do not have to do this. Ask your dealer.

Applying the Stain

Directions for applying stain will vary from manufacturer to manufacturer, so it is important to read and follow the instructions carefully. But on oil- and water-based stains, they all boil down to the same thing. Stain is applied with a brush. Let it soak in for a certain amount of time, then wipe it off to whatever degree you wish—the longer it stays on, the deeper the color. To wipe it off, use either a cheesecloth or a staining pad (Fig. 10-4); neither will leave any lint on the surface. To deepen the color, you can apply additional coats of stain within a certain time, say, 10 h on an oil-based stain. If you want to lighten the color or take it off completely, use the appropriate solvent: water for water-based stains and paint thinner (mineral spirits) for oil-based stains.

There is a time limit on your efforts, however. In general, with water-based stains, you have up to 1 h to remove the stain by wiping with copious quantities of water. With oil-based stain apply a lot of mineral spirits to remove it, and you have a lot more time.

Figure 10-3. Testing stain color.

Figure 10-4. Stain applicators. (*Left*) Staining pad. (*Right*) Cheesecloth.

After this, the stain becomes too dry—it is cured. What happens is that the surface is sealed, and no more stain will penetrate. The existing stain will act as a film and repel it. To remove such stain, more aggressive methods will be required, as discussed below.

An interesting and useful product that can be used outdoors and indoors is an oil stain containing wax (Fig. 10-5). It is applied just as regular stain is, but after application it does not require any further protection. It has a hand-rubbed look. You can also apply a clear coating over this type of stain. Behr makes such a product, called *Scandinavian Oil Wood Stain.*

Protection

As mentioned, standard stain is just color, and it has to be protected with a clear coating of some sort. Years ago, these coatings were generally known as *varnishes;* but these have given way to a new group of clears, generally known as *polyurethanes* today.

Regardless of the name, these products share some features. They dry clear into a hard, durable film—as durable as paint. Polyurethanes are mostly used on raw wood, though specially formulated ones for metal and masonry can be had. These coatings are used because while they protect, they also allow the beauty of the wood to show through. Clear coatings are used to protect surfaces that have been stenciled, and sometimes they are used over wall coverings to keep them color-fast.

Clear coatings come in two forms, oil-based and water-based.

The end (or greatly reduced use) for oil-based clears is near. Because they contain solvents, which have been cited as damaging to the environment, oil-based clears may ultimately be eliminated.

Types of Oil-Based Clears

There are a number of kinds of oil-based clears, and they differ in formulation—the kinds of resins as well as the solvents and driers used. Depending on how

Figure 10-5. Oil stain for indoor and outdoor use.

these are combined, the clear dries more slowly or quickly, has different gloss, resists mars differently, and has different cleanability and chemical resistance.

Alkyds are the most common oil-based clear sold. These varnishes are both flexible and hard; the flexibility helps make them useful for exterior use, although I would put, as discussed in detail later, severe restrictions on their use.

Alkyds have a warm, amber glow and are preferred by many people. Like all oil-based clears, they do yellow, but not as fast as other types. Alkyds are characterized according to the amount of oil in their resins, something called *oil length* in the coating industry. An alkyd is called *short* if it contains less than 15 gal of oil per 100 lb of resin, *medium* if it contains 18 to 25 gal per 100 lb, and *long* if it has 18 to 25 gal/100 lb.

The long oil varnishes are more flexible and softer than other oils, and they take longer to dry. Because of their flexibility, they offer better weather resistance and adhere well to all but alkaline surfaces. Note that applying a varnish or polyurethane outside is a maintenance-intensive job.

Short oils are harder, more brittle, and very resistant to acids and alcohol. Because they are brittle, they are not used on floors. They have a "rubbed" or hand-finished look and are easier to work with than long oils because the sandpaper does not gum up as you work. Medium oil is very good for trim as well as furniture and floors.

Urethanes

As with other clears, there is some confusion of terminology when it comes to urethanes. True urethanes are two-part materials which are mixed before use. The catalyst is something called *isocyanate,* which is a poison and volatile. Anyone mixing urethane has to wear a mask rated to protect against it.

Most urethanes are not sold for painting, nor are they readily available. They are thought of as industrial coatings and are used as well for boats.

Oil-Modified Urethanes

The urethanes used in painting are not true urethanes (not two-part materials) but are described by coating manufacturers as *alkyd-modified urethane.* Indeed, the commonly available urethanes are much more akin to alkyd than true urethanes are.

Even more common than urethanes are polyurethanes, which are simply another kind of urethane.

For the painter, what the product delivers is, of course, more important than understanding its chemical makeup. Of all the clears or varnishes, urethanes are the hardest, resistant to scratching as well as heat, abrasion, water, and chemicals. Because of their hardness, they are often used on floors—they do not peel, chip, or flake. They work quite well on trim, and most adhere well to both wood and ceramic tile and a host of other materials.

Limitations

Before you apply any oil-based clear to a surface, read the label on the container. Many clears can be used over stain (and paint), but most urethanes cannot be applied over or under shellac. Also urethanes should not be used over sealers containing polyvinyl acetate or shellac. Certain urethanes should not be used over fillers that contain stearates; these can act as a soap and prevent good adhesion. Finally, some urethanes should not be used over lacquers because they create white spots or "blush."

Urethane comes in two basic forms, water-based and oil-based. There are distinct and important differences. Oil-based polyurethane thins and cleans up with mineral spirits, and it generally requires overnight drying.

As time goes by, all oil-based varnish, polyurethane, or derivatives turn amber or yellow. Indeed, some people like it because it does give wood an aged look.

Coming on strong in the world of clear coatings is a group of products generally known as water-based polyurethanes. Water-based polyurethane dries quickly—in under 1 h—thins and cleans up with water, and does not turn amber. If you want a stain color to remain true, water-based polyurethane is the answer. It is also good to use over wall covering and stencils that you want to keep true to color. Also, because of its quick drying time, you can complete the job in a single day, whereas oil-based polyurethanes require at least a couple of days.

Water over Oil

Oil-based polyurethane and varnish may be used over oil-based stain and can, in general, be used over water-based stain; they can be applied after the oil-based stain has had 2 or 3 days to cure. Note that not all manufacturers allow water-based polyurethane over oil-based stain, or vice versa, so it is important to read the directions carefully.

Both water- and oil-based polyurethane comes in satin, semigloss, and high-gloss finishes. The finishes are comparable to paint finishes. The satin has a soft eggshell sheen, the semigloss is slightly shiny, and the high-gloss is very shiny.

As with paints, the higher the gloss, the more the imperfections show. For cabinets and trim, most people opt for satin or semigloss, although a few choose high-gloss. But remember that if a high-gloss finish is used, the substrate must be perfect. Any little ding or mar will be magnified.

Sanding Sealer

Just as wood conditioner prevents stain from penetrating unevenly into wood, sanding sealer does the same for a clear coat. It is made in water- and oil-based formulations, and it is essentially a thin coat of the finish polyurethane. Hence, it penetrates well into the wood, providing good holdout for the polyurethane. In some cases manufacturers recommend two coats of sanding sealer with light sanding after the first coat is dry.

If you use a water-based sealer, do not use steel wool. A small section could get caught on the wood; when the solvent in the polyurethane contacts the steel wool, rust can form. Steel wool can be used on oil-based material.

Whenever sanding is done, the dust must be removed. If the finish is oil-based, a tack cloth can be used; but if it is water-based, a damp cloth is appropriate. A cold tack cloth leaves an oily residue which can interfere with the adhesion of the topcoat.

Mixing and Application

Treat polyurethane gently when mixing. Shaking is a no-no. It can produce air bubbles which will be evident when the material is applied.

The best tool for applying polyurethane is ordinarily a brush. If you are using a water-based polyurethane, the polyester or nylon brush works well; if oil-based, a natural bristle brush works best.

But do check the label. Some manufacturers recommend short-bristled painting pads such as Padco makes. These can be particularly useful for doing large, flat surfaces, say, a door. You wipe on the polyurethane and that is it. The finish produced is glass-smooth.

Just dip the brush in the polyurethane, and flow the material on with a light touch. It should level itself. Generally, light coats are recommended. A heavy coat can lead to sagging and poor drying.

If you are applying polyurethane to something like a door, you can do this in the same way as you would paint a door. Apply it to sections of the door, then lay it off with upward strokes that overlap.

If you have a choice and it makes sense timewise, remove cabinet and other doors, and lay them across sawhorses, and apply the polyurethane horizontally. The material is much easier to control.

Stain and Clear in One

In recent years at least one manufacturer, Minwax, has brought out a product that is both stain and clear in one. Both oil-based and water-based versions are available. The former is called *Polyshades* (short for polyurethane and stain) and is available in a variety of wood colors such as mahogany, pine, and maple. Its water-based counterpart, called *Polycrylics*, works the same way. But it is used with water as a solvent.

Polyshades and Polycrylics are applied in thin coats with the same applicator that you would use for a clear coating. Full instructions for use can be found on the can, but essentially a series of thin coats is applied with slight sanding between coats with 220-grit or finer sandpaper. In other words, you handle it just as you do polyurethane.

Lacquers

Like some other finishes, lacquers come from a product in nature, the sumac tree, which grows in Japan and China. The sap of these trees is gathered, strained clear, and mixed with a volatile solvent.

Classic lacquer dries almost instantly to a nonyellowing, clear, hard finish. But today's lacquers have many different chemicals blended into them so that they can be sprayed or brushed, dry hard or relatively soft, and dry very quickly or more slowly. Most lacquers still dry quickly. They also have a strong odor and are volatile.

Lacquers can only be applied to new wood or wood previously coated with lacquer. They will cause other coatings to lift because of the solvents they contain. Lacquers are difficult to brush; the key is not to brush the same area twice. Use a 50-50 mix of lacquer and solvent.

Because of their formulation and their high VOC content, lacquer is on the endangered list. It is already banned for use in some states.

Shellac

Shellac is manufactured from a secretion of the lac bug in India and Burma. The secretion sticks to the soapberry and acacia trees on which the bugs live, branches are removed and washed, and "seed shellac" results. The shellac is then made into thin sheets, dried, and converted to flakes.

To produce orange shellac, the flakes are dissolved in denatured alcohol. To produce white or clear shellac, the flakes are bleached and then dissolved. The ratio of shellac to denatured alcohol provides the "cut," with each cut capable of certain things. For example, two pounds of shellac flakes dissolved in 1 gal of alcohol produces a 2-lb cut, 3 lb in 1 gal creates a 3-lb cut, and so forth.

Years ago, shellac was *the* material for finishing floors, because it dries to a smooth, hard, mirrorlike finish. Today it is used mostly for furniture and trim on raw or stained wood. One of its attributes is that it levels very readily. It also sets up quickly, so the painter who is using it on woodwork must work quickly.

Water and Shellac

While water can damage shellac, it is not as susceptible to damage as is widely believed. Plus, application of a wax will provide all the protection that is necessary.

Alcohol and shellac definitely will not mix. Alcohol will damage it badly.

Other Finishes

As discussed in detail in Chap. 7, a number of products such as gel stains, oil stains, and artist's colors can be used on wood.

Wipe-On Finishes

These finishes are sometimes used on trim and cabinets made of raw wood. While many of the products used are called oil, such as Danish oil or tung oil, they may be and usually are a blend of varnish and tung oil. Indeed, that is what gives the finishes their gloss. They are wiped on and impart a yellowish cast to the wood. Although users are instructed to rub in most of these products, it is an exercise in futility because after the first coat is on, the surface is sealed.

Paint with a Grain

Antiquing kits have pretty much gone by the wayside, but there is at least one product left. It is called *One Stroke,* and it is a goppy kind of paint which is brushed on somewhat as a gel stain, but has a sort of built-in grain. It comes in a variety of colors. It is expensive, but it can be used indoors and outdoors and might be good in some applications, such as a door.

Supernatural

The latest in clear coatings is Supernatural from Bio-Wash. It is much more expensive than standard clears (at about $60/gal), but it imparts a hand-rubbed look to interior and exterior trim. Because of resins in it which were developed by NASA, it will last years longer than other materials and not be subject to the same degradation that other clears are when used outside.

11
Removing Paint
and Stain

Occasionally the painter is asked to strip interior wood of paint or a clear coating and perhaps to lighten or bleach stained wood or raw wood.

Topcoat Removal

Actually, there are two kinds of coating to attack here: a film and a penetrant. While the film is on the surface, nothing can touch the stain—that is its purpose. Hence, the film has to be removed.

There are three ways to take off a film—through sanding, heat, and the use of chemicals.

I do not favor sanding indoors simply because the kind of sanding that would be required to take off, say, paint would be too rough for the moldings or other trim, which are likely to be relatively delicate. Moreover, it would take a lot of sanding, and much sandpaper would have to be used.

Heat

Heat is a better means of removing paint. But as popular do-it-yourself manuals point out, any tool that comes with 10 pages of instructions on its use is something to be wary of. There are a couple of reasons for this.

For one thing, heat could cause a fire. Many heat guns, also called hot air guns and electric paint strippers, operate at temperatures in excess of 1200°F. That is hot enough to set paper, wood, and cloth on fire and to burn you badly.

When you use a heat gun, keep it moving, directing it at the material only long enough to soften the paint so it can be stripped; then move on.

When you are stripping next to glass, you must take care to preheat the glass to protect it. A device (Fig 11-1) is available for keeping the heat from glass.

Unhappily, anything that is combustible behind the molding, such as insulation or framing members, can catch on fire even minutes or hours after the heat gun is used. A fire extinguisher should be kept nearby.

Hot Nozzles

You must also be careful of heat from nozzles. It can take 20 min or more before they cool down. After you have finished using the tool, lay it down on something inflammable until it cools down.

Lead-Based Paint

This is another potential problem if a heat gun is used where paint was applied prior to 1976. In 1976 lead-based paint was banned, but there is no way to know what was applied before this date. If the paint was applied before 1950, it is reasonable to assume that it is lead-based paint.

Stripping this type of paint with a heat gun is hazardous, and I believe that a heat gun should not be employed if you have any suspicions that you are working with lead-based paint. Aside from the hazardous fumes that heat can create, you must wear suitable clothing, go through quite an extensive cleanup procedure, and check with the local official environmental group to learn how to dispose of the material properly. It hardly seems worth all the trouble.

Using a Heat Gun Indoors

If you have decided to use a heat gun indoors, the following tips should help. Direct the heat at the surface with the nozzle 1 or 2 in from the surface. As soon as the paint starts to soften, push it off with a sharp-bladed scraper. (Use a flat scraper for flat areas and a round one for round.) It is a question of timing. If you do not get the paint while it is soft, it will not come off readily.

Also, the scraping tool should be kept clean and sharp. Use some sort of metal tray with a sharp edge, such as joint compound tray, to wipe off and collect the removed paint from the scraper as you go.

There may be multiple coats of paint to strip. If so, do not try to do it all at once. It is better to do one or two layers at a time.

As you hit bare wood, take care. If you scorch it, the scorch mark will be difficult to remove.

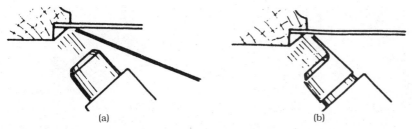

Figure 11-1. Stripping next to glass. (*a*) Barrier to protect glass. (*b*) Special protective device. (*Courtesy of MHT Products, Inc.*)

Chemicals

The third way of removing paint and clear coatings, through the use of chemicals, has a number of advantages over the first two methods. It is quick and, assuming that you take precautions, fairly safe. It will not change the configuration of the wood, as sanding can, and the danger of fire is much less. In addition, this method can remove some of the stain, which is, of course, soaked into the wood pores, if this is your goal.

Three kinds of chemicals are available.

Strongest Strippers

The strongest of all are strippers containing *methylene chloride*, a powerful chemical which has been the core chemical in strippers for many years (Fig. 11-2). The problem with methylene chloride is that it can be harmful to your health. For someone with a heart condition, methylene chloride metabolizes into carbon monoxide, which makes the heart pump harder to get oxygen to the body. Persons with heart conditions should not use methylene chloride.

Methylene chloride is also suspected of being a carcinogen, although this has not been definitely established.

If it is used—by anyone—it should be in a well-ventilated area, which means that there should be cross ventilation. Although a mask can be used, it should not be totally depended on. Ventilation is fail-safe.

Methylene chloride comes in various strengths. The strongest of the methylene chloride–based strippers are known as *acid-fortified* or *alkali-fortified*. When an acid or alkali is present, the stripper's strength is increased. The alkali is usually ammonia, and the acid is oxalic acid.

The acid-fortified methylene chloride stripper is a strong but unstable mixture, so it is usually found only in automotive and boat stores, where it is sold as marine stripper. Strippers with alkali in them are available in paint stores, home centers, and the like.

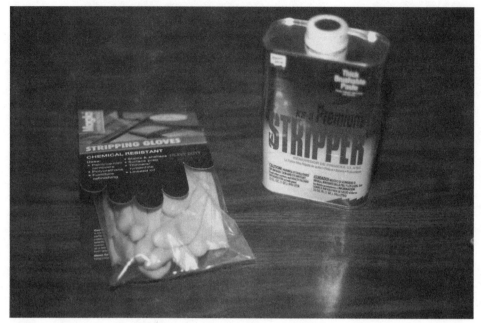

Figure 11-2. Paint stripper and protective gloves.

The health hazards have been mentioned. These strippers are also more expensive than others, but they will remove just about anything including epoxy, polyurethane, polyesters, and boat and car finishes.

Methylene chloride–based strippers may stain hardwoods such as oak, mahogany, cherry, and walnut. The ammonia in the stripper combines with tannic acids in the woods, solubilizes them, and draws them toward the surface, much as water draws tannins from cedar. But there are ways to deal with this problem, as suggested later. Typical products are Klean Strip's Paint Remover, Parks' ProStripper, and Bix' Tuff Job Remover.

Next-Strongest Strippers

The widest variety of strippers available is those whose strength is somewhat below the strongest removers. These contain methanol. They are cheaper than the strongest methylene chloride–based strippers, but are still relatively costly. They are capable of removing all kinds of paint and clear coatings, except epoxy and polyester. Brands of this type of stripper include Superstrip, Zip Strip, Jasco Paint and Epoxy Remover, Zar's Paint & Varnish Remover, and Super Strip.

Weakest Strippers

The weakest of the methylene chloride strippers are those formulations in which methylene chloride methanol is diluted by the addition of acetone and toluene, which reduces the cost. Check the label to see what coatings the products will remove. Although they are relatively weak, these strippers can still remove most paint. Examples of these are Kutzity's Paint & Varnish Remover, Klean Kutter by Klean Strip, Parks' Liquid Strip, and Strypeeze's Paint & Varnish Remover.

Liquid or Paste?

Methylene chloride–based strippers are available in liquid and semipaste form. The liquids are for use on horizontal surfaces. Painters likely use the semipaste version most because it adheres to vertical surfaces, such as trim, and allows the chemicals to work.

The solvents in methylene chloride strippers evaporate rapidly, so to retard this, manufacturers have added paraffin wax. When the stripper is applied, this wax rises to the surface and supplies a sort of shield against evaporation. Hence, when the stripping process is complete, this wax is left on the surface and must be washed away with paint thinner or naphtha.

Other Strippers

There exist other types of strippers, some of which work as well as methylene chloride–based ones. One such is a group containing acetone, toluene, and methanol, or ATM strippers for short. There are two kinds of ATM stripper. One is a semipaste that works much as methylene chloride–based strippers do; some work just as well as methylene chloride types.

The effectiveness of these strippers, which are semipastes, is due to the wax in the formulations. This wax holds the stripper on the surface until the chemicals can work.

The big plus of ATM strippers is that they are cheaper and are not potentially hazardous to human health. On the negative side, they are very flammable, and some will stain hardwoods. Examples of the ATM type of stripper with wax are BIX' Stripper, UGL's Paint Remover, and Klean Strip's Semi-Paste Paint Remover.

Refinishers

The other type of ATM stripper is generally characterized as a refinisher. This type of stripper is much thinner than the semipaste form, containing no wax or fillers. Because of this, though, the solvents evaporate so quickly that they do not penetrate the finish, but rather soften it. Although they cannot be expected to remove varnish and paint, they are effective against lacquer and shellac—once these films are softened, they can be scrubbed off with fine steel wool. Once you are finished, there is no need to clean the wood with paint thinner because no wax remains.

As mentioned, ATM strippers are based on blends of toluene, acetone, and methanol which are present in toxic amounts. These also can be dangerous to the human central nervous system. Observe the same safety precautions as you would with methylene chloride strippers.

Safer Strippers

The latest strippers to come along are relatively safe in terms of their toxicity. There are two kinds, NMP (*N*-methyl pyrrolidone) and DBE (dibasic esters) strippers.

Of the two, NMP strippers work better. They are slower than ATM strippers, but they remove all but the most stubborn kinds of finishes. The problem is that they cost almost twice as much as methylene chloride–based strippers.

The DBE strippers cost less than the NMP ones, but they take a lot longer to work. Although instructions on the can promise a quicker time, it can take overnight to blister paint, shellac, and lacquer. This could put the water in the stripper in contact with veneers on cabinets, say, and lead to delamination. The contact can also leave the wood rough and require that it be heavily sanded before finishing. (And when manufacturers suggest you scrub the surface with a coarse pad and strong detergent, the damage can be increased.)

Stripping Techniques

When you strip molding and cabinets, there are a number of procedures to follow—and you must wear the proper gear. Wear clothing that protects you. Wear a long-sleeved shirt, safety goggles, and butyl or neoprene gloves to protect your hands. (Many strippers eat through ordinary rubber.)

Work in a well-ventilated area. As mentioned earlier, this means cross-ventilation. Also turn off sources of flame if instructions advise.

If cabinets have hardware that will interfere with stripper application, remove it.

Shake the stripper, then open it slowly to let the pressure bleed off, and pour the liquid into a wide-mouth metal can. Do not use a plastic bucket—stripper can eat right through it. Mask off surfaces that you do not want the stripper to touch.

You can use an old brush to apply the stripper. Lay on a generous brushful one way. Do *not* brush back and forth, as this tends to make the solvents evaporate more quickly and dry up, and the stripper is not working when it is dry.

Keep it wet, and after 5 or 10 min—or longer (up to 45 min for individual strippers)—check to see if the film is lifting. Do not start scraping until you can see raw wood. When the film lifts, start to scrape. Deposit the excess stripper in a metal coffee can.

If the molding has grooves or other turnings, use brushes designed for this or use strippers or pads. If you have to get into certain areas, use sharpened dowels, even toothpicks, to do the job.

Strong strippers can take paint and the like off in one application, but repeated applications may be necessary. Apply as much stripper as it takes to remove the film. To remove any residue, apply more stripper and then brush it out with soft-bristled brass or plastic finish brush.

If the stripper is a kind that contains a wax, wash it away, as mentioned earlier, with paint thinner or naphtha.

Problems

Sometimes, the stripper simply does not work, and there are some reasons for this. For one thing, the coatings in place may be too strong for the stripper being used. The answer is to use stronger stripper. This resistance, by the way, can occur halfway through a job. The stripper may remove four layers of paint, but not the bottom two layers.

Sometimes the temperature is wrong. If it is below 65°F where the stripping is being done, the stripper will take longer to work. If it is above 85°F, the solvents could be evaporating so fast that the stripper does not have time to work. If that is the case, you can slow the evaporation by applying the stripper and then enclosing the treated area with sheet plastic. For example, if you are stripping a window, apply the stripper, then tape a sheet of plastic over the affected area.

Another problem arises when you assume that a clear coating is completely off the wood when it is not. Allowing this to remain is not an option because the stain will *not* penetrate. To be sure that a clear finish is completely removed, carefully examine the wood. It should have the look and the feel of raw wood, even though it still has a stain coloring it.

Not All the Paint Comes Off

Sometimes flecks of paint will remain deeply embedded in the pores of the wood. This can happen with both latex and oil-based paints.

What is happening is that these kinds of paint, which do not dissolve but swell and blister, are trapped. The stripper softens the paint, but since it cannot swell or blister, the paint just stays there. Here, the answer is to brush it out while it is wet. After the stripper has had time to work, work the brush over the surface. Wipe out the residue with rags or newspaper.

In some situations, such as on softwoods like poplar and pine (which a lot of painted trim is), the stripper will be able to take the paint out. You can try a number of things.

Make a solution of warm water and lye (where available), but you must take care in using it. Lye can cause severe burns on human skin. Be sure to wear appropriate protective clothing; then make a solution composed of $\frac{1}{4}$ lb lye to 1 gal of water. Always pour the lye into the water; if you do the opposite (pour water into lye), a boiling chemical reaction can result.

Brush only enough of the solution onto the surface to remove the paint. Lye is caustic and can damage wood, so lye should be used carefully and sparingly. When the paint comes off—you can scrub it away—apply vinegar to the surface to neutralize the lye, to stop it from working. Otherwise, the lye can continue to work and damage the wood.

Slaked lime can also be used as a stripper. This is not as potent as lye, but it is strong, less caustic, and therefore safer to use.

If lye does not work, which is unlikely, you will have to use an electric sander or, failing this, compensate for the failure of the stripping efforts by covering the wood with a paste wood filler, glaze, or gel stain. If all else fails, the wood will have to be repainted.

Of Special Note

One stripper and stain remover worth special note is Organic Strip, a product of Bio Wash. This does not contain any methylene chloride, and when applied, it strips not only a film finish like polyurethane or paint but also the stain.

The secret to Organic Strip's success is that it stays wet up to 36 h. It is a yellowish substance with the consistency of honey, and it smells lemony—because it is made with all biodegradable products.

Sometimes the job is done quickly, sometimes it takes longer. Any residue can be wiped away with a little paint thinner.

Bio-Wash also makes a nonmethylene chloride product for exterior paint removal. Rinse or Peel has a caustic base (so does Organic Strip), and is biodegradable. You can put it over the paint, then peel the paint or rinse it off. The product residue will not harm the environment.

These products are relatively new and have not been tested by the author, but the company has a good reputation and it's safe to assume that they work as advertised.

PART 4

Exterior Preparation

12

Preparing the Surfaces

Preparation of surfaces for exterior painting is just as important, of course, as for interior ones. The exterior of a home is susceptible to many more problems than the interior simply because it is subject to more stress. Wind and rain and perhaps snow lash it, the substrate expands and contracts, and various forms of unwanted life, such as mildew and algae, take up residence on it. And then, of course, there is the sun beating down on it and the ultraviolet rays which help to break down the finish very effectively.

Indeed, preparation work on the exterior can be quite extensive, and many pros feel that 75 or 80 percent of the job is preparation. And when paint fails, it is usually not because of the paint, but because something has not been done that should have been done in preparation.

Here a variety of what might be called commonplace problems, preparation steps which are normally required on many, if not most, jobs, are covered. Chapter 28 discusses in detail how to handle a number of other problems which are less common.

Cleaning the Surface

As has already been stated several times, paint will not stick to a surface that is dirty or greasy. If the dirt or grease or whatever is left in place, then the substrate is not the siding or trim, but the foreign matter. And when the foreign matter comes off, so will the finish adhering to it.

Scrubbing the Surface

There are various ways to clean a house, but first you must determine whether it has mildew (Fig. 12-1). This is normally seen as clusters of black dots, as mentioned in Chap. 5, but mildew can be green, red, yellow—you name it.

Test to see if it is mildew. Dab pure household bleach on the suspicious spots. If bleach makes the spots disappear, it is mildew. If not, it is dirt.

If it is mildew, make up a solution that consists of 1 qt of household bleach to 1 cup of nonammoniated detergent (bleach and ammonia combined make a gas as potent as mustard gas) to 1 gal of water.

Working out of a large bucket, use a scrub brush on a stick to wash the affected areas and the house itself. This will kill any hidden mildew.

It is not necessary to scrub terribly hard, nor to make the cleaning an all-day project. The bleach in the solution will kill the mildew. It should take 15 or 20 min or less to do one side of a house. If you need to go high, you need not get on a ladder. As mentioned in Chap. 1, there are extralong poles to which you can attach a threaded scrub brush.

As soon as a section is finished, rinse it off with a garden hose; do not allow it to dry. Bleach can damage wood. It is best to work from the bottom of the house upward. If you work from the top down, rivulets of a dirty water can stream down over clean areas.

Figure 12-1. Mildew on siding.

Figure 12-2. Washing painted wood. (*Courtesy of Armor All*)

If there is no mildew, simply scrub the house with a strong household detergent. An extra benefit of scrubbing a house is that the process also removes chalk, which can cause adhesion problems (see Chap. 16).

Chemical Solutions

In the last year or so, a number of products have been introduced that manufacturers say make the cleaning process even easier. For example, one company, Armor All, put out a product called Armor All Painted Wood Wash Kit that contains two 24-oz bottles of cleaner and a sprayer (Fig. 12-2). The sprayer is attached to one of the bottles, and the garden hose attaches to the sprayer. The chemical is sprayed onto the surface. After 5 or 10 min, the water is fed through the sprayer to rinse. The company says it sprays up to 25 ft high and washes away mildew, mold, and dirt.

If you find mildew, suggest to the client that the cause of the problem should be corrected, whether it is bushes or trees shielding surfaces from the sun so that mildew can thrive, or leaky gutters or downspouts or perhaps ice damming that is creating a moisture-laden environment where mildew can thrive. (For additional information on mildew, see Chap. 5.)

Power Washing

Another way to clean a house is with a power washer, a gas or electrically operated machine that drives water against a surface at high pressure and in great volume. A power washer is capable of everything from removing the damaging effects of sunlight which turns wood gray to blasting paint off the substrate. Since it is a powerful machine, however, you must take care with it.

If you are just cleaning a painted surface and suspect there may be mildew, use a siding wash that includes bleach in its formula and thus kills mildew (Fig. 12-3). And do buy the product ready-made. Manufacturers who put bleach in their products also put in anticorrosive agents. Without these, the bleach could destroy the internal rubber parts of the machine.

If you are power-washing asbestos cement shingles, or vinyl siding, or metal siding, or other nonwood products, just spray away, with pressure at about 1000 lb/in² and using 2 to 3 gal/min of water. However, if you are power-washing

Figure 12-3. Power washing of siding.

Figure 12-4. Score or hammer marks on cedar siding.

a soft wood, such as cedar or redwood, you have to be extremely careful not to score the wood (Fig. 12-4). Use low pressure and work up to a pressure that you can see will not score the wood. The score or hammer marks in cedar siding shown in Fig. 12-4 are the result of spraying with too much pressure up close. Some people use 1000 lb/in² and others use 2000 lb/in² and even more. But the key is to keep the spray far enough away so as not to score the wood.

If you want to remove peeling paint, you can do it. It is best to hold the wand so that it hits the paint from the side rather than dead on.

Power washing transfers a tremendous amount of water to the surface, so make sure the wood has a couple of days to dry thoroughly before you apply primer or paint.

You can hold the power washer wand as close as needed to get the job done, but if the siding is clapboard or wood shingles, angle the spray so that water does not drive up under the courses or shingles. This can set up a moisture-laden environment that is ripe for mildew formation. Spray from a ladder or scaffolding to guard against this.

A professional housepainter should own a power washer. There are hot and cold water models. The hot water model will do a better job of removing baked-in dirt. Various wands are available, and these are invaluable for focusing the stream whichever way you want it. Regarding pressure, you need the capability to go to 3000 or 4000 lb/in². Such pressures work well in cleaning some masonry; you would have to be very careful if using them on wood.

Incidentally, washing a house sometimes reveals that it does not need a paint job—grime and mildew can be that bad.

Power washers are also prime movers, as it were, when you want to remove blackness and grayness from unpainted wood. This is discussed in the chapters on exterior staining and clear coating.

Caulking

Caulk is used to fill the seams of the house. A number are available, as mentioned in Chap. 1. Silicone is the best caulk you can buy.

Before you caulk, scrape out all old material with an opener or the like. The new material will be only as good as the material under it.

Use an old brush or a dust brush that is made for the job to get out any material that has crumbled. Crumbled caulk does not make for a solid surface.

To apply caulking from a gun, cut the tip at a slant so that a slanted opening in the nozzle of the cartridge allows a ⅜-in bead of caulk to be extruded. Puncture the inner seal on the cartridge with a long nail or a slim piece of wood.

Insert the cartridge in the caulking gun, then put the tip of the nozzle on top of the area to be caulked. Squeeze the trigger with even pressure, and draw the gun down along the crack in one continuous motion, extruding a bead that is one-half as deep as it is wide. The bead should be concave. To ensure this, draw a spoon along it, or simply use your forefinger.

In some cases, the gaps will be so deep that a bead of caulk alone will not do—a filler material of some sort has to be inserted. This can be something like Mortite, which comes in long, beaded strips that can be stripped off as needed. Just press the material in place with your fingers—it will stick—and then apply the caulk. You can also use fiberglass insulation or foam-backed rod.

If the gaps are very big, something like a foam in a can such as Great Stuff can be used to partially fill the crack. This is squirted into the gap, and as it dries, it expands greatly. Foam should be applied sparingly until you get a sense of how much is required, because a little, when dry, can go a long way. (For example, a spray can contains 2½ gal of hard foam.)

Peeling Paint

Paint that is peeling must, of course, be removed to provide a sound base for new paint. There are various types of scraper on the market. In most cases, a stiff-bladed 3-in scraper will do the job (Fig. 12-5a). If the surfaces are peeling fairly heavily, a hook-type scraper (Fig. 12-5b), as described in Chap. 1, may be used. This scraper consists of a handle with a double-edged blade assembly that attaches to the handle by tightening down on a screw in the center.

To use the tool, grasp it firmly and pull it down the siding, applying pressure as you go; this should pull off the paint. Some models of this scraper also have a knob on top for gripping with one hand and providing even more pressure.

As you go, examine the surface for areas where peeling may take place—the paint is bubbly or raised—and scrape them off. You can test suspicious areas with tape. Cut through the paint film with a utility knife, place tape or a Band-Aid over it, and pull the tape sharply away to see if the paint adheres. If it does not, it should be removed.

When you scrape in this way, you are often left with a shallowly cratered surface. Here, you can use exterior spackling compound to fill in the craters, or at least apply it along the edges and feather the compound out so the edges are not noticeable.

Sanding

For large peeling areas, you must sand the peeling paint. For this, a heavy-duty industrial sander using two kinds of paper, 16-grit and 60-grit, is a good choice. The 16-grit sandpaper is for removing all the peeling paint down to the bare wood. The 60-grit paper is for smoothing the grooves left in the wood by the 16-grit paper. It is important not to allow any paint to remain on the surface— it will clog the pores of the 60-grit material.

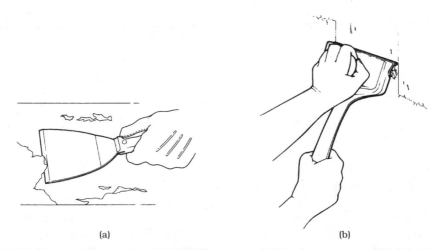

(a)   (b)

Figure 12-5. Removing loose paint with (a) stiff scraper and (b) hook-type scraper. (*Hyde Tools*)

The idea in sanding is to leave a surface on which the new paint will adhere as well as one that looks good. In some cases, you have to sand only where some of the paint needs to be removed.

The sander used is a rotary type, and it is capable of heavily scoring the surface if you do not watch out. Turn on the machine, and bring it to the surface of the work while it is moving. Move it along the surface, holding it a few degrees (up to 10°) off the surface. Do not press it flush to the surface, because it will tend to pull out of your hands and will be hard to manage.

This action will quickly take the paint off down to raw wood, but it will also leave some grooves. Hence, finish-sand it with 60-grit paper to smooth the wood.

Holes

Wood siding and trim can be susceptible to a variety of holes. Small holes can be filled with exterior spackling compound and then touched up with a coat of the finish paint, allowed to dry, and painted.

Any protruding nails can be countersunk with a nailset and hammer, and the depressions filled with compound (Figs. 12-6 and 12-7). If the hole is small and a clear coating is going to be applied over it, then a wood filler is recommended. While there is no such thing as a perfect match, fillers are available in a wide variety of wood colors (see Chap. 10) and are easy to apply with a putty knife.

Sometimes metal substrates get holes in them, and there are a number of products, most based on epoxy, that you can use for repair. For example, Oatey Epoxy putty comes as a soft material which you knead together before use, and liquid solder is used for filling small holes in gutters and the like.

Also available is aluminum adhesive-backed tape which can be wrapped around such things as downspouts. Caulk can also be used on metal, assuming the hole or crack is small enough.

Rot

If the hole or gap is large and there is rot present, say, on a window frame, then spackling compound is not enough. A product that fills the hole and prevents further problems is needed. One such is Minwax Wood Filler. First, scrape out the rot with a stiff putty knife or the like; then mix the filler, a two-part material, and apply it to the damaged area, just as you would any filler. After drying—it dries very hard—sand, prime, and paint it.

Another standard wood filler for exterior (and interior) work is Durham's Rock Hard Water Putty. This comes as a yellowish powder that is mixed with water into a thick paste, which is then applied and dries into a rock-hard material that

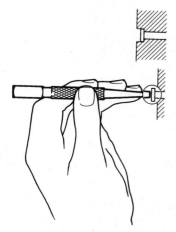

Figure 12-6. Countersink for loose nails.

can be sanded, primed, and painted. Mix it in the same way as plaster is mixed. Pour it into a container, such as a tin plate, use a trowel to depress it in the center, and pour water into the crater. Then use the scraper to fold the water and putty together, mixing it completely. Add water sparingly until it is the right consistency. If you add too much water, just add more powder to thicken it up.

Avoid air pockets in the patch. To do this, push in the patcher with the scraper, or use your fingers to work it in.

Another patching material that is quite good, perhaps the best material for the job, is made by Arbatron. See the discussion of wood putty in Chap. 1.

Priming Wood

You can use the same techniques for applying primer as you would for applying paint. (See Chap. 6.) A number of primers are available for priming wood and painted wood. Use the simplest material you can without sacrificing quality. For example, if a particular material allows a choice between latex and oil-based primer, use latex primer because it is easier to work with.

In the following situations, wood needs to be primed.

Painted Wood

If you are making a dramatic color change, say, going from yellow to green, a primer is a good idea. A latex primer will work quite well, assuming that the wood is a nonbleeding type such as pine. To ensure that the topcoat covers better,

Figure 12-7. Filling nail holes with compound. (*Courtesy of Wm. Zinsser & Co.*)

tint the primer with universal colorant. Normally, up to 4 oz/gal of color can be added without causing the color to streak. A primer will, of course, provide an excellent base coat for the topcoat.

If portions of the paint film have been removed, exposing bare wood, spot-prime these first, allow them to dry, and prime the entire house.

If you are painting new woods of a nonbleeding type, then latex primer can be used.

If you are painting patched areas on bleeding woods, such as cedar or red-wood, standard latex primer is not recommended for the reasons previously stated: The water in the primer can solubilize tannins in the wood and send them to the surface, where they will discolor the primer and may not be covered by the topcoat.

An oil-based primer is recommended for bleeding woods because the oils in it will not solubilize the extracts in the wood. One water-based primer, Bulls Eye 1-2-3, is a good interior as well as exterior primer which is also said to be good on bleeding woods.

Water-Repellent Preservatives

Before applying primer or paint, you can extend a job considerably by using a water-repellent coating, such as Woodlife. This sinks into the pores of the wood and protects the wood from heavy accumulation of water from rain and dew and, therefore, rot. In tests done by the Forest Products Laboratory, the application of a water repellent prior to painting was said to have a significant salutary effect. It is particularly important for species such as southern yellow pine.

Water repellents can be applied by brushing or dipping. Lap and butt joints and the edges of panel products such as hardboard and particleboard should be especially well treated since paint tends to fail in these areas first.

After you apply the repellent, allow at least 2 warm, sunny days for drying. If enough time is not allowed, any paint applied over the treated areas may be slow to dry, or discolor, or dry with a rough surface that resembles alligator hide. If the wood has been dipped, allow it at least one week to dry, if the weather is favorable.

Prime the wood as soon as possible after the repellent is dry.

Pith and Knots

If the wood is exuding pitch or has knots, a stain-blocking primer is recommended. One such is BIN, the shellac-based primer which can be dabbed on and works well. But BIN cannot be used as a whole-house primer outside—it is just for the knots.

Plywood

If the plywood is raw, a latex primer and paint system is recommended. Plywood can expand and contract and make a rigid paint, like oil, fail sooner rather than later.

Rust

The exterior of a home has a variety of metal surfaces that must be prepared for paint. The main enemy of metal is rust, which is created when raw metal and water meet. You may have heard the saying, "Rust never sleeps." It is true. Every speck of rust must be removed, or it must be neutralized in some way, or else it *will* return.

Wrought-Iron Fencing

One of the main areas where rust is found is on wrought-iron fencing. For whatever reason, the paint cracks and peels, and once water contacts bare metal, soon rust is on its way.

If the rust is slight, remove it with a wire brush. These brushes come, as noted in Chap. 1, in various configurations, so it should be easy to get at the rust. If the rust is extensive and accessible, you can also use a metal sanding accessory that is chucked into a drill. One such is made by 3-M. It consists of a hard, webbed disk, and it takes off rust and flaking paint quite readily. There are other types. It is important, whatever type you use, to wear safety goggles. Specks of sanded material or material from the sanding disk can fly into your eyes.

Sand down to metal that is clear of rust, and before priming, wipe down the metal with lacquer thinner, which is a good cleaning solvent that dries very quickly.

Bare spots should be spot-primed. Oil-based primers work well, and so will Bulls Eye 1-2-3. There are also primers that allow you to leave rust on the surface and to not worry about it bleeding through.

With these products it is suggested that you remove all flaking rust and/or peeling paint, then apply the primer to the smooth, though still rusty, areas.

Different types of primers are designed for different surfaces. For example, Rust-Oleum's Light Metal Primer is designed for surfaces which are bare of rust to lightly rusted. It comes in white and a khaki color, in brushable as well as spray forms. The white is recommended for lighter paints while the khaki is for use under darker paints.

For heavily rusted areas where it is difficult to remove all the rust—it might be embedded in the surface of the metal—Rust-Oleum offers Rusty Metal Primer, which is essentially a fish oil and is designed to be applied to heavily rusted areas only. The fish oil penetrates the rust and makes it inert. Rust-Oleum also makes a liquid that is applied with a brush and makes the rust inert.

Another product I have used successfully is Extend, which does essentially the same thing as Rust-Oleum primers. It comes in spray and liquid versions. The spray is black while the brushable material is a tan color. Hammarite is yet another coating.

Metal windows and other items made of steel and iron can be handled in the same way as cast-iron fencing. Metal is metal.

If you wish, you can remove rust from hard-to-sand spots with Naval Jelly. This is a thick, pinkish liquid that is dabbed on, allowed to work for 30 min, and then washed off with water.

Raw Galvanized Steel

Raw galvanized steel must be handled differently. It contains an oil to which paint will not adhere. The galvanized steel must be allowed to weather 6 months; or it can be washed off with lacquer thinner, followed by a prime coat of a zinc-rich primer specially geared for galvanized steel, and then painted with latex paint.

Preparing Concrete

There are two basic kinds of concrete that can be painted—concrete that is painted and concrete that is raw; it may be on the floor or on the walls.

Raw Concrete

The first step in preparing concrete for painting is to clean the surface. Use a broom to sweep the floor clean or a shop vacuum or an air compressor to blow off grit and dirt. If you use the latter, you must wear safety goggles.

Any stains on the floor must come up. Grease stains are usually relatively easy. First, use a putty knife to scrape up any grease deposits. Then use a heavy-duty solution of water and cleaner or degreaser to remove the stains that are left, scrubbing as needed and rinsing carefully. Paint will not adhere to grease, no matter how small the spot. If the grease does not come up when the degreaser is used with water, it may be necessary to use it full-strength.

Oil

Oil stains are worse than grease because oil penetrates into concrete, and the longer it stays, the more deeply it penetrates. Hence, to remove it, you need something to penetrate deeply into the concrete.

If there is surface oil, soak up as much as you can with a rag. Resist the temptation to wipe. The result will be a bigger stain, and the oil will be driven deeper into the concrete. Once you have finished with a rag, dispose of it by sealing it in a 1-gal can filled with water; oil-soaked rags can spontaneously burst into flames.

To remove the rest of the oil, there are a couple of options. You can purchase a powdered floor-drying material at a local automotive supply store; or you can sprinkle Portland cement on the stain, allow it to stay on the stain for 24 h, and then pick it up. Repeat the procedure until all the stain is gone. Another option is to purchase a commercial cleaner.

Rust Stains

A rust stain is not rust; it does not keep growing, as rust does. So if you are painting it, it is a simple matter to cover it with a coat of stain-blocking primer. However, if you are using a clear sealer of some kind, you must remove the stain.

The material to use for this is oxalic acid, which comes as a powder and is available at paint stores, woodworking supply stores, and drug stores. The powder is mixed with water in a ratio of $\frac{1}{4}$ lb of acid to 1 qt of water. Apply the mixture to the rust stain, allow it to stand for 1 h or so, then rinse it off with clear water while scrubbing it with a clean, stiff-bristled acid brush. If not all the stains come off after one application, repeat the procedure.

Etch Concrete

No concrete should be painted until 90 days after it has been poured. Why? It leaches alkalies which can interfere with the adhesion of the coating.

It is also a good idea to "etch" the concrete—roughen it so the coatings applied adhere better. A number of companies make concrete etch.

Concrete Patches

Concrete may have gaps or holes in it, and these must be repaired before any painting is done. If the hole is in the wall and there is no water leakage, ordinary concrete patcher may be used. You mix this powder with water. Just follow the directions on the box, mixing it and then applying it with a putty knife, scraper, or trowel.

If it is a narrow crack, it should be widened and made into a V, with the bottom made wider than the top. This will provide a key for the material.

Floor Holes

If there is a hole in a concrete floor or spalling or cracks, these must be repaired. Concrete patcher may be used. It is a good idea to allow at least 30 days to pass before you paint these patches, to make sure that they have given up all the alkalies.

Preparing Stucco

Pure stucco is not painted, and your goal in preparing it for painting is to not paint unless you have to. Unpainted stucco can last for years. Painted stucco will require periodic redoing, just as other exterior surfaces do.

The first step in preparing it is to clean it. You can do this with some detergent and water and a rough nylon-bristle brush. Once the soil is removed, the stucco may be clean and bright—it will not need repainting.

In some instances you will also find mildew, efflorescence, and peeling paint. Peeling paint can be removed with a wire brush. It is not a good idea to power-wash stucco heavily because you can knock down its texture. However, there is nothing wrong with a light washing. If there are gaps in the stucco, you can patch them with an acrylic latex caulk.

13
Exterior Painting

Painting the exterior of a building or home is usually more difficult than doing the interior, simply because often you have to work from extension ladders or other equipment. The up-and-down aspect is physically taxing, as is moving the ladder. You also must be careful not to spill paint and must be mindful of safety, avoiding falls and electrical hazards. Also there is simply more involved—more scraping, more sanding, and more priming.

When doing an exterior paint job it is best to stay in the shade as much as possible. It is better for the painter and for the paint, because direct sunlight on freshly applied paint can lead to a malady called *wrinkling*, where the top of the paint film dries while the bottom does not. Painting in the shade is not always possible; if you must paint in the sun, try to do it early in the morning, when you and the substrate are not getting the direct rays and the wood is cool.

It is also a good idea to take breaks, drink plenty of cool liquids, and just not overexert.

The procedures here focus on the painting of a house with a brush or roller. But when you can—when it is practical—a paint sprayer can be much faster. This is described in detail in Chap. 17.

In painting a house or other building, the idea is to work from the top down. The theory is that if any paint drips, the drip will be painted over as the job progresses.

Most painters do the siding first and then the trim. The reason is that a lot of paint is applied when siding is done, and there are bound to be some drips and spatters onto the trim. If so, the drips can be covered when the trim is painted.

Doing it this way will mean having to lean a ladder against freshly painted siding. This is not usually a problem if the ends of the ladder that lean against the siding are covered with ladder mitts. If worse comes to worst, a spot could be touched up as the ladder is moved.

Drop Cloths

Canvas drop cloths work best for covering up (Fig. 13-1). As mentioned in Chap. 1, they drape over things more easily and will not flutter away in the wind. Cover anything anywhere you figure the paint may fall and anywhere you are likely to walk. Be particularly careful to cover asphalt roofing and concrete. Because these items are porous, getting off all the paint can be a problem.

Getting paint off screens is difficult as well, hence it is always a good idea to remove the screens or to drape cloths over them.

Try not to cover plants, flowers, and bushes for too long. Being covered by drop cloths is not a natural occurrence for vegetation, and the sooner you allow air and sunlight in, the better. If bushes and plants are brushing against a wall, cover them with drop cloths and tie them back a bit with rope, or just hold them back with your back as you slither through.

Masking Off

Some painters mask off certain areas when they paint, and others do not, thinking it will take them a lot longer.

Figure 13-1. Canvas drop cloths.

I have concluded that masking off is a good idea, but do *not* use masking tape on a painted surface. It can strip off paint. The better idea, as discussed in Chap. 1, is to use painter's tape, which looks like and works the same as masking tape but strips off easily. Use it around doorknobs and light fixtures (Fig. 13-2*d*), along a roof line where you will be cutting in siding, such as where a dormer cuts into a roof, around posts mounted in concrete (Fig. 13-2*a*). In other words, put tape wherever you need a sharp, clean line, where the painted surface meets the unpainted.

When painting these cut-in areas, I have always found it best to use a *dry brush*—one that has paint on it but does not drip (Fig. 13-2*b*). Even though the painter's tape protects the surface, you do not want paint to run down into it.

Wait until the paint is dry before you strip off the tape. This way the paint will not come off with the tape.

Painting Siding

The easy way to paint siding is to do as much of it with a roller as you can (assuming you are not spray-painting). Not all sidings allow this; some are made so that a roller cannot get in all the surfaces easily. On siding of this kind, a brush or a painting pad will work well.

In any case, some of the siding around windows, doors, and other things protruding from the siding (such as vents and pipes) will have to be cut in somewhat before the roller is used. Cut in first; then use the roller to get as close as you can to the obstruction.

Following is a lineup of siding types and some methods that might be employed to paint them. Note that if conditions are right, the easiest method of all can be to spray-paint them using an airless sprayer.

Asbestos Cement Shingles

This is definitely a job for a roller. One that has a $\frac{3}{4}$-in nap will do a good job, but I know one painter who swears by $1\frac{1}{2}$-in nap, saying that since it brings so much paint to the surface, the job goes more quickly. One criticism is that it can leave a textured kind of finish, but backrolling (going over painted areas with an undipped roller) would solve this.

Concentrate on getting a generous amount of paint on the surface, applying it in W or M patterns, in a 3-ft strip that goes from the bottom to the top of the siding. Do an adjacent 3-ft strip in the same way, and then come back with a dry roller (one empty of paint) and backroll the applied paint in the first strip until it is smooth.

Figure 13-2. Masking off (*a*) to protect masonry from paint dribbles; (*b,c*) for cutting in; and (*d*) to protect doorknob.

Cedar Siding

If it is the flat type of cedar siding, you can paint it with a roller. If it is striated, use a cut-down brush or a pad (Fig. 13-3).

Painting this type of siding is basically a wipe-down job. You dip the brush into the paint, jam it up under the shingles and wipe the paint on with a downward stroke. Old-time painters often use a "stub" brush for this, which is a cut-down or worn, old brush; but a paint pad can work well. Padco, for example, sells pads with thick, fluffy naps that might work as well as one with a rough texture and a turned-over fabric on it. The turned-over portion is designed to be jammed under a course of shingles, and then the paint is wiped on.

Clapboard

This clapboard in Fig. 13-4 is a little too configured to paint totally with a roller. The best bet here is to cut in with a brush and then paint the faces of the boards. Some painters like to use a 3- or 4-in-wide roller on a long handle to paint the faces.

Figure 13-3. Cedar siding. (*Courtesy of Dutch Boy*)

Figure 13-4. Clapboard siding.

Vinyl Siding

You can paint this the same way you'd paint wood using an acrylic latex paint. Use a fluffy roller on it as much as possible. Tip: When painting vinyl you should stick to lighter paints to avoid a darker paint that absorbs so much heat from the sun that it starts to warp the siding.

Aluminum Siding

Aluminum siding has a hard, baked enamel finish. Here, I would cut in with a brush, then apply the paint with a 7-in roller with a $\frac{3}{8}$-in nap.

Do as much of the siding as you can while working on the ground. The more you can do this way, the quicker the job will go. This means securing the roller to a pole. The standard one-piece pole is 4 ft long, but they come longer, as noted in Chap. 1.

I would not go higher than 10 ft. Beyond this, the pole becomes unwieldy and heavy. Control of the pole is poor. The best bet, I believe, is to use the 4-ft pole and then work from a plank set on ladder jacks.

Using a 5-gal bucket of paint with a grid insert is most efficient. Just roll the roller in and out on the grid and apply the paint.

In applying the paint, concentrate at first on getting it on, just as you would with a room. Then go back and forth over it to smooth it out.

Painting Difficult Areas

Not all houses are ranch style and simple to paint. Some have all kinds of angles and such that make painting some spots difficult. For example, one difficult area is the sides of dormers or similar configurations. The roof slants, so there is no way to stand on it and feel secure. One way to rig the ladder for painting dormers is shown in Fig. 13-5. Hooks on top hold the ladder to the roof.

One solution is to first lay a drop cloth or drop cloths along the roof next to the side of the dormer. Then lean an extension ladder against the side of the house and climb up. Place half of the extension ladder or stepladder so that it lies flat on the roof and its feet rest against the top of the extension ladder. As long as a helper holds the bottom ladder solidly, the ladder lying on the roof cannot slide down. If you have no helper, use blocks or tie the ladder solidly so it cannot move.

One way to paint a sloping roof that is fairly low is to simply lay an extension ladder along it, with the feet of the ladder dug into the ground. Use another ladder to climb up on the first, as shown in Fig. 13-6.

Painting above a Porch

Another difficult spot is above a porch or an overhang of some sort, because if you set the ladder so that it is above the trim, you will not be able to reach the

Figure 13-5. Painting dormers.

Figure 13-6. Painting a sloping roof.

siding. The best solution here is to cover the porch roof or overhang with drop cloths and to work off the overhang. You may not be able to reach the very top of the siding; just lay a closed stepladder against the wall, using it as a small extension ladder.

Painting Trim

Exterior trim is painted in the same way as interior trim. Dip the brush about one-third of the way into the paint, tap off excess paint on the inside of the can, then apply it, brushing it out.

Paint from the *dry into the wet:* Start each succeeding brushful of paint about 1 ft away from the last brushful, and paint back toward it.

Use plenty of paint. If you keep dipping the brush in one-third of the way, this will not be a problem. Avoid excessive brushing; apply the paint, then lay it off, as with interior painting, smoothing it out. Every now and then, look back, check for sags, and brush these out. Good paint is self-leveling and turns out fine with minimal effort.

As you go, there are sure to be drips on adjacent siding. Either wipe them off with a rag moistened in thinner, or swipe them flat with the tip of the brush.

Painting Windows and Doors

I cannot tell you how many times I have seen numbered sequences for painting certain parts of doors and windows in a certain order. For me, this is overkill. There are just a few things to remember.

Paint a window from the inside out. That is, open the window a few inches on top and bottom and paint it; then open both halves (assuming a double-hung window) so that you can paint the portions of the rails that are exposed.

When the windows themselves are finished, paint the frame, again using the dry-into-wet method. When the window is finished, take a look at it. Check for any missed spots or sags in the paint. Use the tip of the brush to brush them out. Be particularly mindful of the window sill; paint can run down over the window and collect on it.

Painting Doors

To paint a door, open it completely, first being sure that a clean, dustfree drop cloth is pulled underneath to protect the interior from paint spatters. How you paint depends on whether the door is paneled or flush, but the key concept, as with trim, is the laying off. Apply the paint and then brush it out smoothly.

On a flush door, dip the brush about 1 in into the paint, tap off excess paint on the inside of the can, and paint the hinge edge of the door with sweeping strokes. When the paint is applied, bring your dry brush across it with upward strokes.

Get in the habit, a few minutes after you apply paint, of checking for sags, and brush these out with gentle laying-off strokes.

Also when you are painting a narrow edge, do not push the brush against it so hard that the brush touches the sides. This can lead to a brush malady called *fingering*—clumps of bristles are separated—and will ruin the brush.

Paint the other edge, then the face of the door.

Do it in quarters, first applying the paint horizontally, then vertically, and finally laying it off with light, upward strokes. Paint an adjacent quarter the same way, then the bottom quarters, making your final laying-off strokes overlap the previously applied paint.

If you are painting a paneled door, first paint the edges, then paint from the inside out: the perimeters of the panels followed by the rails, then the stiles.

Paint the door, then paint the trim. Leave it open awhile until the paint dries enough that the door can be closed without marring the paint.

Painting High Up on a Peak

Another difficult spot can be high up on a peak. There may be no way to rig a ladder so that you can paint this spot safely. In this instance, I would suggest using a brush clamped into a brush holder. This will enable you to get into virtually any area of a house. The brush holder may be angled and locked in position with thumbscrews as needed (see Chap. 1).

Procedures for Stopping Work

Stopping Temporarily

At times during the job, you will stop for a break or lunch, and it is a good idea to safeguard tools then. Just immerse the roller in the paint and put the paint in the shade.

You can lay a brush flat, first wrapping it with plastic wrap. It is not a good idea to put the brush in a pail. This puts stress on the bristles and could slightly deform them. However, one manufacturer, Hyde, makes a device which can be used to temporarily hold a brush straight in a can. It attaches to the can and has a magnet against which the ferrule on the brush is placed, to hold the tool in position.

Finishing for the Day

When you are finished for the day, there are a number of procedures to follow. First, take down ladders if they are in such a position on the house that someone could accidentally walk into them or if they are located where children play.

When you stop, it should be at a structural break, say, the end of a wall or up to the edge of an addition or the like. Avoid the situation where you are midway through painting a wall and when you pick up, your strokes of freshly applied paint overlap the existing dry coat and leave a lap mark.

Cleaning Brushes and Rollers

The big idea in cleaning brushes and rollers properly is to remove as much of the paint as you can before cleaning with solvents. For brushes, you can proceed as follows.

Lay the brush on a sheet of newspaper, then push down on the bristles with a scraper or joint compound knife, squeezing out as much paint as possible.

Following this, use a comb brush to comb the paint out of the bristles down near the ferrule. As noted elsewhere, paint can collect there.

When you have removed as much paint as possible from the brush, the next step is to wash it. If the brush was used with latex paint, immerse the bristles in a solution of water and mild soap. Sometimes the soap is forgotten, but this is not a good idea; it is crucial to cut down on rinsing and do a better cleaning job. Knead the bristles with your hand, then rinse in clear, running water. Finally, mount the brush on a spinning tool and spin it inside a large box so the liquid from the brush does not fly all over the place. Wrap the brush in newspaper or its original package or its "keeper," if you have it, and hang it up.

If the brush is used with oil-based paint, follow the procedure above to remove as much paint as possible; immerse the bristles in a can of mineral spirits, kneading them with your finger (you can wear rubber gloves if you wish), then immerse it in another can containing paint thinner and repeat the process. Next, immerse it in thinner again and wash. As a final step, use the spinning tool.

Safety Precautions

Ladder Safety—and Efficiency

Every year, hundreds of people are killed or injured while using ladders. For the painter the risk is increased, and the simple fact is that improper use of a ladder results in less efficiency.

Ladder safety is partly a function of using a good-quality ladder. This was covered in Chap. 1, and it is good advice to follow.

The following points should be noted:

- Inspect ladders on a daily basis. This is an exercise not in advanced science but in common sense. Are rails split or broken, is something bent, are bolts loose? If you have any questions about the equipment being totally safe, do not use it. Wrap masking tape around the ladder, write on it "Don't Use," and take it out of service. If you have a busy shop where many ladders are used, ones that are out of service should be chained together so someone cannot use them inadvertently.

- If a ladder cannot be repaired (and good-quality ladders can be), discard it. But first destroy it by running over it with a truck or cutting it up. You do not want someone at the dump to pick up such a ladder and use it.

- When you are using the ladder, do not stretch (see Fig. 13-7). Paint only what you can easily see and easily reach. This may mean moving a heavy extension ladder more often than you would like, but the alternative is to take a chance on falling. Of course, some stretching will be required from time to time, but do not put yourself in jeopardy.

- Do not "jump" the ladder—move the top of it—from one position to another while you are standing on it, just to reach a missed spot.

- Get help if you cannot manage the ladder. Once I had to move a 40-ft steel extension ladder by myself along the side of a house, and it was a miracle that it did not fall through one of the windows. I should have gotten help. You should, too, if you believe that you cannot move a ladder without its toppling over.

- Do not make the ladder lean too much—or too little. The rule when you are leaning an extension ladder against a house is that the bottom should be one-quarter of the ladder height away from the house (Fig. 13-8). Sometimes bushes

Figure 13-7. Safe position for painting on a ladder.

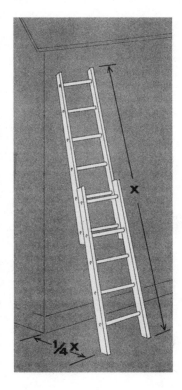

Figure 13-8. Correct ladder placement.

and other obstructions interfere with this theory, but adhere to it as much as possible. If the ladder is set too steeply against a wall, it could topple backward; if it is positioned too far from the wall, the front end could slide down the siding.

- Make sure the legs cannot slide out. Do not set the legs of the ladder in soft earth. Sometimes you can solve the problem of soft earth by banging homemade pegs into the ground in front of the ladder's feet. If the ground is not soft, put weight there—a pair of concrete blocks—or, if necessary, tie the legs in place in some fashion.

- Make sure the ladder cannot fall sideways. This can be a problem when you are painting a house on rough terrain. The legs may not be on exactly level terrain, and a shift in weight can send it toppling.

To level them, use C clamps to lengthen a board to make it level with the other. Commercial extensions are also available.

Figure 13-9. Potentially dangerous work arrangement.

- Do not stand on the top step of the ladder to reach something. Get a taller ladder.
- Do not work on a ladder in front of an unlocked door (Fig. 13-9). This is an accident waiting to happen. Neither the board nor the painter should ever go on top of the ladder. Someone could come out, the door smacks into the ladder, and down you go.

- Do not work outside when there's a strong wind or lightning.

- Overall, the best procedure when you set up a ladder is to climb up on it a few steps and see if it is stable, before you climb higher.

- If you are using an aluminum or wood ladder, by all means be careful that you are not in danger of tipping or falling into an electrical line. If the line is frayed, the shock could easily kill you.

Other Good Safety Ideas

There are a few other ideas that can help painters do a faster, safer job.

- Use scaffolding, a scissor lift, or an aerial boom whenever possible. Such equipment makes working high up safer. Such equipment will cost extra, assuming you rent it, but the labor saved may well justify it.

- Properly schedule work. Perhaps the site is in the midst of construction work or the like, and painting amid a lot of chaotic activity is an invitation to an accident. It is better to reschedule the work until the site is less hazardous.

- Use "extenders" when possible. The more you stay off a ladder or any high equipment, the better. As mentioned earlier, very long poles are available for applying paint by roller, and comparable equipment—wands and poles—is available for spray painting. For example, a ceiling can be painted with a short extension and shield. An 8-ft pole gun can be used for vaulted ceilings.

- Scaffolding and other aids are discussed in Chap. 1.

14
Stains

Perhaps 10 years ago, paint was just about the only thing available as a coating for exterior wood. But stains are becoming quite popular, and in certain situations they are, in my view, just flat out better to use than paint.

The Look

Paint and stain differ in many ways and certainly in looks. Paint provides a dense, opaque finish that hides the surface underneath, while stains are subtler. There is some color in what is classically regarded as a stain, but not so much that it does not allow the wood grain and color to show through, along with the texture. Opaque stains are available, but these, in our view and as discussed later, are really paints.

On the Surface

Paint and stain act very differently on the surface of raw wood. Stains penetrate raw wood like sauce on a sponge cake—an average $\frac{1}{8}$ in, depending on the wood species and its condition. Paints bond to the wood as a film with little or no penetration.

Because stains penetrate rather than form a film, they are less likely to peel. When moisture—one of the main causes of peeling of coatings—trapped in the wood pushes to get out, it pushes against the film, and this leads to blistering and then peeling.

Stain is semipermeable, however, so that when moisture pushes against it, the stain bleeds through, hits the surface, and evaporates.

Reduced Maintenance

This suggests that stains offer a significant maintenance advantage over paint in the long run. Although the surface has to be recoated more often, preparation for restaining is much easier than that for repainting. Merely clean dirt and mildew from the stain surface, and apply fresh stain. There is no need to scrape, sand, and prime, as with deteriorated paint.

Stain Formulations

Stains vary, of course, and the differences among them are based on the amounts and types of vehicle, pigment, resin, and additives.

Vehicle

The oil in stains gives them their superior penetrating ability, because oil molecules are very small. Some stains contain pure oil; others are made from modified oils. Pure oils are suspended in mineral spirits and must be cleaned up with a petroleum solvent such as turpentine or paint thinner. Modified oils are chemically changed into water-soluble emulsions so they can clean up with water.

Both pure and modified oils give off volatile organic compounds (VOCs) because they are based on petroleum products. So far, the amount of the VOCs has been limited because manufacturers have increased the solids content, pigment, and resins compared to years ago.

Low-VOC latex and water-based stains are available, but they do not have the penetrating capability of oil-based stain because the molecules are larger. They form a partial film, as paint does, and may be vulnerable to peeling.

Pigment

Pigments do a number of things in stain. For one thing, they provide color, of course. But they also protect the wood against degradation by the sun's ultraviolet rays. The more pigment on the wood, the better the protection. For this reason, use two wet-on-wet coats of stain when possible.

Resins

Resins give the stain its durability. Made of long-molecular-chain polymer chemicals, they cure to form a tough protective surface. Manufacturers formulate the resins in stains for different purposes. For instance, a deck stain which is subject to foot traffic is given harder curing resins than a stain for siding.

Additives

High-quality stains contain ultraviolet (UV) blockers to provide further protection from the sun. UV blockers either absorb or reflect UV radiation, to prevent pigments from fading and to protect the wood surface for a longer period.

Exterior stains also contain wood preservatives which are not found in interior stains. Preservatives help prevent insect infestation and stave off weathering.

Fungicides may also be present. Not all stains contain them, but the better ones do. Airborne fungi, such as mildew, are always present outdoors, and left unchecked, they can damage wood and discolor any finish. Check the label for a phrase that says the stain is mildew resistant to see if fungicides are included.

Semitransparent stains come in a wide variety of colors with the most popular being the earth colors—browns, blacks, reds, and greens. But lighter colors, such as beige and even white, are available as well as nonearth colors such as blue.

Semitransparent stain, as mentioned before, is transparent, but applying two coats to the wood makes it less transparent and the color more intense, simply because of the addition of pigment. Two coats are usually good only on rough-textured or weathered wood. Smooth, new wood often can only absorb one coat of stain before becoming saturated. The excess will lie on the finish, and unless it is wiped away, it can form a film which can peel as paint does. Pay attention to what the manufacturer says about application, but be aware of possible consequences.

Bleed-through

Take care, when you are restaining, that the color of the wood and the color you are applying are compatible. If you stain over a darker color, the darker hue will show through. You can, however, cover a lighter transparent stain with a darker one, say, a beige with a dark brown.

Also make sure that the stain is formulated—has the resins—for the area you are doing. Some manufacturers make an all-purpose semitransparent stain that can be used on siding, fencing, decks—anywhere. However, others make a stain designed for only a specific area, such as siding. Just check the label.

Not for Hardboard, etc.

Because they are designed to work by penetrating, semitransparent stains do not work on hardboard, waferboard, oriented-strand board, or other composition materials. These products are manufactured with glue, waxes, and additives that stain cannot penetrate. For that same reason, you cannot use semitransparent stain over paint or solid-color stain; neither will absorb.

Like semitransparent stains, solid-color stains dry to a flat finish. But aside from the way they work—film versus penetrant—since they contain much more pigment (are thicker), the thin film they form can peel, although the likelihood of peeling is less than with paint.

Because of their filmic nature, you can use solid-color stains to coat composition products such as hardboard and for surfaces which are painted.

Formulations

Solid-color stain is available in oil and latex acrylic-based formulations. Acrylics are better products than oil-based stains primarily because they are less likely to peel. In any film-building coating, acrylic polymers are more elastic and adhere to the substrate's surface better than oil-based polymers, which are more brittle and tend to crack.

For many years, manufacturers have formulated solid-color stains for use only on vertical surfaces such as siding and fencing, because they could not be made strong enough to stand up to foot traffic. However, one company, Behr, has a formula for decks that the company claims holds up, because of the toughness of the acrylic resins used.

Solid-color stains come in a rainbow of colors. You will get longer life with multiple coats. In fact, for woods such as cedar, cypress, and redwood, manufacturers recommend using a stain-blocking primer under acrylic finishes. The primer prevents tannins in the wood from discoloring the finish.

Note that the more solid-color stain is applied, the more the natural look—or texture—of the wood is lost. At least one manufacturer, Cabot, makes a semisolid stain that is a cross between a semitransparent and a solid-color stain. Cabot says the stain penetrates as a semitransparent stain but has good color coverage, as a solid-color stain, yet with more texture showing through.

Applying Stains

The first rule for applying any semitransparent stain—any coating for that matter—is to thoroughly read the instructions. Individual manufacturers allow different application methods. If you have any doubt, call the 800 customer-service number of the company to get details.

In general, though, you should observe the following.

- Coat new wood as soon as possible. Conventional wisdom used to have it that new wood, particularly pressure-treated wood, had to weather awhile, to drive out moisture and provide a roughened surface before coating. This has been found to be emphatically not true. In fact, studies by the Forest Products Laboratory in Madison, Wisconsin, have determined that coatings should be applied as soon as a wood surface is dry. Doing this will increase its life span by an average 20 percent. In other words, a deck that could be expected to last 20 years without a coating could last 24 to 25 years with a coating.

- Clean all wood surfaces before applying stain. If the wood has turned gray or black, power-wash it. You can also use one of the commercially available types.

- Check that the batch numbers on the cans are the same. The numbers are on the top or bottom of the cans. This means that the stain was mixed and packaged at the same time, and color discrepancies from can to can in the same batch are less likely. Even so, pour all the stain you are using into a 5-gal can and work from it. Stains, like paints, are available in 5-gal containers, and when bought this way, they are a little cheaper than if bought in 1-gal containers.

- The color of stain in the store will not be the same on the siding, deck, or wherever you put it. As mentioned in Chap. 4, many things affect color.

  To ensure you will like the color, buy a small amount of it—1 qt, if you can—and apply it under a railing or in some other spot where it can be hidden to see if you like the color.

- Stain must be stirred frequently as it is applied, because solvent tends to separate quickly from color and you want to use it at full strength for a true color.

- Use a good brush. It is the best applicator for any stain. In Fig. 14-1a, stain is applied and then backbrushed, and areas where the roller cannot reach are brushed. Brushing drives the product deep into the wood surface. It can also be used in conjunction with other equipment. If you spray on a semitransparent stain with a low-pressure sprayer, backbrush it—brush out the applied stain to make sure it is spread properly and is worked into the wood—penetration is the key. You can also use fluffy pads for semitransparent stain; rollers work well for solid-color stain which, as mentioned, is essentially a flat paint. Brushes are used on fences (Fig. 14-1b), a time-consuming process. Stain pads could be used on parts of the fence.

- When you apply a semitransparent stain, be aware that it dries quickly and you will have to do a couple of things to avoid lap marks—flash drying on one already stained area which is then overlapped by a second gives the effect of two coats—and a lap mark.

(a)

(b)

(c)

Figure 14-1. Applying wood stain with (*a,b*) brush and (*c*) roller. (*Courtesy of Flood*)

- Stain is thin and dries quickly—a central idea to keep in mind no matter where you apply it. Hence on a deck, do a board or two at a time, keeping a wet edge and working your way down the length of the board or boards until finished (Fig. 14-1c). You should try to do top work in the shade, or early in the morning when the sun is hot and flash drying is not promoted.

Removing Stains

At times it is desirable to remove stain from a deck. It may have been overapplied, or someone wants a color change.

Until relatively recently, there was not much the painter could do, short of using a floor sander to take it up, thereby removing wood from the deck, or waiting for it to weather out, or perhaps just painting or applying a solid-color stain to it.

Happily, that is no longer the case. A new group of products now allows you to remove the stain—and more—completely. Four manufacturers familiar to me are Flood, Thompson, Wolman, and Bio-Wash, but there are surely others.

A distinction should be made between the stain removal products and wood cleaners. Cleaners are just that: They are formulated to remove dirt and mildew and grayness from wood. But they have no appreciable effect on stain.

The new products emphatically do. Now the painter has the capability of removing semitransparent as well as (in the case of at least one manufacturer, Bio-Wash) solid-color latex stain and polyurethane.

The general idea is that the older the stain, the better the product works (Fig. 14-2). If the coating on a deck has been battered by weather, the wood is better able to absorb the stain lifters, so they get under the existing stain and lift it off. I tested one product, Bio-Wash's Stripex and Stripex-L, and they worked very well.

First, surrounding vegetation is sprayed down with water to protect it, even though Bio-Wash's products are biodegradable. Stripex is applied to the deck with a roller, then a mist or spray of water is applied. This turns it into a gel-like substance (which, by the way, is very slippery underfoot). The product is agitated by brushing with a brush on a stick and allowed to work for 5 or 10 min; then a chisel or other tool is used to scrape a test area to see if the stain is loosened and lifting. If it is, a power washer is used to drive it off the stain. One pro who has used the product extensively suggests a 25° tip at 2000 lb/in². Of course, you have to be careful not to score a softwood.

Use of the product tends to darken the wood, so after stripping apply a wood brightener—Natural Wood Brightener—which is packaged with the product as a powder and is mixed with water for use. This is scrubbed on the stripped deck, then power-washed off.

Figure 14-2. Stain removed from deck.

While Stripex is designed to remove stain, and Stripex-L to remove solid-color latex and polyurethane, Stripex-L has been used on decks to remove stain, because it is stronger. Stripex is good to use on vertical rails because it is a gel and tends to stick better.

Either product could be used to remove stain from siding. At this writing Bio-Wash Stripex goes for about $30 per gallon retail, which includes a powder packet of Natural Wood Brightener. Stripex-L costs a bit more. Coverage is 100 to 150 ft²/gal. Sometimes multiple applications are required.

Specific Stains

Wood, particularly decks, is subject to a variety of stains from such sources as barbecue sauce, wax, and vegetation. These stains must be removed prior to application of a finish coating. Following are some causes of stains and ways to remove them:

Lumber Grading Stamps

There is no way to effectively remove these, although they can be primed and painted. The solution here is to use sandpaper to wear off the letters and numbers.

Algae and Moss

These leave green stains and are difficult to remove completely. They develop a root structure which penetrates the wood and can regrow. The only way to control them is to apply bleach full strength as needed.

Rust Spots

Use a 5% solution of oxalic acid in water directly applied to the stain. You will likely need two applications. Rinse the area well before applying any finish.

Wax

When citronella and other candles are used in and around a deck, there are often wax drippings. Place a mineral-spirits-saturated rag on the wax spot, and keep it wet until the spot is absorbed into the rag.

Barbecue Sauce, Grease, and Fats

Clean these with water-rinsable automotive degreasers and carburetor cleaners. Do not apply these removers when the surface is exposed to direct sun—use only in the shade.

Leaf Stains

Wash with 1-to-1 solution of household bleach and water.

15
Clear Coatings

As mentioned throughout this book, whenever wood is exposed to the elements, whether it be a deck, gazebo, fencing, or siding, it should be protected to maximize its life. Even cedar, redwood, and pressure-treated lumber will suffer the effects of weathering—graying, cupping, checking, cracking, and ultimately decaying—unless the wood is protected.

There are various ways to protect wood. But if you want to protect it and preserve its natural color as much as possible, the best thing to use is a clear penetrating sealer. Unlike polyurethanes and varnishes, which give wood a clear, thick coating that is subject to cracking, peeling, and other deterioration, penetrating clear sealers do not crack. Instead they penetrate into the wood and coat the wood fibers with a water repellent.

Some clear protective finishes also protect against mildew, fungi which promote decay, and the damaging effects of the ultraviolet rays of the sun.

Water Repellents Plus

When you shop for clear sealer, you will find that there is one attribute that they can all claim: the ability to repel water. It is important protection. Clear sealer keeps water out of wood, but lets the wood's beauty show through (Fig. 15-1). When beading does not occur anymore, it is time to recoat. Without it, the wood goes through a wetting-drying cycle that leads to warping, checking, and cracking which leads to more decay. That is, when wet, wood expands and when dry, it contracts; it gets wet, then dry repeatedly.

The common water repellents used in clear sealers are paraffin waxes, waxy substances like aluminum stearate, oils (mineral and linseed), and acrylic polymers. Because neither rain nor snow can penetrate the wax, oil, or acrylic coating, it beads up and is shed.

Figure 15-1. Water beading on sealed wood surface.

Repelling Water

Clear sealers rely on solvents to draw water repellents into the wood. Common solvents include mineral spirits, oil, water, and increasingly some combination of these. Most experts favor traditional oil- and mineral-spirits-based sealers for their proven ability to penetrate wood. However, many of these formulations are disappearing because they release large amounts of volatile organic compounds (VOCs) which, as has been pointed out, contribute to deplete ozone or increase smog. So state and local governments, abiding by federal mandates, are outlawing products with excessive amounts of VOCs.

As a result, at this writing manufacturers have been striving to create formulations which do not rely heavily on high-VOC solvents. For oil-based finishes a common method is to decrease the solvent and increase the solids content. However, this can affect the sealer's ability to penetrate the wood and can make these formulations rather harder to apply without creating lap marks.

Another approach to VOC reduction is modified-oil emulsions, which break down oil into small enough droplets to suspend in water. This eliminates most of the bad solvents and allows soap-and-water cleanup, but it also reduces penetration.

Newer yet are water-based acrylic coatings. These clears are easy to apply, and they clean up immediately with soap and water. However, acrylics have a tendency to form a film on wood surfaces that is vulnerable to the destructive effects of sunlight and abrasive foot traffic.

Still, these and other VOC-compliant formulas are the future. Although they require a bit more care when you apply them and may need to be renewed more often, they offer protection for exterior wood without negative environmental consequences.

Blocking the Sun

Sunlight—actually UV radiation—is a natural enemy of wood. It breaks down the cells on the surface of the wood and the lignin that connects the wood fibers, graying the wood and eroding its surface over time. You cannot prevent this process, but water-repellent finishes with UV protectors can slow it down.

Two kinds of UV inhibitors are used in clear finishes: organic and inorganic. Organic UV inhibitors are carbon-rich compounds that bind to the wood's surfaces. They absorb UV radiation and chemically change it to heat on a molecular level. Because the inhibitors are sacrificed in the process, UV protection declines over time.

Inorganic inhibitors usually block UV radiation. They are made of iron oxides ground to an ultrafine consistency. Although the finish is virtually transparent to visible light, it is opaque in the UV range, creating a protective layer. You can tell if the sealer uses inorganic blockers because the blocker imparts a slight color, usually pink or reddish. A sealer that uses organic inhibitors is almost water-clear.

Whether a UV inhibitor is organic or inorganic is not an important factor in its protective effect. You cannot even tell the type used in the formula by reading the label. The only sure way is to see if the finish has any color.

UV protection does not last long, despite what manufacturers claim on the label. Figure 1 year or so at most on sunny surfaces. On vertical surfaces in the shade you might get 2 years.

If you want to keep the wood its natural color—something usually desirable with lovely woods such as cedar and redwood—you have to redo it every year or so. But even with this kind of maintenance, the wood will fade and will have to be renewed with cleaner periodically.

Picking Clears

Of the two types of clear, pick a formulation that contains a UV inhibitor. Also, in all but the direst desert climates, choose a coating that contains preservatives—mildewcides and fungicides. This is especially important if you are coating a deck that is close to the ground or protecting an area which is constantly sheltered from wind and sun. Preservatives do a better job of protecting.

Not all clear sealers have preservatives. And some that do may not use the word *preservative* on the label because to do so is an expensive registration process (it costs $1 million) with the Environmental Protection Agency. Because of this, even companies whose products have mildewcides and fungicides in them do not use the word. Instead they use phrases such as "preserves the natural beauty of wood" or just claim to be "mildew-resistant." The section "How to Read a Label" contains tips on how to tell if a clear contains a preservative.

For a pressure-treated deck, toners that use a small amount of pigment are available to make the wood look more like redwood or cedar.

Of the two kinds of sealers available—solvent- and water-based—solvent-based will give longer protection, but emulsions and water-based acrylics offer easier cleanup.

Applying Clears

Applying clear sealers is relatively easy, but it is not the same as applying paint. Although instructions vary from brand to brand—and you should read the instructions on the label—the following should work.

First, make sure the surface is clean. If you see black, green, or red dots, they may be mildew. To test, dab a little bleach on them. If they are mildew, they will disappear; if not, they are dirt. For hints on identifying and removing other stains, see Chap. 14.

Coat Quickly

Coat new wood quickly. Allow a week or so of dry weather, especially on pressure-treated lumber; then apply the clear. As has been said before, the longer you wait, the greater the checking and the more natural color you will lose.

Use a brush to apply the clear. A brush drives the product into the wood better than anything else. If you wish, you can also use a fluffy pad on the end of a stick, such as Padco's.

Work with the grain. Some companies suggest using a roller or sprayer (Fig. 15-2). If you use a sprayer, though, be aware that it is easy to overapply the product. The material is milky white in the can, but it dries clear.

Back-Brush

After spraying, back-brush the applied material. Keep a wet edge to avoid lap marks. It is best to do three or four boards at a time, going from end to end or to a natural break, such as at a fence.

Figure 15-2. Applying clear with a roller. (*Courtesy of Flood*)

Avoidance of lap marks is facilitated by applying the material when the wood is cool and not in direct sunlight.

The biggest mistake made in applying clears is to apply too much. The logic goes that if some is good, a lot will be better. But this is not true. Some clear coatings are designed to be applied in only one coat. What happens is that the wood becomes saturated with the product, it does not fully penetrate, and it lays on the surface in a puddle. It can stay that way for weeks, wet and sticky. Eventually it does dry, but to a film, and then it peels.

Some manufacturers do recommend two coats, but where this is the case, it should be a wet-on-wet application.

Using Clear Films
Outdoors

Clear coatings of conventional spar urethane or marine varnish are film-forming finishes and are not generally recommended for exterior use on wood. Ultraviolet radiation penetrates the transparent film and degrades the wood underneath it. Regardless of the number of coats applied, the finish will eventually become brittle as a result of exposure to sunlight, develop severe cracks, and peel, often in less than 2 years. Photochemically degraded fibers peel from the wood along with the finish. If the finish does not require a long service life or is protected from direct sunlight by an overhang or porch, then the north side of the structure can be coated with exterior-grade varnish. In these areas a minimum of three coats is recommended, and the wood should be first treated with a paintable water-repellent preservative. The use of a varnish-compatible pigmented stain and sealers as undercoats will also contribute to a longer life for the clear finish. In marine exposures, six coats of varnish should be applied for best performance.

There are two other types of film-forming transparent coatings, but neither works well in exterior applications. Two-part polyurethanes, the first type, are tougher and perhaps more resistant to ultraviolet radiation than other transparent film-forming coatings, but they are expensive, are difficult to use, and usually have a short life as conventional varnishes.

The second type, lacquers and shellac, is not suitable for exterior application, even as sealers and primers because these coatings have little resistance to moisture. They are normally brittle and thus crack easily. However, specially pigmented knot scaler primers such as BIN do work outside and the like.

Clears on Wood

If you are going to use a clear, it is best to get the wood back to its natural color if it is discolored in any way. How to do this depends on the kind of wood, the degree of discoloration, and where the stain is located.

If the wood is cedar or redwood and has mildew, the only way to remove it is with a bleach-based product. There are a wide variety of commercial cleaners available with bleach in them.

Spray this on the deck or the siding, wait 15 min, and then rinse it off. This will kill the mildew. Do not leave it on too long, because it could bleach the wood to some degree.

If the wood is just gray or has brownish stains, an indication of tannins or extractives leaching from the wood, they can be removed by application of an oxalic acid–based cleaner and brightener. Just spray this on, scrub it in a bit, and

Figure 15-3. Power-washing wood. (*Courtesy of Wolman*)

power-wash it off. Oxalic acid pulls the tannins from wood and restores it to its original color.

Pressure-treated wood may be treated with a bleach-based solution, then rinsed and power-washed. Power-washing a deck will restore it to its natural color (see Figs. 15-3 and 15-4).

Tips for using a power washer are given in Chap. 12 on exterior preparation. What you want to be chary of is accidentally scoring redwood or cedar, which is quite soft (cedar is softer).

Once the wood has been rinsed, let it dry in the sun for a couple of days; then apply the clear coating.

Figure 15-4. Partially power-washed deck. (*Courtesy of Wolman*)

Figure 15-5. Process of UV protectors and preservatives are indicated on the label.

How to Read a Label

To evaluate what kind of clear-finish water repellent to buy, pay attention to these key features on the can's label to ensure getting the protection you want.

- *Water resistance.* Look for the term *water-repellent* or *water-resistant.* You will not be able to tell exactly what process the products use. If the sealer's formulation is oil-based, it uses either paraffin wax or some kind of oil, such as mineral or linseed, to protect against water. If the finish is water-based, it probably uses an acrylic polymer. The best type of clear to get is one that protects against sun and water and is also a preservative (Fig. 15-5). This should be stated on the can.

- *UV protection.* Look for any terms that use *UV,* such as *shields UV rays, screens out UV rays,* or *UV protection.* If you do not see the word *UV* on the label, the finish will not offer protection from the ravages of sunlight.

- *Mildew and fungal protection.* Look for a term such as *resists mildew* or *mildew-resistant.* Also look for the words *wood preservative* or *preserves wood.*

16
Paint Problems

Exterior coatings are subject to a number of problems. The following are representative.

Mildew

Mildew plays no favorites—it can affect exterior as well as interior surfaces, as suggested in Chap. 12. Mildew is probably the most common cause of discoloration of housepaint as well as of solid-color stains, semitransparent stains, and natural finishes. It can also cause uncoated wood to discolor.

The term *mildew* applies to both the fungus (a type of microscopic plant life) and its staining effects on the substrate, consisting of the wood and the coating on it.

Unlike wood-rotting fungi, mildew grows on the surface of the wood and does not degrade it. But it is very unsightly. It is usually black, but it may be red, brown, green, pink, and other colors.

Mildew can be found anywhere on the house, but it likes dampness, darkness, and dirty surfaces outside as well as inside. It is most common where the climate is warm and humid, and while it can be found on any portion of the building, it is usually located behind trees and shrubs where air movement is restricted.

Mildew may also be related to the dew pattern on a house. Dew will form on those parts of the house that are not heated and that tend to cool rapidly—eaves, the ceilings of carports and porches, and the wall area between studs. Dew acts as a moisture source for the mildew.

Detecting Mildew

Mildew can be distinguished from dirt with a simple test, as mentioned earlier. Apply pure bleach to the stain. If it disappears, it is mildew; if not, it is dirt.

Sometimes you can detect mildew by its appearance. In its growing stage, when the surface is damp, mildew appears threadlike. In the dormant stage, when the surface is dry, the fungus has many egg-shaped spores. By contrast, granular patterns of dirt are irregular in size and shape.

More-Susceptible Paints

Some paints are more vulnerable than others to attack by mildew fungi. Zinc oxide, a common paint pigment in topcoats, inhibits the growth of mildew (that is, acts as a mildewcide) while titanium dioxide, another common paint pigment, does not resist mildew well.

With oil-based paints, mildew grows more rapidly on exterior flat house paint than on exterior semigloss or gloss enamel. These and other paints which contain linseed oil are very vulnerable to mildew.

Of all the water-based paint available, acrylic latex is the most resistant to mildew. Porous latex paints without a mildewcide and applied over a primer containing linseed oil can develop severe mildew problems in warm, humid climates.

The label on the paint usually indicates if the paint contains a mildewcide. Or you can buy mildewcides in packets and jars, and these can easily be added to paint. Note that they are caustic and must be handled carefully.

Removing Mildew

Before any wood is finished, or refinished, any mildew must be removed. If it is not, it can grow on or through paint and ruin the job.

A number of commercial solutions and sprays are available to kill mildew, and they all depend, to one degree or another, on bleach, or sodium hypochlorite. You can make an effective solution by mixing 1 cup of household detergent with 1 to 2 qt of household bleach to 2 to 3 qt of warm water. Note that the household detergent must *not* contain ammonia; mixing bleach and ammonia can create lethal fumes. To kill the mildew, scrub the surface, or sponge it with the solution.

If mildew has formed on an earlier coat of finish and subsequent coats have been applied without first cleaning the surface, mildew can grow through the new coating. In this situation it is nearly impossible to control the mildew; the paint and mildew must be removed and fresh paint applied.

For new wood surfaces in warm, humid climates, mildew can be prevented by using topcoats containing zinc oxide and mildewcide over a primer coat that also contains a mildewcide. For mild cases of mildew, just use a paint containing a mildewcide.

Peeling and Cracking

There are various kinds of peeling and cracking that painters should know how to deal with on an exterior paint job. While the reasons may be many, the solution is usually the same: Remove all peeling paint and repaint, as described in Chap. 12 on preparation.

Intercoat Peeling

This term describes separation of the new paint coat from the old, indicating that the bond between coats is weak. Intercoat peeling usually results from inadequate cleaning of the weathered surface prior to painting. It can be prevented by good cleaning and painting practice, and usually it occurs within 1 year of repainting.

Intercoat peeling can also occur on freshly painted wood if too much time elapses between the primer coat and topcoat. If more than 2 weeks pass before the topcoat is applied to an oil-based primer, soaplike materials may form on the surface and interfere with the bonding of the topcoat. The surface must be scrubbed before the second coat is applied. If the prime coat is applied in the fall, do not wait until spring to apply the topcoat. If the time lapse is unavoidable, the old primer should be washed and the surface reprimed before painting.

Multiple-Coat Peeling

This occurs when a number of existing layers of paint, over which new layers are applied, start to peel (Fig. 16-1). Moisture is often the cause of multiple-coat peeling.

Moisture may come from a number of sources, but it is the main reason why paint fails (Fig. 16-2). One cause could be a lack of a vapor barrier, so moist air gets behind the exterior paint and drives it off. It may be coming from the house, where vapor emanating from the kitchen, bath, and laundry room goes through walls and condenses on the back side of siding during the winter and freezes there. In the summer the vapor changes to water, soaks the siding, and then migrates through to the outside of the siding and drives the paint off.

Moisture may also be wicked up by siding from a damp or wet foundation or siding whose bottom edges are very close to the ground. Indeed, often peeling occurs 18 in or so off the ground, which is an indication that water is getting behind the paint film. In Fig. 16-3, moisture wicked up through the wood and drove off the paint. When moisture is the culprit in paint failure, it usually takes off all paint down to the bare wood.

Multiple-coat peeling may also be caused by untrimmed shrubbery, which is periodically wet from rain, resting against the siding or an uncovered crawl space.

One other cause is that older coats of paint have lost their ability to withstand the expansion and contraction of the siding over the seasons, as temperatures change.

Figure 16-1. Multiple-coat peeling.

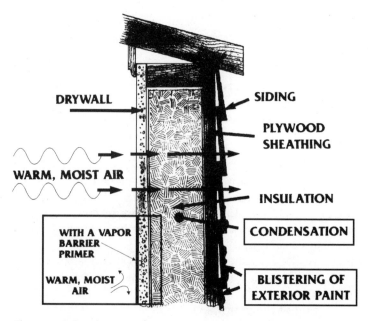

Figure 16-2. Absence of a vapor barrier promotes exterior paint blistering.

Figure 16-3. Result of moisture being wicked up behind the paint film.

Water may also enter the butt ends of siding boards and window frames—wherever water can get to the ends of the boards. The water is then wicked in, and it pushes out—the result is peeling.

Anywhere caulk is loose or missing is another access route for water. Loose window putty can do the same thing. Water gets in through the cracks and into the wood.

Such conditions must be corrected and the peeling areas, again, primed and painted.

Water in the form of rainwater or melting snow can get in behind the fascia boards and into the unpainted side of the boards if the roof does not overhang at least 1 in. The fascia boards must be replaced; then prime and paint them front and back before installation. Additionally, the roof overhang should be extended with flashing so water cannot reenter.

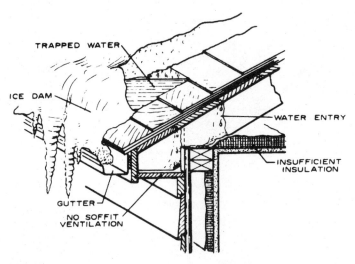

Figure 16-4. Ice dam.

Ice Dams

Ice dams are the bane of a house, and the problem should be corrected because they can cause severe damage to both the inside and outside of the house.

Ice dams are caused by a combination of improper ventilation and insulation (Fig. 16-4). When there is snow on the roof and inadequate ventilation and insulation, warm air from inside the house melts the snow, and water runs down the roof. When it reaches the coldest parts of the house, water partially freezes; as time goes by, more and more of it freezes until eventually there is an ice dam. Water collects and starts backing up—and then under the shingles, which are made to handle water flowing down, not up. Eventually water can soak through the roof deck and down into walls, where it will make paint peel on the interior and exterior of the house.

Customers should be advised that the only way to solve the problem is to have adequate ventilation put in the soffits and roof of the house and adequate insulation to ensure that the outside temperature is about the same as that on the underside of the roof.

Tip: To see if water is penetrating into the house from an ice dam, remove the first four to six courses of shingles. If there are water marks or they are wet, then water is penetrating. This can be alleviated by installing what is known as an *ice belt*—a membrane about 3 ft wide that is self-adhesive and is installed directly on the deck. The shingles are then carefully reinstalled. Although the nails penetrate the ice shield, it is self-sealing.

Peeling on Specific Materials

Peeling may also occur on specific materials for various reasons.

Hardboard or Composition Siding

Being made of what is essentially compressed wood fibers, this material is highly susceptible to damage from moisture, particularly moisture that penetrates through the edges. Once water gets into this material, it swells and fails rapidly (Fig. 16-5).

This type of siding comes primed, but the primer is often not adequate. When it arrives, it should be primed again with an oil-based primer. Give the edges a double coat before a topcoat with latex or oil is applied.

Once peeling—likely from moisture penetration—has occurred, it is very difficult to deal with. Hardboard does not sand well. Sand off as much of the peeling paint as possible, spot-prime with an oil-based primer, and repaint.

Figure 16-5. Water damage to composition board.

T-111. This is a very popular and common material for siding and other homes. But it can and does peel, sometimes because it has a grain that expands and contracts in the weather, producing a series of fine cracks that lead to peeling.

T-111 must be carefully sealed on the face and the edges to minimize problems. When cracking occurs, sand smooth, prime, and repaint.

Cross-Grain Cracking

This situation develops when the paint film becomes too thick. The problem often arises in older homes that have been painted several times. Normally, paint cracks in the direction in which it was brushed onto the wood—with the grain. The cracks run across the wood and paint. Once cracking has occurred, the only solution is to remove all the old paint and apply new paint.

To prevent cross-grain cracking, follow the manufacturer's directions concerning the rate of spread. Do not repaint areas that are sheltered from the weather such as porch ceilings and roof overhangs as often as you would other areas. Paint them only as they weather and require it. If painting is needed, clean the area first with a bristle brush to remove water-soluble extractives, let it dry, and then paint. (Latex paints, based on either vinyl or acrylic polymers, have not been known to develop cross-checks.)

Blistering

Blisters, one might say, is one stage in the development of peeling. Blisters form, and when they burst, the paint peels and fails. There are a number of types.

Temperature Blisters. This malady usually only occurs with oil-based paint, and usually where darker paints are used. It also occurs on only the first coat of paint. Temperature blisters are swellings of the paint film ballooned with solvent vapors.

They form because of the sun. As it beats down on the freshly applied paint, the rapid rise in temperature turns the solvent under the freshly applied paint to vapor, which cannot escape from underneath the paint film and so instead lifts it.

To avoid temperature blisters, avoid painting areas where the sun is due to strike shortly and avoid painting in direct sun. Follow the sun around the house, painting areas where it is not. The north side should be painted early in the morning, the east side in the late morning, the south side well into the afternoon, and the west side late in the afternoon.

If blisters form, they should be scraped off, the edges of the area feathered with sandpaper, and painted.

Moisture Blisters.   These types of blisters have water trapped inside them, and the water can come from a number of places. For one thing, rain may saturate the ends of boards, migrating down the board and pushing off the paint film.

Another factor is poor construction, particularly on the lower courses where splashing rain can enter the ends of open boards. Moisture blisters such as the above often appear after the house has been lashed by spring rains.

Moisture blisters can also be formed by moisture migrating, as it naturally does, from inside to outside the house. The water may be produced by leaks in plumbing, but also simply by vapor generated by humidifiers, dryers, and just normal living. If there is no vapor barrier inside the house, nothing stops moisture from moving under the paint film and causing blisters to form.

Moisture blisters usually affect all coats of paint down to the wood. After the blisters appear, they dry out and collapse, leaving a roughened surface; in severe cases they may peel. Some small blisters may disappear completely.

Another cause of moisture blisters is a high level of humidity inside the house. This is a likely cause if blistering is seen on walls outside the kitchen and bath, where most water vapor is generated, and is even more pronounced on the outside of an upper floor. In multistory buildings, there is a chimney effect. Warm, moist air is trying to vent outside (heat transfer), and eventually the moisture travels out through the siding.

Paint failure may be more noticeable near electrical outlets of other breaks in the vapor barrier. Drier air enters the house through cracks on the main level; therefore paint failure caused by high humidity is usually not a problem on the main level.

Condensation on the windows also indicates excessive humidity in the house. An expensive but efficient solution to high levels of humidity is to install an air-to-air heat exchanger. Here, warm, moist air gives its heat to the incoming fresh, dry air.

The most likely blisters to peel are those of oil-based paint. Old, thick coatings of paint are usually too hard to balloon and form blisters, but they can move to the point of cracking and peeling.

Elimination of excessive sources of moisture and the use of a vapor barrier are the only feasible ways to prevent moisture blisters. Ventilating devices from Hyde Company (Fig. 16-6a) are pushed in, pushing out the siding so that trapped moist air can be released (Fig. 16-6b). Figure 16-7 shows good house construction that will keep paint from failing.

Peeling can also be caused simply by dirty siding. The soil on it interferes with the paint bonding, and it fails. Prior to painting, as noted elsewhere, siding should be power-washed or cleaned with detergent and a stiff-bristled brush.

Another cause of peeling is that the weather was too humid when the painting was done.

When water-based paints are used, the water should evaporate as fast as or faster than the solvents in the paint. After the water has evaporated, the paint

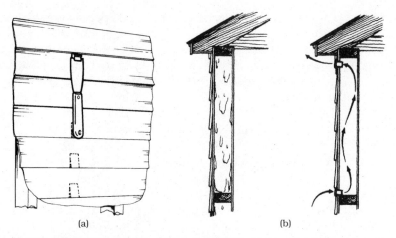

(a)   (b)

Figure 16-6. Installation of (*a*) a ventilation device allows (*b*) moisture to be released. (*Courtesy of Chade Tools*)

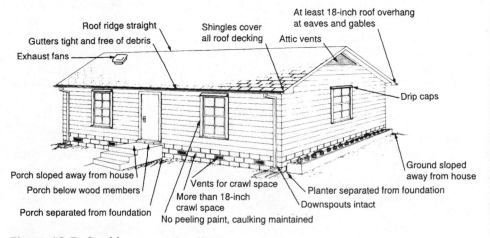

Figure 16-7. Good house construction.

will shrink to nearly its final shape: The paint chemically reacts to form a hard material. However, when it is too humid, the water cannot evaporate, and so the solvents may evaporate first, causing the paint to cure while still in a water-filled state. The only solution is to remove all the paint. Oil-based paints will also fail if the weather is too humid.

There are a variety of other reasons for paint failure on wood.

- Wood was wet when painted. If only the surface of the wood was wet, then only one sunny day is usually needed for drying prior to painting. If the wood is saturated with water, several sunny or windy days are necessary for drying prior to painting.

- Unfinished siding was exposed to several weeks of sunlight before painting. Sunlight, as noted earlier, degrades an unfinished wood surface, so it will not hold paint as well as fresh wood. If the unfinished wood was exposed to the sun for more than 3 or 4 weeks, lightly sand or power-wash the surface to remove the thin layer or degraded wood before you apply paint.

- Surface was too cold. Paint must be allowed to cure at the proper rate. To ensure this, oil-based paint should be applied when the temperature is 40°F or more. Latex paints should not be applied below 50°F, and in both cases the temperature should stay above those figures for at least 24 h.

  Also when you pretreat the wood with a paintable preservative (a recommended practice, as noted earlier), the best results are achieved when temperatures are higher than 70°F.

- Wood was painted when the temperature was too high. Painting should not be done when the temperature is above 90°F, or else temperature blisters can occur.

Peeling from Masonry

As with wood, there are a number of reasons why painted masonry peels (Fig. 16-8). One may be that the paint was applied to a surface that was chalky. This, as noted elsewhere, is like applying the paint to a powdered surface, and no paint will stick to a powder.

The solution is to scrape off as much paint as possible from the wall, using a stainless-steel brush; then wash the powdery areas with a 5% solution of muriatic acid or undiluted vinegar. Rinse thoroughly and let dry; then prime the exposed areas with a good latex topcoat. When this is dry, paint the entire surface. *Note:* It is important to rinse thoroughly. If any traces of efflorescence are left, they can absorb water later and make the paint peel.

Another reason for peeling is the deterioration of the brick itself. The brick starts to scale, spall, or fragment. An examination of the peeled paint will show if this is true. Pieces of brick will adhere to the peeled paint or be loose and flaky. The solution here is new brick, or perhaps a parge coat of masonry.

Figure 16-8. Paint peeling from masonry.

Peeling of Alkyd Paint

Masonry is an alkaline substance, so before it is painted, it must be etched to remove this alkalinity. Otherwise, peeling can result because the alkalies in the masonry chemically react with the resins in the paint and create soapy deposits, known as *saponification,* mentioned earlier, which will soften the paint and make it unstable.

Peeling from Metal

When paint peels from metal surfaces, it can have a number of causes. The surface may not have been cleaned or cleaned properly, or a proper primer may not have been used.

Wire-brush the peeling paint, and prime the areas with a dab of finish paint. Let this dry completely; then repaint.

If rust is the problem and you do not want to scrape it all off, you do not need to. As noted in Chap. 15, other products are available for making a rusty surface inert so that you can paint over it without worrying about the rust bleeding through.

Discoloration

Mill Glaze

This is a problem with the wood rather than the paint. It can occur on smooth, flat-grained western red cedar siding and occasionally other species, such as redwood. While there is controversy over what causes it, it seems to be the result of using dull planer blades at the mill and is heightened by the difficult-to-plane flat-grained surface of the lumber.

Nevertheless, the result is that water-soluble extractives are brought to the surface of the wood and create a hard, varnishlike glaze. As these extractives age, particularly in direct sunlight, they become insoluble and difficult to remove. If the glaze occurs prior to final planing, this last step usually removes it.

Whatever the reason, mill glaze cannot be penetrated by stains or clear coating and must be dealt with. If you suspect it, the easiest way to determine if it is mill glaze is to sprinkle some water on the spot. If the water does not penetrate, then you know it is. Sanding it lightly will remove the glaze and solve the problem. There is also a solution you can use to solve the problem.

Wax Bleed

Wax bleeding is discoloration on the surface of composition siding. A variety of factors contribute to the condition, but before doing anything, you should be sure it is wax bleed. So, dab a little laundry bleach (5% sodium hypochlorite); if the discolorations are not affected, it is likely wax bleed. You can help confirm this by sprinkling some water on the discolorations. If it beads up, it is wax. If the condition is particularly bad, you may even be able to feel an oily substance on the siding.

The condition arises from a variety of situations. Wax, or petrolatum, is used in the manufacture of composition siding; its purpose is to protect the siding against moisture. But for various reasons it migrates to the surface.

The wax can be made "mobile" when temperatures are high. In a sense, it melts. Darker paints, which absorb and retain more heat, are more vulnerable to wax bleed than light paints.

It may be that the film of paint in that particular area was not thick enough.

Another factor is cheap paint, containing a low amount of binder and/or nonvolatile vehicle. This paint tends to be porous and draws the wax to the surface.

Finally, exposure to the weather may affect the condition. The southern and western sides of a building are usually more susceptible to wax bleed than others.

You can usually remove the wax with some detergent and water if the condition is moderate. If the wax is heavy, use mineral spirits, soaking the material in them and changing them frequently.

In either case, allow the siding to dry; then prime with an oil-based primer and follow with two coats of latex or oil-based finish paint.

To prevent wax bleeding, do the following:

- Paint the hardboard within 30 days if unprimed and within 90 days if factory-primed.
- Use an oil primer.
- Use two topcoats, either oil-based or latex.

Surfactant Bleeding

Surfactants are soapy substances in latex paints. They are a component of the paint, but not part of the finish film. They may emerge as time goes by but not be noticed, because they wash away. However, sometimes—in low temperatures and condensation moisture—they will emerge rapidly and form a buildup.

The best solution is to do nothing. As time goes by, the surfactants will be washed away by weather.

Stains from Metal

Sometimes the chemical extractives in wood react with flashings, air conditioners, faucets, and other metal items, and the result is darkish stains below the item.

Use a mild solution of detergent and water to remove the stains. Rinse and when dry, recoat with the stain or clear used originally. To keep the problems from recurring, use a good-quality caulk in the joint where metal meets wood.

Rust Streaks

This is usually a problem when the wrong kind of nails has been used or when they have not been primed or painted properly. Water is in contact with the heads, rust forms, and water washes it down.

Ideally, aluminum, galvanized-steel, or stainless-steel nails should be used. If steel nails are used, the primer that goes over them should be rust-inhibitive.

Removing rust stains is not easy. The best bet is to prime with a rust-inhibitive primer, such as Bulls Eye 1-2-3, and repaint. The heads can be countersunk and filled with caulk or putty.

Fading

It is inevitable that all paints fade. There are a number of causes, not the least of which is that the paint is not of the highest quality. The only solution is to repaint. For maximum color retention, the use of a high-quality acrylic paint is recommended, with the surface properly primed first.

Chalking

Many paints chalk; that is, some of the resins and pigment collect in a fine powder on the surface of the paint and are washed away by weather. In most instances this is fine because as this powder washes away, it keeps the paint fresh-looking.

The problem arises when the paint chalks excessively. This is particularly bad if the surface beneath a painted area that is chalking is a different color, say, white siding over red brick. Then the chalk can leave unsightly streaks on the brick.

If this is not the case, ordinarily you can tell if the chalking is excessive by rubbing your hands on the painted surface. If a powder appears on your fingers, chalking is excessive.

If there is chalk, it must be removed prior to the application of any paint. Paint will not adhere to powder.

Scrub off chalk with detergent and water, then rinse thoroughly. Prime these areas with a top-quality oil-based primer or a stain-blocking latex primer such as Bulls Eye 1-2-3.

You can also use a detergent-and-water solution and a scrub brush to remove chalk that has washed down onto other surfaces. Rinse thoroughly when you have finished scrubbing. Also, the chalking will gradually weather away, assuming the problem was corrected.

Two Types of Discoloration

Discoloration actually occurs in two general forms. There is what is known as *diffused discoloration,* which is caused by rain and dew that penetrate a porous, thin paint film. It can also be caused by rain and dew that penetrate joints in the siding or from faulty roof drainage or gutters.

The other type of discoloration is streaking. This is commonly caused by the backs of the siding becoming wet. The water migrates into the wood and solubilizes the extractives, and they migrate to the surface. This solubilization can also occur during cold weather when water vapor inside the house moves to the outside of the house, condensing on walls, clothes dryers, humidifiers, and showers; and cooking produces moisture that does this. Then in the warmer months the ice turns to water and gets into the siding.

Water can also get into the siding from leaks, from faulty gutters, and through louvers in vents.

Streaking discoloration can be stopped or reduced by stopping moisture migration into the siding.

If a house is being remodeled or a room added, or even when a house is being built and walls are accessible, the problem can be reduced or eliminated by installation of a vapor barrier (such as a continuous 6-mil sheet of plastic) along the insides of all exterior walls. If this cannot be done, then a vapor-resistant paint should be applied on these walls.

Moisture can also be reduced by reduction of vapor generation within the home. Kitchens and baths should be vented to the outside as should clothes dryers, rather than to the attic or crawlspace.

Also, condensation in the attic (where the weather is cold enough to cause this) can be prevented by installing adequate insulation and providing proper ventilation.

Outside, water vapor can be reduced in a number of ways. If there is a crawlspace, cover it with 6-mil plastic sheeting so vapor cannot rise and enter the living areas. Also rainwater can be kept out by proper roof and gutter maintenance. Condensation in the attic can be prevented by installing adequate insulation and proper ventilation. For gable roofs, vents should be provided in the gable ends and should be about 1/300th the ceiling area. Also, air movement, as mentioned above for ice dams, is necessary, and this is provided by proper venting.

If the stains already exist, they will usually weather away in unprotected areas in a matter of months. However, if they are in protected areas, they can become more difficult to remove as time goes by. In such cases the discolored areas should be washed with a mild detergent soon after the problem develops. A solution containing 4 to 16 oz of oxalic acid per gallon of water may be effective.

Water Stain

Wood siding can become water-stained, particularly if it is left unfinished or a natural finish has started to break down.

Water stains are most common on a house in certain areas, that is, where rainwater runs off a roof, hits a hard surface, and splashes back onto the side of the building. Water will cause a finish to deteriorate quickly in this area. If the finish is not replaced (or if there is no finish to begin with), the water can leach out water-soluble extractives in the wood and create the stain.

Water stains can also be seen where gutters overflow. Whenever possible, good construction practices should be followed to prevent water stain.

The best way to guard against water stain is to treat it regularly with water-repellent coating. If stains are present, they can be very difficult to remove. Sometimes scrubbing with a mild detergent and water is effective. Light sanding may work on smooth surfaces. And bleaches such as household bleach or oxalic acid solutions have been used with varying degrees of success.

Blue Stain

This type of stain is caused by microscopic fungi that commonly affect the sap-wood of all woody species. Although microscopic, the fungi produce a blue-black discoloration. Blue stain does not normally affect a wood structurally, but conditions that favor stain development are also ideal for serious wood decay and paint failure.

Blue stain may be in wood being used, and nothing detrimental will happen as long as the moisture content is kept below 20 percent. However, the wood is exposed to moisture from rain, condensation, or leaky plumbing; the moisture content will increase; the blue stain fungi will develop further; and decay may even follow.

To prevent blue stain from discoloring paint, customers should be advised to keep wood as dry as possible. Provide an adequate roof overhang and properly maintained shingles, gutters, and downspouts. Window and door casings should slope away from the house, allowing water to drain away rapidly. In northern climates, a vapor barrier inside the exterior walls will prevent condensation. Also, vent clothes dryers, showers, and cooking areas to the outside, and watch the use of humidifiers.

Additionally, treat wood with water-repellent preservative; apply a nonporous primer and a topcoat containing a mildewcide.

The application of a 5% solution of sodium hypochlorite (liquid household bleach) sometimes removes blue stains, but it is not a permanent cure. The moisture problem must be corrected to obtain a permanent solution

Brown Stain

The knots in many softwoods, particularly pine, contain much resin, and it can sometimes cause paint to peel or turn brown. In most cases this is not a problem, though, because the resin is locked into the wood by the high temperatures used in the kiln drying of lumber.

Good painting practice will stop brown stains before they start. Use a primer followed by two topcoats.

Exuding of Pitch

Pine and Douglas fir can exude pitch or resin, while cedar species except western red cedar can exude oils. Usually, pitch and oils are not a problem because manufacturers produce lumber at certain kiln drying temperatures which lock the resin in place. Occasionally, however, it can be a problem.

If the boards are new and the pitch is dry, you can use a scraper to scrape it off; then follow by sanding. If the pitch is soft, use rags saturated with denatured alcohol to wipe away as much as you can; then sand. If the wood still exudes pitch after this treatment, treat it again.

If wood is exuding pitch after painting, it might be best to leave it alone until it is time to repaint. At that time the pitch can be scraped off and the areas sanded and primed. But if the paint has peeled badly, it might be best to replace the boards before repainting.

Pitch can continue to exude from boards for literally years, and there is no way to stop it. The condition is usually exacerbated during months when the weather is hot.

PART 5
Spray Painting

17

Spray Painting
Indoors and Outdoors

Spraying paint can be a boon for the professional housepainter because it makes the job go more quickly. It is estimated that spray-painting a surface is twice as fast as painting it with a roller. Spray painting started out as a tool in industry for painting irregular shapes and items, but because of its speed in some situations its use spread to both the inside and outside of houses.

Sprayers

There are three kinds of spray painters available: conventional, high-volume low-pressure (HVLP), and airless.

All systems use air to atomize the paint, but the conventional system, also called the *cup-and-gun* system, atomizes it into a very fine mist and expels it from the spray gun by using compressed air. In airless systems, a pump is used, and the droplets are much heavier (Fig. 17-1). With the airless sprayer, most often used by painters, there is little overspray, and it can be used inside.

Each system will work only on certain materials. The thicker the material in the conventional system, the more it will have to be thinned. Hence, lacquer- and oil-based paints work well with cup-and-gun sprayers, but in order to spray heavier materials, such as latexes, the paint must be heavily cut. For example, conventional sprayers require that the paint be chemically stable, but evaporate mainly in the spray cone as well as dry on the surface being sprayed.

Paint applied with a cup and gun is often so thin that one or more additional coats are required. And because of the thinness of the paint, the spray mist can carry, making it impractical for many interior and exterior uses, unless a

(a)   (b)

Figure 17-1. Airless sprayer being used (*a*) inside and (*b*) outside. (*Courtesy of Graco*)

controlled situation exists. Think of this system for fine work such as furniture and the like. The main tool of the painter is the airless sprayer.

Airless Sprayers

Airless sprayers do not atomize the spray in the same way as cup-and-gun types do; airless sprayers do not require that the paint be atomized to work well. They are airless. They depend on pressure—from 1200 to 3000 lb/in^2—to drive the paint through a nozzle, an orifice where it is broken up into particle size, and deliver a thick, airless wet film where you want it. Unlike conventional sprayers, which require that a guard be used when spraying, these do not: An experienced painter can paint close to other areas without shielding them or masking them off. In some instances, spray guards are useful. They are about 3 ft long and 12 in wide, are made of plastic or metal with a handle, and resemble a huge fan.

Airless sprayers are faster than conventional guns. A good airless sprayer can apply 1 gal of paint in 3 min. That is equivalent to 20 gal/h of paint. Usually, painters work out of a 5-gal container; the paint is drawn up into the spray gun via a hose.

Another plus of an airless sprayer is its *transfer efficiency*—the amount of paint that is actually transferred from the sprayer to the surface and that is not overspray or wasted. The paint emerges from the tip and is atomized.

Great caution is necessary with an airless spray gun. Because of the tremendous pressures, it can cut through flesh with ease.

HVLP Sprayers

The high-volume low-pressure sprayer is the newest kind of spray equipment available. It looks like a conventional cup-and-gun sprayer, but the significant difference is that the HVLP sprayer only requires 10 lb/in^2 of pressure to operate as opposed to 80 to 130 lb/in^2, and the difference allows far greater control of the spray. The HVLP sprayer is good for fine work, but is not powerful enough to do large areas such as rooms or houses.

Spraying Techniques

Using the Spray Gun

The best way to apply paint from a spray gun is to make overlapping patterns (Fig. 17-2), much as you would in mowing a lawn. To paint a flat surface, such as plywood walls or asbestos cement shingles, apply a band of spray, then another that slightly overlaps the first. Try to limit the degree of overlap: All you need is enough to close any gaps between bands. Going too far can result in too large a paint buildup.

When spraying, position your body parallel to the surface being painted and keep the gun parallel to the surface as you go (Figs. 17-3 and 17-4). Hold it 6 to 8 in from the surface. A common error is to apply the paint in sweeping arcs. This results in a buildup of paint that's heavier in the middle and thinner at the edges.

Each time you turn off the gun and start a new band, have the gun moving before you turn it on. Then there will not be a heavier buildup of paint where you start compared to other areas.

Use the same technique at the end of the stroke. Turn off the gun while your arm is moving. If you stop moving the gun, there will be a big paint buildup there.

Spraying Corners

Spraying, of course, is not only for flat surfaces. The average job also calls for the spraying of inside and outside corners.

To spray an inside corner, hold the gun 6 to 8 in from the corner (Fig. 17-5). Then just move the gun back and forth across the corner as if it were a flat surface. The spray will overlap the corner, but there will be no excessive paint buildup. Remember to have the gun moving before you turn it on, both before and after the strokes.

To spray outside corners, also locate the gun 6 to 8 in from the corner. Turn the gun 90° and then spray, moving the gun along vertically. As you do, the spray pattern will overlap both walls that are adjacent to the corner.

Clapboard and Other Lap Siding

If you are painting clapboard or other siding that overlaps, it is best to do it in a few steps. Keeping in mind the advice to keep the spray gun moving, paint the bottoms of the four courses. (It is important to catch it all; otherwise, the siding can wick in water, and the paint can fail.)

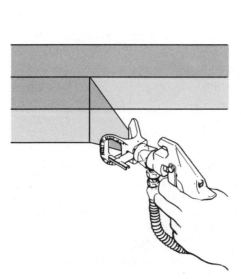

Figure 17-2. Spraying paint in overlapping bands. (*Courtesy of Graco*)

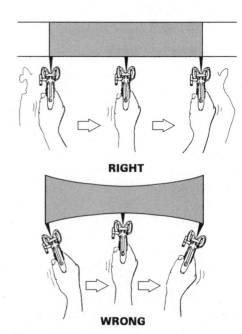

RIGHT

WRONG

Figure 17-3. Correct way to spray paint. (*Courtesy of Graco*)

Figure 17-4. Painter holds gun parallel to surface. (*Courtesy of Graco*)

Figure 17-5. Spray-painting an inside corner. (*Courtesy of Graco*)

(a)

(b)

Figure 17-6. Applying stain. (*a*) Spraying. (*b*) Back-brushing.

Next, holding the spray gun slightly down and moving it downward vertically, spray the bottom edge of each board. Finally, draw the gun across the face of each board horizontally.

If you are painting rough surfaces, paint the bottom of the courses as suggested above, then the faces. Rougher surfaces are less likely to need backrolling—at least the first coat—than smooth surfaces.

When you are using stain, spray on the material, then back-brush it into the surface (Fig. 17-6). A spray wand is helpful for reaching out-of-the-way places and for keeping the spray parallel to the surface (Fig. 17-7). When painting siding, hit between courses first, then paint faces (Fig. 17-8).

Figure 17-7. Using an extension wand. (*Courtesy of Graco*)

Figure 17-8. Painting siding, hitting overlaps first. (*Courtesy of Graco*)

Hints for Successful Spraying

To minimize glitches and reduce problems of spray-painting, follow these hints:
   Cover everything that could possible get oversprayed, such as bushes, lamps, windows, and doors. This preparation takes time, but since spray-painting goes

so speedily, it is well worth the effort. If there is the slightest wind, do not spray. Any wind at all can carry the paint all over the place.

You may not want to paint if setting up scaffolding will be a problem, such as for a house on rough terrain. To spray-paint properly, scaffolding is sometimes required, and this is difficult to install on such terrain.

Before you use paint—particularly the cup-and-gun system—strain it through a paint bag to remove all potential clogging bits. Spray tips are extraordinarily sensitive to clogs.

Use Floetrol in latex paints to be sprayed and Penetrol in oil-based paint. These products are paint conditioners; they make the paint flow better and keep a wet edge longer. While they can be used with the brush and the roller (and are recommended), they allow the use of lower pressures in spray painting and, therefore, better control of the job.

Safety Measures

It is important to protect yourself when spray-painting. A respirator is recommended (see Chap. 1) so that you do not breathe in the fumes. Also wear goggles to protect your eyes (the wraparound kind is best in this situation). A pair of cotton gloves and a long-sleeved shirt are needed, too. Wear clothes that you will not mind discarding when the job is done. Or you can use disposable coveralls which are inexpensive and lightweight.

Spray Paints

It is sometimes convenient to apply paint from an aerosol can. They are simple to use, but there are some things to observe to ensure the best results.

Many different kinds are available, from clear polyurethane to rust-proofing primers. Indeed, today you can get both solvent-based and latex-based paints. Aerosol spray paint, no matter the type, consists of the coating and the propellant. The latter may be one of two different kinds: carbon dioxide, which is a compressed gas, and liquid hydrocarbons. The most common propellant is lightweight hydrocarbon. It usually consists of around 23 percent of what is known as the *fill ratio*—the ratio of propellant to paint in percent. For example, you might see 78/22%, which means that 78 percent is paint and the rest is propellant.

Most spray paints dry to the touch in 10 min or less, but there are exceptions.

Before starting to spray, you must shake the can vigorously to activate the ball inside. This mixes the paint for application.

Application

The way to succeed with aerosol spray cans is to apply multiple light coats rather than one heavy coat. One heavy coat leads to paint buildup and sagging...and having to start over.

Hold the can at whatever distance the manufacturer suggests in directions on the label. This is usually 12 to 16 in from the surface. Hold the can straight up and perpendicular to the surface. Hold it a few inches away from the item, and move it across the face of the item, thereby having the spray fully on by the time it coats the surface; this ensures an even coat.

Once you reach the end of the item, come back and paint another strip, slightly overlapping the first and keeping the spray can moving.

The first coat is known as the *tack* coat. You can normally apply (see directions on the can) a second coat before the first is dry, but usually you must wait until the second coat is completely dry before applying subsequent coats.

Clogging

The bane of aerosol spray painting is the clogging of the tip. It happens more than occasionally. There are several ways to clean a clogged tip. One way is to simply rotate the tip back and forth a half turn. Paint sometimes collects and dries inside the can around the stem, and this will break it and allow paint to flow freely.

If rotating does not work, pull off the spray tip and use an X-acto knife or some other narrow-bladed tip to clear the V groove in the stem.

Replace the tip, making sure the arrow indicating the spray direction points away from you. Otherwise, you could be spray-painting yourself!

If this does not work—the tip is badly clogged—remove it and soak it in mineral spirits for about 30 min. Then brush or wipe off the loosened paint.

It is *not* a good idea, by the way, to clean any of the orifices with a needle. The opening might be inadvertently enlarged such that it emits too much paint.

To ensure that a spray tip is cleaned, take it off after a job and put it on a WD-40 spray can. Then fire a few blasts. This will clear it of paint that might clog it.

Tip Wear

In operating spray equipment, it is, of course, important to maintain the equipment so that it gives maximum service and production, just as you maintain brushes and rollers.

When problems arise in operating the equipment, some of them, such as a punctured hose, a leaky pump, or a clogged filter, are relatively easy to spot. However, one problem that is often overlooked—because it does not have dramatic symptoms—is tip wear.

There are symptoms. If the spray runs, sags, or tails, it may well be a worn tip that is at fault. Because there is a tendency to increase the pressure to correct these conditions, a lot of extra stress is put on the pump, which could burn it out. Even if this does not happen, by using a worn tip you'll be using more paint and more time to do the job.

To keep the system functioning smoothly, check for tip wear every 100 gal of paint or so. Do you notice significant changes in the spray pattern?

Essentially, as the tip wears, the orifice from which the paint is fired becomes enlarged, and the fan pattern decreases. Essentially, it seems as if you are using the wrong size tip for the job. A worn tip provides less control of its narrower fan pattern, so it takes more passes to cover the area.

For example, a 515 tip (a Wagner product) will produce a 10-in fan pattern at 2500 lb/in^2, when spraying latex paint 12 in from the surface. The flow rate here is about 1 qt/min. But the same tip, when worn, becomes a 0.017 size tip, so under the same spraying conditions (12 in away, latex paint), the flow rate increases to almost one-third of 1 gal/min, or 1½ qt/min—50 percent repaint.

When the tip is larger, it gets even worse. For example, a tip that is increased to 0.021 will use approximately ½ gal/min of paint, or 2 qt/min. You will be using twice as much paint as with the original tip.

PART 6
Hanging Wall Coverings

18
What Is Available

Hanging wall coverings is as much a part of a painter's job as painting, and it is a skill that the professional should master. The first step is to become aware of and understand the variety of wall coverings available.

The first thing to understand is the name, *wall coverings*. Years ago there was just wall*paper*, but with the advent of a wide variety of other papers including ones that had vinyl facings to grasscloth and foil, the word *paper* no longer was accurate. Not all were pure paper, so the term *wall coverings* came into use. But *wallpaper* is still used, often to describe a wall covering that is not pure paper. So, too, one speaks of *paper hanging* and *hanging wallpaper* when, in fact, wall covering is being installed.

How Wall Coverings Are Sized

Wall coverings are sold by single roll in U.S. or metric sizes. The former range from 12 to 24 ft long and 18 to 36 in wide, containing 34 and 36 ft^2.

The metric sized roll, covering between 27 and 30 ft per roll, is commonly sold 20½ in wide by 16½ ft long. Rolls cover from 27 to 30 ft^2—about 25 percent more than the U.S. roll—and can range from 13½ to 16½ ft long and 20½ to 28 in wide.

Wall coverings are priced by the single roll, but standard coverings usually come in a double or, less commonly, triple roll. Some heavy industrial coverings come 48 or 54 in wide.

Double and triple roll sizes are based on the assumption of use on a standard 8-ft-high wall. If it were sold by the single roll, the installer would constantly be splicing cut sections or have a lot of waste. (See Fig. 18-1 to figure how much wall covering is needed.)

Measuring Guide

Measure the height of the ceiling and the distance around the room. Check the chart below to determine the number of single rolls needed for the walls. All patterns come in double rolls. Deduct one single roll for every two ordinary-size openings, such as windows and doors.

Ceiling height	8 ft	9 ft	10 ft	12 ft
Distance around room in feet	Single rolls			
40	14 (13)	18 (14)	18 (17)	22 (19)
44	16 (14)	18 (15)	20 (18)	24 (20)
48	18 (15)	20 (18)	22 (19)	26 (23)
52	18 (17)	22 (19)	24 (20)	28 (24)
56	20 (18)	24 (20)	26 (22)	30 (26)
60	22 (19)	26 (22)	26 (24)	32 (28)
64	22 (20)	26 (23)	28 (25)	34 (30)
68	24 (22)	28 (24)	30 (26)	36 (32)
72	26 (23)	30 (25)	32 (28)	40 (34)

This chart can be used for both 20½- and 27-in-wide rolls. The numbers in parentheses are for 27-in-wide rolls.

Figure 18-1. Guide for measuring wallpaper. (*Courtesy of Gencorp*)

Types of Wall Coverings

Wall coverings, as mentioned, come in a number of types:

- *Paper.* This paper has the pattern and color printed directly on it and has a very thin coating of vinyl to protect it somewhat. But it is not normally used in areas such as the bath or kitchen, where it has to stand up to excessive amounts of soil or moisture.

- *Vinyl-coated.*   This paper has a coating of vinyl sprayed or otherwise applied during manufacture. It is highly washable and comes in a huge array of colors and patterns.

- *Solid-sheet vinyl.*   This is a backing of paper to which a solid sheet of thin vinyl is glued, on which the pattern and color are imprinted. This wall covering can be installed anywhere and is easy to clean.

- *Foil.*   This is composed of thin sheets of aluminum foil, which contains the color and pattern, adhered to a paper or cloth backing known as a *scrim*. There may also be a layer of polyester between the foil and backing to prevent water in the wall covering paste from contacting the foil.

- *Commercial vinyl.*   These are heavier coverings, composed of a vinyl facing on a cloth backing. They are usually 48 to 54 in wide and come in various weights. Type 1 weighs 7 to 13 oz/yd^2; the cloth backing is called a scrim. Type 2 weighs 14 to 21 oz/yd^2, and its backing is a heavier cloth called an osnaburg or drill. Type 3 weighs 21 oz/yd^2 or more and has an even heavier drill than type 2.

- *Flocked.*   This is wallpaper with a raised-pattern finish which might be silk, rayon, nylon, or cotton. The base of flocked wallpaper may be cloth or paper.

- *Felt.*   This has a nappy surface which looks like the leather made from a goat.

- *Suede.*   This also simulates leather.

- *Raised vinyl.*   This is also known as *heated vinyl,* and it consists of a vinyl film which has had raised patterns embossed in it with heat. It is mounted on a paper backing.

- *Mylar.*   This is a trade name of du Pont and refers to a certain kind of polyester film that has been combined with aluminum or vinyl sheeting. It is applied over decorative wallpapers with a variety of backings.

  Mylar is sometimes confused with foil. The chief difference is that while foil will not burn, Mylar will.

- *Moiré.*   This usually resembles solid-sheet vinyl, but when light is reflected on it, it can look like a wood grain or texture.

- *Grasscloth.*   This is made by hand. The raw material used is a native vine called arrowroot that comes from Korea. The material is made on looms in vertical strands of string, known as *warp threading.* Across this the vine strips are woven; this is known as *weft threading.* Together the warp and weft are known as the *netting.* The netting is laminated to a paper backing and dyed.

- *Rushcloth.*   This resembles grasscloth and is made from strands of rush, a kind of plant, woven together.

- *Hemp.*   The raw material of this paper also comes from a plant, in this case the hemp plant. It looks like grasscloth.

- *Reedcloth.*   This is also made by hand. It consists of reeds interwoven with vertical cotton threads (called the *warp*), and the reeds are of different thicknesses and colors.

- *Stringcloth.*   Here, delicate threads are laminated to a backing. The paper is available in a variety of colors and sizes. It differs from grasscloth in that the seams are not prominent.

- *Jute.*   This is made with coarse fibers which are sometimes blended with cloth and laminated to a backing.

- *Paper weave.*   This looks like grasscloth but is not. It is made of paper which has been cut into strips and then pulled to make hanks of material. Companies make the yarn into a weave, and then it is laminated to a paper backing.

- *Hand-screened prints.*   Silk screening is used in making this wall covering. The process may be done by hand or by machine or by both. The print itself is bonded to a paper backing as solid vinyl wall covering is.

- *Hand-printed mural.*   A mural is created by hanging individual strips of wall covering that are installed in a certain sequence.

- *Liner paper.*   This is thin material that comes in rolls, as wall covering does, and may be fiberglass, polyester, or canvas. It is designed as a base for wall coverings which are being installed over particularly rough walls. Details are given in Chap. 5.

Dye Lot Numbers

On each roll of wallpaper, a manufacturer will imprint a *dye lot* number, which indicates that all the material was manufactured at the same time. When dye lot numbers differ, it means that each lot was manufactured at a different time. This is significant because there can be small differences in the look of the paper, the inks used were slightly different, the amount of vinyl coating varied ever so slightly, or the embossments differed. When installed, the strips can look slightly different and may mar the overall look of the job. Hence, it is important to only hang wall coverings from the same dye lots.

Wall coverings are commonly shipped to stores in the same-dye-lot numbers. If you have trouble getting enough paper with the same dye lot numbers from one outlet, check others or contact the manufacturer.

Borders

These are, as the name suggests, materials used to go around something, in this case to accent wall-ceiling lines, doors, windows, and the like.

They come in a wide variety of styles and colors, both plain and prepasted, and can be used, like wall covering, on papered or painted walls. They are available in 5- and 7-yd spools and continuous rolls.

Prepasted—or Not

Some wall coverings come plain and are installed by applying an appropriate paste or adhesive. Others are prepasted—their backings are coated with a factory-applied dry adhesive which is activated with water or a product called an *activator,* which is really a thinned-down clear paste.

The paperhanger will likely rely on only a few adhesives, but it is good to know about them all. Following is a roundup.

Wheat Paste

This is the old standby of pastes, a powder that is mixed with water to form the paste. Actually, wheat paste is only one of a number of pastes which are in the starch adhesive family. These include corn, sago, tapioca, and potato.

Like any paste that must be mixed, wheat paste is relatively inconvenient to use because it must be mixed until it reaches a smooth, lumpfree consistency. But it works well in hanging paper and paper- and cotton-backed coverings. Preservatives are usually added to it to prevent mildew.

Clear Premixed Adhesives

These adhesives come in a thick, syrupy consistency and can be applied directly to the paper without mixing. They are made from wheat pastes, which have been cooked with acid or steam, and do well in hanging paper and paper-backed products as well as others.

While not strictly speaking clear—they will leave a haze if left on wall coverings—clear premixes are easy to clean and work with. Clear premixes can be unforgiving. For example, if applied too heavily, it tends to stretch and dry out and interfere with adhesion.

Clay-Based Adhesive

This gets its name from the clay which is added to the starches used to make the adhesive. The clay gives the adhesive greater tack and makes it dry much more quickly than other types of adhesives. In other words, the job goes faster.

Clay-based adhesives may also have vinyl-to-vinyl adhesive mixed in and are used as a sizing. This shortens the work time even more, and the acrylic resin make the adhesive stronger.

Clay-based adhesives also shrink less than other types, making them useful when covering must be stretched around corners and shrinkage is critical.

It also should be used whenever a nonbreathing wall covering is installed over an oil-based primer sealer. Regular adhesive can take a relatively long time to dry, which gives mildew more time to form, while clay-based adhesive dries so much faster that this is not likely to happen. If the wall covering is breathable, this mildew should not be a problem.

Clay-based adhesive is more difficult to clean than other types of adhesives, and any wrinkles which are formed during installation tend to stay that way because of the clay in the adhesive.

Vinyl-to-Vinyl Adhesive

This is the preferred adhesive for hanging borders over other wall coverings. It is the strongest wall covering adhesive available. It is primarily composed of acrylic resin and very little water; the latter is good because it vastly reduces the possibility of mildew forming.

Prepasted Adhesive

This wall covering comes with a thin film of dry paste on it. Drawing it through water or otherwise wetting it activates the paste.

Some paperhangers prefer to apply an activator prepasted wall covering rather than water alone. Sometimes, depending on the manufacturer, there can be gaps in the dry paste and, therefore, possible points of failure. The activator is essentially a thin glue and ensures that this does not happen.

19
Preparing Walls for Wall Covering

Preparing walls for wall covering is just as important as preparing them for painting. Wallpaper will adhere better and not be subject to a number of problems, such as mildew, which can affect its durability and looks. You should make the following preparations.

Clean Walls

Walls should be free of grease and dirt. Use a nonpowdered cleaner (a residue of powder can interfere with adhesion) such as equal parts of water and ammonia.

Sand and Patch

The walls should be smooth, so all dings and mars should be sanded out with a coarse sandpaper and the walls sanded smooth.

Cracks as well as lumps and bumps should be dug out with a scraper or other tool as necessary and then filled with a water-based patcher (check the label for this). If the holes are deep, check how deep the patcher can be applied without risk of cracking. Some cracks require multiple shallow coats.

If there are broad areas that need smoothing, a skim coat should be applied. (See Chap. 5.)

Patching is made easier by using scrapers or compound knives with flexible blades, as suggested in Chap. 1. The patcher should be made smooth without sanding, though sanding should be done (100-grit paper) as a final step to remove very minor imperfections.

After patching and smoothing, view the wall from the side with a 150-W light; areas that still needs patching will show up. For additional information on patching, see Chap. 5.

Mildew

Mildew is a spore that lives in the air, and when it alights on damp surfaces—it needs moisture to survive—it grows. It comes in a variety of colors, usually black but also green, yellow, brown, pink, and purple.

Household bleach—a 50-50 water and bleach mixture—works, or you can buy any of a variety of mildew killers, such as Mil Klean.

After you remove the mildew, wash the affected area with warm water and let it dry before proceeding with any other step.

Peeling Paint

Any paint that is peeling or otherwise damaged must be removed, the surface sanded, and patcher applied as needed. For shallow depressions joint compound works well. It can be applied in thin coats (two coats may be needed) and has tenacious sticking power.

Large Holes and Cracks

Holes and cracks may be repaired as described in Chap. 6. Remember that a surface that is not smooth can reflect through some wall coverings and mar the job.

Priming and Sizing

Before wall covering is applied, make sure the walls are also primed and sized as needed. The wall is primed so there is no bleed-through of color and/or through the wall covering.

Sizing is a coating applied to ensure that the wall surface is sealed, so that the paste on the wall covering will not penetrate unevenly and possibly lead to failure. It also provides better tooth or gripping power for the wall coverings. Sizing has one other goal: to make it easier to take off the wall covering in the future.

Today there is a number of materials that are primer and sizing in one, such as Shieldz, Muralo Adhesium, and others. You can roll either of these products on like paint.

Preparing Walls of Nonstandard Materials

There are a number of materials over which you may want to install wall covering that are not considered standard walls. Following is a roundup of these and how to do the job.

Masonry

By its nature, masonry is rough, whether it is poured concrete or block. The first step before deciding to install wall covering is to make sure that there is not a moisture problem. Once this is decided, then the work can proceed.

Assuming the walls are unpainted, apply an acrylic-based primer sealer. When this is dry, install a heavyweight liner paper horizontally, using the adhesive specified by the manufacturer. This material will be able to bridge the cracks. When this is finished, the liner may be primed and sized and the wall covering installed.

A good trick after the liner is installed is to view it against the light of a 150-W bulb, which will show any imperfections. If there are some, patch them.

In some cases, the wall will be so rough that not even a heavy liner paper will cover it all. If wall covering is still desired, it may be necessary to have the wall furred out and to install drywall.

Paneling

Wall liner may be used over paneling and is also good for preparing grooved paneling for wall covering.

It is neither necessary nor desirable to first fill the grooves with spackling compound. Indeed, this can cause the spackling compound to shrink, marring the job.

First, repair the paneling as needed, making sure it is tight and straight. Wash down the paneling with a solution of half warm water and half ammonia. Make sure all grease, oil, and wax are off; a stripper may be necessary.

Use 80-grit sandpaper to scuff-sand the walls, wiping away dust with a damp rag as needed. Prime the paneling with an acrylic-based primer, making sure all edges near doors and windows are also primed to keep moisture from penetrating.

Install medium-weight liner paper horizontally. Use the lightbulb as suggested above to check depressions and mars. Spackle as necessary.

To be on the safe side, prime the liner paper with an acrylic-based primer.

Sand or Textured Walls

These types of walls are too rough to install wall covering on as is. Steps must be taken to remove the texture or sand, to create a dead flat surface that will enable the wall covering to adhere to the entire wall, rather than to just the high point of the sand or texture.

You can remove such walls or cover them over. Removal can be done by chemical means or sanding. For sanding, a belt sander is desirable. As you can imagine, this, too, is an extraordinarily messy job. Wear a good respirator and hang plastic, secured with painter's tape, over openings such as doors and the like so the dust cannot float into other rooms.

Take care not to score or gouge the walls. If this happens, patch them with drywall compound before you proceed.

You can also cover the wall. There are three ways to do this. You can skim-coat it, as detailed in Chap. 5, install thin Sheetrock, or install wall liner. If you have a good hand, the skim coat is the way to go. A liner would be next. The $\frac{1}{4}$-in Sheetrock would involve more work than the other coverups.

Ceramic Tile Walls

Here, as with block and concrete, a heavyweight liner is the best. First, clean the walls thoroughly with a 50-50 solution of ammonia and warm water, then scuff-sand them, wipe away dust, and prime with an acrylic-based primer. Install heavyweight liner paper on the tile, as with concrete and masonry.

Plastic Laminate and Glass

Wall coverings can also be installed over plastic laminate and glass. Wash the surface thoroughly, scuff-sand with 80-grit sandpaper, prime, and size it.

Sheetrock

All raw Sheetrock requires is a prime or sizing like Shieldz or Muralo Adhesium.

Existing Wall Covering

When installing wall covering over existing wall covering, the main thing to remember is that the old wall covering acts as a base for the new material, and therefore it must be as solid as if the wall covering were being installed on a wall.

Check the seams of the paper. If they are lifting, secure with seam adhesive. Use a roller to make sure it will adhere. If there are open seams, also apply spackling compound to these. If seams are overlapped and have a slight bump, spackle these.

If there are bubbles or other loose spots in the paper, open them up with a razor knife and affix adhesive, or cut out and spackle the area.

Checking for Inks Bleed

The design on wall covering is made with different inks, and it is important to know if these are a type that run. If so, they could bleed through the new wall covering. The problem is particularly prevalent with vinyl papers with metallic inks.

To find out, dab a 50-50 mixture of ammonia and water on the color. If it runs, then the paper must be primed with a shellac-based primer.

Other Problems

A variety of other problems may occur regarding wall covering. If the wall covering being applied has a transparent quality, the walls should be primed with acrylic primer to ensure that the problem areas do not show through.

If the existing wall covering is a solid vinyl or a nonbreathing type, this should be addressed one of two ways: (1) If regular adhesive is used, install liner paper first. This will absorb much of the adhesive used and will help avoid a situation where the glue takes a long time to dry and mildew is created. (2) Use vinyl-to-vinyl adhesive. This has such a small amount of water in it that the chances of mildew's forming are remote.

Finally, if a wall covering is being hung over an existing solid vinyl, check the vinyl wall covering to see if it feels a little sticky. If so, this means that it has plasticizers on the surface, and it should be washed thoroughly with mineral spirits before an acrylic primer is applied.

20
Removing Wall Coverings

The professional painter who hangs wall coverings as well as paints is occasionally called upon to remove existing paper or wall covering. Sometimes this will be easy. If it is a cloth-type paper, just grab a corner of the paper and pull it off. It comes off in one strip. Then wash any residual glue off the wall with a cleaner (more about this later).

In doing this, however, you must guard against damaging the wall surface. If it is plaster, there is little chance of this. However, drywall has a kraft facing paper, and this could be pulled off—and perhaps gypsum with it. It all depends how the person who hung the wall covering prepared the walls; often they are not prepared that well.

Hence, it is a good idea to use a scraper to gently lift one corner and then pull off the paper, with the peeling paper just about parallel to that on the wall. Avoid pulling it straight out.

If it does not peel off, then one or two methods should be used: chemicals or a steamer. If you expect to remove a lot of paper, the steamer is likely the cheaper method.

Whichever method you employ, remember that both methods remove wall covering by attacking—weakening the adhesive that bonds—the covering to the wall. Once this is softened, the covering can be stripped easily from the wall.

Steaming

Essentially, the steamer consists of a flat-metal steam plate, about 8 in by 11 in with holes in it, like a clothes iron. The plate is connected by a long hose to what

275

is essentially a pressure cooker, where water is heated and turned to steam; the steam travels through the hose and emerges from the plate perforations. To use it, hold the plate against the wall covering, saturating it with hot steam. This steam resolubilizes the paste, which is water-based, and the covering starts to loosen.

The chemical method is one of two types. The first uses a liquid, such as DIF, one very common brand, which is added to water and makes enough remover for the average room. The solution is applied to the wall, preferably with a deck sprayer because it saturates the wall, to a 3-ft-wide area going from the ceiling to the base molding. Then additional solution is applied to an adjacent 3-ft strip, and so on down the wall. To keep the wall covering saturated, new solution is applied to the first strips done as the job progresses.

After 30 min, a stiff scraper is used to scrape off the wall covering; then more solution is used to clean excess remaining glue off the wall. Also use the scraper and rags as needed to do this.

Gel Remover

Gel remover is more expensive than DIF, but no reapplication is required. The gel is brushed on the surface. Because it is thick, it sticks there of its own accord, saturating the paper with chemicals and attacking the paste. After a certain time, the gell has penetrated the paper and attacked the paste.

After the paper is stripped, the glue that remains must also be removed.

Some types of wall covering will allow the outer plastic surface to be stripped away, leaving a backing paper in place. Once the plastic is off, treat it in the same way as you would treat paper: Apply and let the solution soak in, scrape, and rinse.

Impermeable Wall Coverings

Many wall coverings, as noted in Chap. 36, are not pure paper but are covered with vinyl or some other material. Chemical strippers will not penetrate this covering, of course. A pathway must literally be cut for it; that is, the paper must be scored.

This can be done in a variety of ways. One way uses the tines of a fork. A fork is simply drawn across the wall covering, and the tines break through the paper to the surface beneath. Another way uses the edge of a scraper, and yet another employs rough-grit sandpaper. In doing this, of course, make sure not to score the surface beneath the paper. If you do, fill in the scrapes before proceeding with new paint or wall covering.

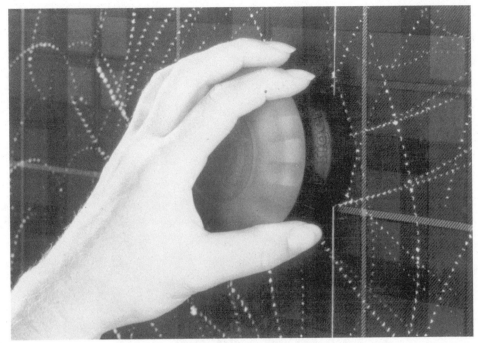

Figure 20-1. Device for removing wallpaper. (*Courtesy of Wm. Zinsser & Co.*)

One method uses Paper Tiger, a product made by Zinsser which has toothed wheels (Fig. 20-1). The device is rolled over the covering with pressure applied, and the wheels score the covering.

Once all the wall covering is off, wash off any residual glue with chemicals or gel.

Removing wall covering is a messy process no matter what you use, and it is a good idea to cover up carefully, using masking tape, plastic drops, and cloth ones. Also remember that plastic is slippery and can be treacherous underfoot.

Removing Specific Types of Wall Covering

Following is a lineup of wall coverings, what you might expect to remove at one point or another, and what is usually involved.

- *Paper.*   No scoring is necessary. Just wet it down and scrape it off gently (Fig. 20-2).

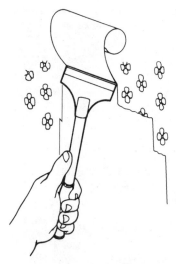

Figure 20-2. Scraping off wall covering with
a razor. (*Courtesy of Hyde Tools*)

- *Solid vinyl.*   Usually, the vinyl surface film comes off by pulling, leaving the backing on the wall; then this can be removed as paper is.
- *Vinyl-coated.*   Sometimes this can be dry-stripped from the wall, and other times it cannot be and will have to be wet down, then stripped.
- *Commercial vinyl.*   These usually can be dry-stripped.
- *Raised vinyl.*   The top vinyl layer can be peeled off, and then the backing is either left on or removed as paper is.
- *Flocked.*   The substrate of flock paper may be paper or scrim. If scrim, the paper can be peeled away. If paper, it must be wet.
- *Foil.*   Normally, this must be scored and wetted for removal.
- *Cork veneer.*   This is usually a two-part procedure. First, the cork veneer is saturated with remover and scraped off; second, the backing is wet and scraped off, or left on for installation.
- *Suede.*   This can normally be removed as cork veneer is.
- *Grasscloth.*   Usually this is a two-part procedure. First the surface netting is saturated and scraped off, then the backing is wet and scraped off.
- *Hemp.*   Remove as you would grasscloth.
- *Reedcloth.*   Remove as you would grasscloth.
- *Paper weave.*   Remove as you would grasscloth.

- *Stringcloth.*   Remove as you would grasscloth.

- *Jute.*   Remove as you would grasscloth.

- *Moiré.*   This may have a paper backing or a light cloth one. If cloth, the strips may be peeled off. If paper, it can be removed as regular paper is, after the top layer is stripped off.

- *Mylar.*   This may have a backing that enables it to be dry-stripped from the wall or the top layer stripped off and then the paper layer removed.

21
Hanging Various Wall Coverings

Just as painters have their own preferred ways of painting, so do they have ways of hanging wall coverings. The following discussion covers one standard way and variations of doing the job.

The first task is to figure out how much wall covering is needed. The measuring guide will help determine this. All calculations are made in terms of double rolls. If what you need falls between one and two rolls, get an extra double roll. You will need more or less material according to the pattern match. As mentioned, all rolls that you buy should have the same dye lot numbers.

Plumb Lines

Most ceilings and floors are not straight, so it is important to first snap a plumb line. Select an inconspicuous corner, such as behind a door, to hang the first strip. Measure (Fig. 21-1) from the corner the width of the roll less ½ in, and snap a plumb line on the wall. For example, if the wall covering is 27 in wide, the plumb line will be 26½ in from the corner; make this mark near the ceiling. Hang the plumb line from the ceiling; when the line stops moving, mark the wall where the line falls, about 2 in above the baseboard. With these two lines as reference points, snap a line that bisects them. As you reach each, snap a new plumb line as suggested.

Measure the wall height at several points, then add 2 in for trimming at both the ceiling and baseboard. (If the pattern is large, say a floral design, hold the roll up against the wall and determine where you want the pattern to fall at the ceiling line, before you cut.)

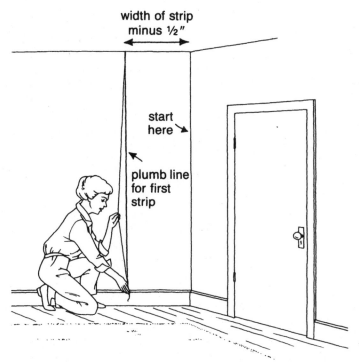

Figure 21-1. Measuring for the first strip of wallpaper. (*Courtesy of Gencorp*)

Lay this strip face on a table or floor, roll out another strip to check for matching; and cut this and then additional strips.

Prepasted and Unpasted Papers

If the strip is unpasted, you can check with your dealer for an adhesive suggestion; also see Chap. 18.

First, roll out the strip along the wall covering table, with the pattern side down. Apply the adhesive to one-half of the strip, using either a $\frac{3}{8}$-in roller or a wide wall covering brush, working from the middle of the strip to the ends and outward, covering it completely. Being careful not to crease it, loosely fold the strip on itself—wet to wet.

Repeat the procedure for the other half, applying adhesive, then folding it back on itself. Next, let it "book"—relax for at least 5 min so the covering fully expands (Fig. 21-2).

If it is unpasted, also book it, regardless of whether you use an activator.

Apply the strip so the edge aligns with the plumb line and overlaps it 2 in at the ceiling and baseboard. Using a sponge or smoothing brush, work from the center out to remove bubbles and wrinkles (Fig. 21-3*a*).

Unroll the lower half of the paper and repeat the procedure (Fig. 21-3*b*). Use a sponge to clean any excess adhesive off the face of the strip.

Butt the first strip against the second, so that there is no overlap and the pattern matches perfectly. Do not stretch the strip to fit—it can shrink back and the seam can open.

Most times when wall covering becomes loose, it occurs at the seams. So it is important to roll them with a seam roller to make sure that the covering is in full contact with the wall and that seams are tight. Gaps mean potential weak spots.

Insurance Against Loosening

As insurance against wall covering loosening at the seams, one painter uses regular paste or activator, as the case may be, but also applies vinyl-to-vinyl paste to the wall at the points where the seams are. Vinyl-to-vinyl paste is very strong and ensures that the seams will not loosen.

Every couple of strips, use a joint knife and a very sharp razor-blade knife (a utility knife or one with breakaway blades works well) to trim off excess paper (Fig. 21-4), using the joint skiff to hold the wall covering tightly in the seam as you trim (Fig. 21-5). As you go, use a roller to make sure edges have good adhesion.

Figure 21-2. "Booking" the wallpaper strip.
(*Courtesy of Gencorp*)

Figure 21-3. Applying the (*a*) first and (*b*) second strips of wallpaper. (*Courtesy of Gencorp*)

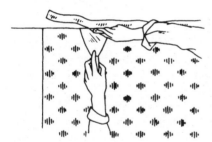

Figure 21-4. Trimming. (*Courtesy of Gencorp*)

Figure 21-5. Rolling the edges. (*Courtesy of Gencorp*)

As you trim, change blades frequently, to avoid pulling adhered paper off the wall with the movement of the blade and to make a sharp cut. As you go, use a clean sponge to clear away any adhesive.

Corners

It might seem easier to handle inside corners by simply "wrapping" the covering into them, but this is not the way to go. It can lead to the covering being slightly awry as the job proceeds.

The best bet is to cut two pieces of wall covering. Measure at three spots along the edge of the wall covering—baseboard, middle, and ceiling. To the widest measurement add $\frac{1}{2}$ in. Cut this width from the new strip, which is A in Fig. 21-6a. You can do this by snapping a cut line. Paste this strip as you did the others, and butt it against the last strip hung.

Take the leftover part of the strip, B, apply paste, and then hang it on the adjacent corner, overlapping the first strip $\frac{1}{2}$ in. The overlap will not be noticeable because it will match the adjacent design very well.

On an outside corner no cutting is required. Just paste the strip and install it as other strips, making sure it is tight and well-adhered.

Openings

When you reach a window or door, the job can be continued in essentially the same way (Fig. 21-7). Cut a matching strip to butt against the last applied strip, but 1 in or so longer. When the wall covering is laid over the window or door, a little more slack is needed.

When the strip is pasted, butt it against the strip and position it over the window or door. Then use scissors or a razor to slice the covering diagonally, as shown in the illustration; then use the joint knife to press it in snugly around the molding of the door or window, and trim off excess with a sharp blade. Use a smoothing brush to work out any bubbles, then trim off excess. Special hypodermic-type needles can be used to flatten blisters (Fig. 21-8).

Ceilings

You can install wall coverings on a ceiling, but there are, of course, some differences in method.

First, work across the short dimension of the ceiling because this will allow you to work with shorter strips, a boon when working above your head. Start on the side of the room where it is going to be as much out of sight as possible, because you will not have a match.

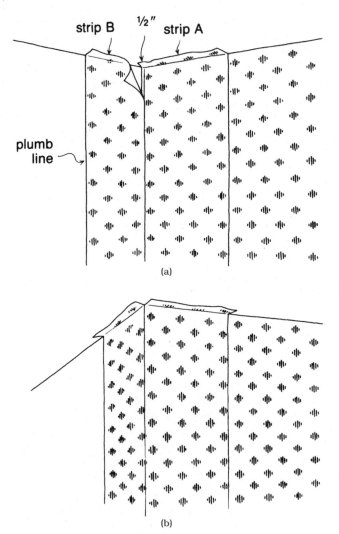

strip B   ½″ strip A

plumb
line

(a)

(b)

Figure 21-6. Rounding an (*a*) inside corner and an (*b*) out-side corner. (*Courtesy of Gencorp*)

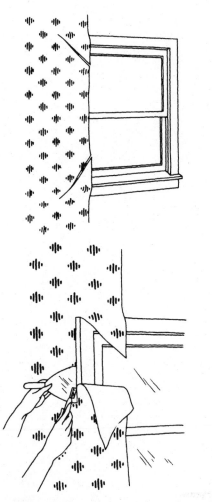

Figure 21-7. Trimming around windows. (*Courtesy of Gencorp*)

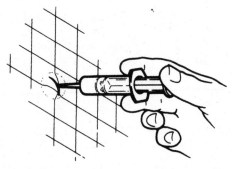

Figure 21-8. Flattening blisters. (*Courtesy of Gencorp*)

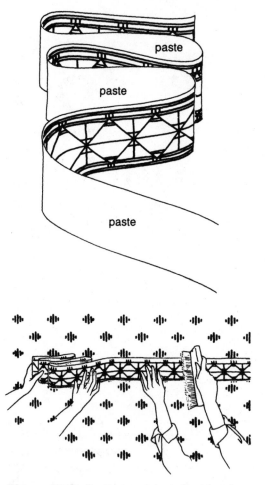

Figure 21-9. Pasting and installing borders.
(*Courtesy of Gencorp*)

Cut the strip a couple of inches longer than needed, apply paste, and set it up in position. To help do this, you can use a broom, and a helper is definitely called for to position the strips. Trim each as you go, and roll out the seams.

When you are finished, wipe away excess glue with a clean, damp sponge.

Borders

The average wall covering border (Fig. 21-9) is 15 ft long. If you are applying it to a painted wall, measure down the length of the roll and make a guide line on the wall. Then carefully paste the rear of the first strip and, following instructions given for hanging wall covering, install the border.

22
Problems with Wall Coverings

There are a number of problems that the paperhanger is called on to solve during the course of a job. Following is a roundup and suggested solutions. As with painting, many of the problems that arise with wall covering relate to improper preparation.

Wall Covering Falling Off the Wall

A variety of things can cause this. One may be that the paper was applied when the temperature in the area was too low—below 55°F. This means that the paste, like paint, could not cure properly and therefore lost its adhesive ability—so the paper came off.

Too high a temperature can create the same problem. At temperatures above 90°F, the moisture in the paste evaporates, and, again, the paste loses its strength.

Another cause is old sizing. Although it is not as prevalent these days, starch-based sizing is occasionally used; and if it is mixed and not applied in a day or two, it can lose its potency.

Another cause is that the wall was not prepared properly. This could be due to a number of different things; perhaps the wall was not smooth enough to accept the paper well.

Primer sealer may be too old—this is a problem of strength.

Areas subject to high moisture can also be a problem. If the moisture gets to the paste, it can resolubilize it—make it liquid—and the wall covering will peel off. If the covering abuts such things as tubs and sinks, there should be a solid bead of caulk to seal the wall covering seams from the moisture.

Wrong primer sealer can also make the paper fall off.

Mildew can cause big problems. It usually forms because of some interaction with the adhesive, and the result is a weakened adhesive—and the wall covering comes off.

Gaps in Seams

There are a number of causes of gaps in seams. You can get a hint of what might be happening by considering how much time has elapsed. If the seam opens up 24 h or more after installation, the problem is likely that the backing of the covering is shrinking too much. This would be particularly noticeable if there were a white primer on the wall and a dark paper.

The only real solution to this problem is to color the openings, using an artist's brush and paint mixed to match the wall covering. In this latter regard, it is a good idea to take a sample of the wall covering and get a quart of paint custom-made to that color. Or perhaps you can find the appropriate color in a smaller amount ready-made.

If the problem occurs during application—the adhesive is still wet—usually too much adhesive is being applied and the drying process is slowed. Often it is because a roller is being used, or a paste machine which has not been properly adjusted. The safest way to control the amount of adhesive applied is to apply it with a brush, rather than a roller.

Another reason for gaps in seams is that the paper has been pushed too far to make it butt tight against previously installed strip. But wall covering is like rubber that has been stretched too far. It dries and pulls back a little—and the gap is created.

Bubbling and Blistering

Bubbles and blisters that develop in wall covering also have a variety of causes.

One possible reason for bubbles forming under the newly applied wall coverings is that the adhesive has been overmixed perhaps with a high-speed drill. This can lead to bubbles, or air pockets, forming in the adhesive; the pockets stay there even after the adhesive is applied. Mixing paste with a slow figure-eight motion is regarded as the best way.

Another possible cause of blisters arises when a water-based primer is applied to a paper that is not impervious to moisture, or to another kind of wall covering where there are gaps, in either rips or tears, and the water in the primer can get to the paste. This resolubilizes it, and the water vapor creates the blisters.

Blisters can stay in wall covering overnight or even longer, but they usually go away on their own. The moisture evaporates, and the wall covering pulls back tight against the wall. This does not always happen, however. When it does, use a utility knife to cut out the blisters. Once the primer is dry, patch the area, reseal, and proceed as usual.

Another way to resecure blisters that fail to contract is with a special wall covering hypodermic needle (see Chap. 21).

Blisters can also occur when a freshly pasted wall covering is installed too soon after the adhesive is applied.

Also blisters form on the kraft paper covering of drywall. This occurs subtlely. The paperhanger removes the wall covering, usually a cloth-backed type, and the angle of removal is severe enough that it pulls the drywall facing loose. When a latex-based primer is applied, the facing expands in the loose spots, just as wall covering would. Such blisters do not pull back on their own. The solution is to cut them out and patch the areas as needed.

Stains

A variety of stains can occur on wall coverings. Following are some stains and their causes.

Excessive water in the paste or too much adhesive could cause stains. The water can penetrate through the facing from the backside and dry to a stain.

On polyester products like Mylar, the water can seep through and cause the ink to bleed.

Another problem is flaking inks. This occurs particularly on wall coverings with dull finishes, and this is usually caused by premixed paste that is left on the surface. It acts to remove the inks, and they flake off as a result.

Delamination is one other problem. This refers to the separation of the backing of the wall covering from the facing, and it usually occurs on grasscloth, jute, and similar coverings because they have been booked too long. Five minutes is normally the maximum amount of time they should be booked.

Glossary

Absorption: Penetration of a porous substrate by resin.

Acetone: A highly volatile liquid used in cleanup and paint thinning. Acetone has a flash point of zero.

Acrylic: A high-quality synthetic binder used in high-quality paints that adds considerably to a paint's wearability and color retention. Acrylic made water-based paints into a high-quality product. Technically, acrylic is known as synthetic acid-based plastic monomer used to create polyester resins. It is often referred to as a latex, which pays homage more to tradition than to accuracy. Purely latex paints have not been around for a long time.

Additives: Chemicals added to paint formulations to impart various desirable characteristics such as mildew resistance, low spatter, and little or no foaming.

Adhesion: The ability of dried paint to remain on the surface—no peeling, etc. Wet adhesion occurs when paint will adhere to a surface despite its being wet. Latex is a prime example, as are some waterproofing paints. They can be applied when a surface is actually wet from dew rain, etc., though there is a point at which they will run. Painters describe adhesion with the term *bonding*.

Advancing colors: These are dark colors or warm colors which make a room or other area painted with them seem smaller than it actually is—the colors advance toward the viewer.

Aerosol spray: Simply spray paint. It is paint and solvent powered from a can by compressed gas. The paint is mixed by shaking the can to activate an agitating ball.

Air cure: One way liquids dry to a film or paint dries. Oxygen combines with resin molecules to make the paint dry.

Air entrapment: Air bubbles trapped in a paint film. This can have a variety of causes, such as applying paint in hot sun. Air entrapment bubbles show up in a finish as it is applied.

Airless sprayer: Machine used to spray-paint. It uses a pump to atomize the paint.

Algae: Brownish or reddish aquatic plants that normally grow in areas of a house or building that are sheltered from the sun.

Alkyd: A blend of oils with synthetic materials which makes for properties not in the original oil, such as faster drying and a harder film. Essentially, molecules in the vegetable oils are replaced with synthetic molecules. Also a type of resin in oil-based paints which contain oil "reacted" to a harder, more durable state than oil alone can provide.

Alligatoring: Form of paint failure in which the paint cracks apart and resembles the hide of an alligator. It is one of the more common forms of paint failure. Essentially it means that the paint is not adhering for one reason or another. When this occurs, the film lifts off the surface, and the stress cracks it. Left alone, the paint will gradually reach the stage where it will peel.

Amalgamate: Chemical used to recondition old paint or lacquer. This chemical is also used to remove from lacquer-coated surfaces the white rings caused by heat, water, or alcohol.

Amide: Epoxy resin-curing agent. Unlike other paints, epoxy does not air-dry but dries by chemical action. It takes longer to cure than standard paint and has generally a very hard, durable finish.

Anatase titanium: Pigment used in alkyd paints to create chalking so the films clean themselves. It is not used much these days.

Aniline dye: Bluish die made from aniline, which is poisonous. It is used in making wood stains.

Anticorrosion paint: Metal paint designed to prevent corrosion.

Antifouling paint: Paint used in marine applications below the waterline to help boats and other marine structures resist the ravages of water.

Aromatic oils: Oils present in some woods such as cypress, teak, and the cedars (except western red cedar) that can cause finishing problems. They can slow down drying of coatings, leaving them sticky, and often cause blistering, softening, wrinkling, and general disintegration. This is mainly a problem caused by the way the wood was kiln-dried.

Back-brushing: Process of brushing out a material applied with another type of applicator.

The classic use of back-brushing occurs when stain or clear finish is applied to raw wood–or finish-compatible stain or clear with a pump sprayer. Without back-brushing, the material may lie on the surface, ultimately "drying" into a sticky puddle and then to a hard film—which can peel. Back-brushing avoids this, because the action of the brush drives the products deep into the wood pores. In a word, they penetrate deeply into the wood and, therefore, cannot peel.

Back-brushing is also commonly done after spraying. The spray gets the paint onto the surface, and the brush is used to smooth it out.

Back-priming: Painting the unexposed backs of material such as house shingles before installation. This is a good idea, because it ensures that moisture migrating from the house into the shingles is minimized.

Back-rolling: Same thing as back-brushing except a roller is used. The classic use is on walls. The paint is applied by roller, the next strip is done, and then the painter comes back and rolls over—back-rolls—the applied paint with a relatively dry roller to smooth it out.

Back-rolling is used in any situation where it is felt the paint is too thickly applied to remain as it is.

Batch code: Method of identifying when and where a particular paint was made.

Binder: Chemical which "glues" pigment particles together while in liquid suspension and also makes paint adhere to a surface. The amount and type of binders in a paint are a very strong determining factor in just how good the paint is. The best binder is acrylic, and the more of it, the better.

Biocide: Substance placed in paint to prevent its contamination by fungi while waiting to be sold.

Bleeding: (1) The appearance of something that has taken on a lighter hue than normal. The usual reason is sunlight. (2) The process that results in material being lighter than normal. (3) An undercoat or patching material which shows through a topcoat. There can be many reasons for bleeding: not priming patches before applying finish coat, not letting primed patches dry, using the wrong primer for the job, and applying paint that does not have good hiding ability.

Blisters: In exterior painting, an expanded part of a paint film, the stage before cracking, then peeling. There are many reasons for blisters, but one of the main ones is that water vapor, migrating from inside the house, gets trapped behind the paint film. As the vapor pushes outward, the paint film gets pushed and lifted off the surface, hence the blister. You can confirm the reason by puncturing the blister and watching to see if water runs out.

Blisters also can occur on wall covering, usually due to the buildup of vapor from adhesive. Sometimes the blisters deflate, and the wall covering readheres to the wall; but at other times it is necessary to prick a hole in the blister to draw out the air and to apply more adhesive.

Block filler: A thick paint which is suggested for application to masonry surfaces which are very rough.

Bloom: Marring caused by high humidity when painting.

Booking: Technique for gently folding (but not creasing) wallpaper that has had paste applied to it. The ends of the strip will be folded over toward the center of the strip.

Booking gives the adhesive time to penetrate deeply into the covering, relaxes it—makes it more supple-and prevents it from drying out (because the glued faces are touching and not in open air) until ready for hanging. Different wall coverings require different amounts of time to relax.

Boxing: Mixing paint by pouring it back and forth between containers. It is the best nonmechanical way to mix paint.

Breathing: The ability of paint to allow moisture vapor to pass harmlessly through a coating without damaging it. Latex paint, for example, breathes while oil-based paint does not, making the latter more likely to peel.

Bristles: Fibers of hair that constitute the working end of a brush. *Bristle* is a term that is sometimes misunderstood, used to refer to a "bristle" brush which implies that the brush is a China, or natural bristle, brush. At other times it is used to describe the bristles on a synthetic brush. Today, then, the term must be seen in context to determine its meaning.

Bubbles: Air pockets that normally form if a paint has been overmixed or there is excessive brushing.

Some materials, such as polyurethane clear coating, can develop bubbles quite readily: These should not even be shaken.

Burnishing: Paint mars, shiny spots, usually on flat paint, which occur as a result of rubbing when cleaning. Manufacturers may champion their paint as being washable, even scrubbable, and it may well be. The problem, though, is that cleaning will leave a mark, which is just as noticeable as a soil mark.

Burnt sienna: Color used in tinting paint; a reddish brown.

Burnt umber: A color that is a fairly dark brown, one of a number of colors painters use to tint paint. Like other colorants, it is available in tubes and cans.

Calcium carbonate: Commonly called *chalk*; a mineral that is used as a colorant and pigment extender.

Catalyst: Chemical which makes drying occur faster in epoxy coatings (and adhesives). Commonly there is a catalyst and a hardener.

Caulk: Flexible material used to fill the seams or joints of a house. It is applied wherever dissimilar materials meet, such as masonry and wood, and where windows, doors, and the like meet. Buildings expand and contract, and without a flexible material to seal these seams, water and cold (and heat) could pass in and out of the house easily, affecting heating and cooling and leading to much higher fuel costs.

Caulk comes in a variety of types, but essentially it is designed for either interior use, in which case it is mildew-resistant, or not, in which case it is for exterior use.

Chalking: Surface of paint film turning to a powder. This occurs when the binder in the paint cannot stand up to the weather conditions.

Checking: (1) Small rupture along the grain of the wood caused by the alternate shrinking and swelling during its life. Low-density (light) woods will resist warping and checking better than high-density ones. For example, low-density woods such as redwood, cedar, and cypress will resist cupping twice as well as high-density hardwoods such as white oak and northern red oak; these have only one-quarter of the resistance to cupping as cypress and redwood. (2) The appearance of paint that is failing. A dense number of squarish cracks appear in the paint film which run lengthwise with the wood grain.

Color chip: Small square of color in paint brochures. Chips are actually made of paint so that you can get an idea of what the color truly is. The gloss or sheen of the chip is also accurately depicted.

Color retention: The ability of paint to hold its color without fading.

Corrosion: Discoloration or deterioration of metal and concrete by chemical or electromagnetic reaction because of exposure to weather, chemicals, or other environmental factors.

Coverage: Area that a paint covers and/or how well it covers. Standard coverage figure given is 400 ft^2/gal, or 100 ft^2/qt, but this is misleading. Perhaps in a laboratory setting this might work out. But in painting surfaces, factors that must be considered are the roughness of the surface, the color being covered, and the applicator being used (roller applies paint more heavily than a brush).

Crackle: A clear material used in decorative painting. A base coat is applied and allowed to dry, and then the crackle coat is applied and allowed to dry and a topcoat is applied over the crackle. The crackle removes water from the topcoat, "crackling" it, opening fissures through which the base coat can be viewed. If the topcoat is applied with a sponge, it will have an alligatored look; if brushed on, a paint-peeled look. In certain circumstances the crackle look can be quite attractive.

Cratering: Small round concave depressions in paint film.

Crawling: Adhesion problem where paint is incompatible with substrate and beads up or otherwise does not penetrate, such as oil on wax.

Cross-checking: Crosswise cracks in paint film.

Cupping: A distortion or twist across the flatness of a board. Wide boards cup more than narrow boards. Boards may also twist from one to the other, deviating from a straight line along the length of the piece; this is also known as *crook*.

Curing: Chemical reaction which occurs as coatings dry.

Cutting in: Using a brush to apply a different color or gloss (or both) of paint to another area without getting any of the new material where it does not belong. Painters speak of cutting in the molding, or windows, or the line where the wall paint meets the ceiling paint.

Denatured alcohol: The solvent for shellac and one of the cleanup materials (the other is ammonia).

Density: How heavy or light wood is; a factor in how it performs and coatings perform on it.

Density varies greatly from species to species. For example, among the softwoods, southern yellow pine is almost twice as dense as western red cedar. This leads to more or less shrinking and swelling, with heavy woods shrinking and swelling more than light ones because of gains or losses in moisture with changes in relative humidity and from periodic wetting caused by rain and dew. Wood in heated homes tends to dry and shrink in the winter as the result of the low relative humidity, then gain moisture and swell in the spring and summer. If the moisture changes are unusual, the excessive dimension changes—the swelling and contracting—can cause early failure of paint.

Diluent: Water, the thinner in water-based paint.

Drop match: In wallpapering, a type of matching of designs where (assuming the strips are level) there will be matching patterns at the ceiling line and an overall diagonal line.

Drops: Short for drop cloths, the painter's cloths used to protect areas from paint. Drop cloths come in a variety of sizes, but usually 9 ft by 12 ft, and in various textures. While the average drop cloth is not waterproof, it will absorb drops of paint and they will not get through to do any damage. Drop cloths also may be plastic, but these are not really regarded as the main coverings by painters.

Dry hide: The ability of paint to hide well once it is dry. Such paint is typically formulated with extenders which work along with the prime pigment to produce a paint that will not hide well when wet but does hide well when dry. However, dry hide paints are not washable.

Drying agent: Compound added to paint to retard or increase drying time.

Drywall: General name for a common building material, also known as wallboard, gypsum board, and plasterboard but perhaps most commonly by one brand name—Sheetrock. Sheetrock consists of panels of gypsum surfaced on both sides with a tough paper material.

Dye lot number: In wallpapering, the numbers assigned to wall covering when it is printed, indicating that all the rolls were printed at the same time.

Having the same dye lot numbers is an important consideration for painters, because if the dye lot numbers are different, there can be a slight variation in the ink, embossment, etc. And dye lot numbers should be recorded somewhere in case more rolls are needed in the future.

Eggshell: The sheen level of a paint, which is roughly that of an eggshell. Also known as *satin flat.*

Emulsion: Coating mixture where oil and water are compatible.

Enamel: Generally a hard, shiny paint. The term is confusing because it also is applied to flat paints. Enamel originally referred to a shiny, oil-based paint.

Epoxy: Usually a two-part system where a hardener is mixed with a resin which dries chemically (not by evaporation) into a hard, durable surface.

Etch: Washing of a surface with acid to roughen it and provide better tooth for primer or paint.

Extender: Ingredient in paint that makes it thicker and more likely to cover. Extenders include clays, calcium carbonate, and silica.

Extractives: Substances in wood that affect its properties. Depending on the species, wood may contain water-soluble extractives, pitch or oil. Each of these substances has its own properties and characteristics. Although they only involve a small percentage of the wood, they are disproportionately important in terms of their effect on a number of wood properties, including color, decay and insect resistance, odor, permeability, density, and hardness. Without extractives, pitch, and oil, many woods would appear essentially identical except for their anatomical features.

   Water-soluble extractives are located in the lumens or cavities of cells in the heartwoods of both hardwoods and softwoods. They are particularly plentiful in woods used outdoors, such as western red cedar, redwood, and cypress, and are found in lesser amounts in Douglas fir and southern yellow pine where heartwood is present. The handsome color, dimensional stability, and decay resistance of many species are due to extractives. However, these extractives can interfere with finishing, both when the finish is applied and later. Because they are water-soluble, water that saturates the woods seeps down and solubilizes them. They then leach to the surface and stain it a reddish brown, something particularly noticeable on white or light-colored paints or solid-colored stains.

Fading: Loss of color due to weather, time, and/or light.

Fat edge: Slang for a buildup of paint at an edge of something such as molding.

Feathering: Technique which describes the smoothing of a patching material so the outer edges blend into nothingness. Also the brush application of paint whereby one brushful of paint, by lifting the last part of the stroke, is blended seamlessly into an adjacent wet edge.

Flash: Flashed areas are those that appear different from other areas because of either inadequate application of paint or one area's being more susceptible to absorbing paint than another. The latter problem usually results because the surface was not prepared properly and offered inadequate holdout.

Flat paint: Paint without any sheen.

Flow: Property of a paint to go on smoothly and level out.

Foots: The solids in paint, such as pigments, which settle to the bottom of the can.

From the dry into the wet: Painter's term indicating the proper way to paint when using a brush, particularly trim. That is, a brushful (or half a brushful) of paint is applied and brushed out. Then the next brushful is applied about 1 ft from the wet edge in a dry area, and the brush is pulled across the dry area and into the wet. This enables the painter to cover the maximum dry area with each stroke.

Glazing compound: The correct name for window putty, used for sealing around panes of glass.

Gloss: The amount of shine in a finish. Gloss paint refers to very shiny paint. A device called a *gloss meter* is used to measure the glossiness of a paint. On the meter the maximum gloss is 69 to 70 degrees, and this surface is like glass. One step down is semigloss, which is 35 on the meter. Below this is eggshell, 20 to 35; and the lowest gloss of all, flat, is below 15. The numbers are arrived at by focusing a specified amount of light onto a surface and then measuring it. Note that one manufacturer may call a paint high-gloss, but according to objective measurements it may be less or more than other manufacturers' high-gloss paints. In other words, one company's semigloss may be another company's gloss.

Grain raising: Swelling or raising of wood grain in raw wood due to the absorption of water or other solvents.

Gypsum board: Another name for drywall.

Heartwood and sapwood: A dark column of wood (heartwood) and outside this a lighter column of wood (sapwood). The sapwood is composed of live cells that carry water and nutrients from the roots to the leaves and that provide mechanical support. The heartwood, which is composed of dead cells, provides only mechanical support.

The heartwood, being already dead, provides a much better resistance to decay than sapwood. Some species, such as southern yellow pine, have a much wider sapwood zone than other species, such as cedar and redwood, and therefore much less decay resistance.

Old or original-growth timber from some species, such as cypress, is notable for its natural resistance to decay and insects. Second-growth lumber contains a much larger amount of sapwood than old-growth lumber and is much more susceptible to decay than old-growth; its heartwood is not as resistant to decay as old-growth heartwood.

Hide: The ability of paint to obscure the color of the stain or paint to which it has been applied. The hide is provided by the prime pigment in the paint. For example, in good-quality white or pastel paints, titanium dioxide is the prime pigment.

Holiday: Slang for a missed spot when painting. The term first surfaced many years ago in regard to applying tar to a boat; a missed spot was called a holiday or vacation, in the sense that it fills a gap in the routine.

Painters say that holidays are much more likely to occur when painting is done at night than in the day; natural light is much better. You can eye paint in artificial light and then view it in natural light, and holidays may show up despite your most careful efforts.

Joint tape: Paper tape used as a base for sealing Sheetrock panel joints. It is embedded in and covered by multiple coats of joint compound.

Isopropyl alcohol: More commonly known as *rubbing alcohol*; an inexpensive liquid that is an outstanding cleaner of silicone caulking.

Knots: Irregularities in wood growth. The presence of knots affects the paintability of lumber and is generally a function of lumber grade.

Knots are mostly exposed on the end grain of wood, end-grained wood absorbs more finish than flat- or edge-grained lumber, and this affects the way the paint looks. In pine, knots often contain a high percentage of resin, which may cause the paint above the knot to discolor. Furthermore, large knots usually check and crack, and a noticeable split or defect occurs. In sum, the higher grades of lumber are better to use for finishing.

Lacquer: Quick-drying clear or colored coating.

Lampblack: Black colorant. It is used many times as a basic color for paint and to tint white paint so that it is slightly gray and covers better.

Latex: Emulsion of synthetic resins, commonly used to describe paint that uses water as the solvent but, in fact, is not latex in the strictest sense. When latex paint was first formulated, latex came from the rubber tree and was used as a binder for the paint. This was before World War II. When the war started, latex became scarce and synthetics were developed, but the name stuck.

Leveling: Capacity of paint to form a seamless surface when dry that is free of brush or other applicator marks.

Liner paper: Blank wall covering which can vary in thickness depending on the job at hand but whose function is to make rough walls, such as block walls, or paneling, or those that have been heavily patched, smooth. Liner paper can be primed and painted. It also serves as an excellent base for wall covering, particularly expensive foils and hand-painted types.

The wallpaper-wide strips are normally installed horizontally with paste, just as ordinary wall covering, and this crisscross installation pattern provides extra strength. Liner is not recommended for installation over individual wood planks because expansion and contraction of the boards can lead to failure of the paper.

There are three kinds of liner paper: polyester, canvas, and fiberglass. They come in various weights. The fiberglass liner is installed on wet paint, and then it must be painted again to seal the seams.

Linseed oil: Vegetable oil obtained by crushing seeds of the flax plant; a basic component of some paints, chiefly the oil-base type. Raw linseed oil is available in two forms: boiled and not. Boiling means it is heated by chemical dryers (years ago it was actually cooked) so that it dries more quickly.

Low luster: A low sheen. Note that what is low-luster paint to one manufacturer is not to another, or vice versa. It is best to check the color chip cards of manufacturers. These show just what the luster is because they are made of paint and are not photographically reproduced.

Mildew: A living organism that forms on and discolors paint under certain conditions.

Mildewcide: Chemical agent added to or formulated into paint which kills mildew.

Oil-based paint: Any paint which thins and cleans up with mineral spirits.

Open time: The amount of time a coating stays workable or wet after it has been applied. The term is frequently used to refer to glazes employed in graining, which depend greatly on the coating's staying workable while it is tooled.

Painter's tape: Tape that comes in a variety of widths and lengths and somewhat resembles masking tape (although some is white and blue), though it differs greatly. Painter's tape is designed to be able to be peeled off a surface without damaging it. Try the same thing with masking tape, and you will tear the paint or wallpaper.

Pigment: Main ingredient in paint, which gives paint its color and hiding power. In light and white paints, the most important pigment is titanium dioxide.

Pitch: In most pines and Douglas fir trees, substance exuded from either the sapwood or the heartwood. It is usually a mixture of rosin and turpentine, a mixture called *rosin*. Rosin is brittle and remains solid at most temperatures. By use of proper kiln-drying techniques, turpentine can generally be driven out of the wood, leaving only the solid rosin. However, for green lumber or oven-dried lumber marketed for general construction, different kiln schedules may be used, and the turpentine will remain in the wood mixed with the rosin. This resin melts at a much lower temperature than does pure rosin, and consequently the mixture can migrate to the surface. If the surface has a finish, the resin may exude through the coating or cause it to discolor or blister. This usually occurs slowly, as temperature changes force the resin outward. The most serious problem occurs when the wood is heated, for example, when the sun strikes the south side of a house.

Once the resin, which is sticky, is on the surface, the turpentine evaporates, leaving beads of hard rosin. If the wood is painted, the rosin will diffuse through the film, discoloring it.

Prime pigment: The main pigment in a paint which imparts hiding ability and color.

Rheology additives: Chemicals added to latex and alkyd paints which increase the paint's ability to flow and to level.

Ring orientation: The way a board is sawn, or manufactured, from a log which affects the orientation of the annual rings and the wood's paintability.

Softwood lumber is referred to as either flat-grained or edge-grained; plain-sawed or quarter-sawed in hardwoods; or a combination of these. Most standard lumber is flat-grained. For example, most board-and-batten and shiplap are flat-grained. Bevel siding and redwood or cedar are generally produced in a flat-grained standard grade and an edge-grained premium grade.

The problem is with the flat-grained wood. It shrinks more than edge-grained wood and has wider, darker bands of latewood. Therefore edge-grained lumber used for siding will usually hold paint better than flat-grained; and quarter-sawed or hardwood paints hold better than plain-sawed boards. But the difference is relatively small compared to quarter-sawed and plain-sawed softwoods.

Substrate: Surface to which coating or wall covering is applied.

Tannin bleed: Migration of water-soluble chemicals to the surface of wood, such as cedar.

Texture: The coarseness of the individual wood cells, often used in reference to hardwoods. Hardwoods are composed of relatively short, small-diameter cells (fibers) and large-diameter pores or vessels. Softwoods, by contrast, are composed of longer, small-diameter cells called *tracheids*. Hardwoods with large pores, such as oak and ash, are poorly adapted to ordinary housepainting because pinholes can form in the coating over the large pores; these holes, as well as being unsightly, can lead to early paint failure. Hardwoods with small pores include magnolia, yellow poplar, and cottonwood; they are low-density and have small pores and are, therefore, the best hardwoods to paint.

Thinner: The liquid used to thin and clean up paint. In oil-based paints the thinner is mineral spirits; in latex paints it is water.

Titanium dioxide: A high-quality white pigment used in the making of pastel-colored paints.

Vehicle: The liquid portion of paint which carries the solids, such as pigment.

Viscosity: The thickness of a paint or stain.

VOC: Volatile organic compound. Carbon compound that evaporates. VOCs are found in oil-based paints; because of their destructive effects on the environment, they have been seriously limited.

Wet edge: A combination of flow and slow drying that allows the paint to be brushed out to a seamless look.

Index

About the Author

Tom Philbin, a former painter, is a respected author with more than 25 books on home improvement, repair, and maintenance to his credit. He is a regular contributor on home improvement issues for various TV and radio shows. Former Home and Shop Editor of *Home Mechanix* and Managing Editor of *Family Handyman* magazines, Philbin writes for such widely respected publications as *Reader's Digest* and *Woman's Day*.